普通高等教育经管类专业系列教材

会 计 英 语

（双语版）

张　倩　黄雨曦　主编

清华大学出版社
北　京

内 容 简 介

本书采用英汉对照的模式编写，主要涵盖基础会计和财务会计两部分内容。全书共十四章，首先介绍了会计理论框架、会计等式、会计循环等基础会计知识，再由浅入深介绍了资产、负债、所有者权益、收入、费用和财务报表等财务会计专业知识。全书每章都提供有理论和实务操作练习题、案例分析题以及本章重要的专业术语的详细注解，以便教师教学和学生学习，并有助于提高学生的会计专业英语的阅读理解能力和实务操作能力。

本书内容新颖，体系完整，结构合理，针对性强，可供高等院校会计、财务管理等相关专业作为教学用书，也可供财务管理人员、审计人员、法律工作者等国际财务会计相关人员作为自学参考书。

本书封面贴有清华大学出版社防伪标签，无标签者不得销售。
版权所有，侵权必究。举报：010-62782989，beiqinquan@tup.tsinghua.edu.cn。

图书在版编目(CIP)数据

会计英语：双语版/张倩，黄雨曦主编. —北京：清华大学出版社，2022.5 (2024.8 重印)
普通高等教育经管类专业系列教材
ISBN 978-7-302-57829-1

Ⅰ.①会… Ⅱ.①张… ②黄… Ⅲ.①会计—英语—高等学校—教材 Ⅳ.①F23

中国版本图书馆 CIP 数据核字(2021)第 057267 号

责任编辑：刘金喜
封面设计：周晓亮
版式设计：思创景点
责任校对：成凤进
责任印制：刘海龙

出版发行：清华大学出版社
    网　　址：https://www.tup.com.cn，https://www.wqxuetang.com
    地　　址：北京清华大学学研大厦 A 座　　　　邮　编：100084
    社 总 机：010-83470000　　　　　　　　　　邮　购：010-62786544
    投稿与读者服务：010-62776969，c-service@tup.tsinghua.edu.cn
    质 量 反 馈：010-62772015，zhiliang@tup.tsinghua.edu.cn
印 装 者：三河市君旺印务有限公司
经　　销：全国新华书店
开　　本：185mm×260mm　　　印　张：19.25　　　字　数：542 千字
版　　次：2022 年 7 月第 1 版　　印　次：2024 年 8 月第 2 次印刷
定　　价：79.00 元

产品编号：081528-01

前　言

"一带一路"建设已进入全面务实合作阶段，这使得我国与沿线国家间的贸易投资往来日益频繁，由此产生的跨境会计问题也日渐突出。在会计国际化趋势背景下，会计人员将面临一系列新的会计问题。因此，仅对我国会计准则下相关会计知识体系的理解与认识已不足以满足会计从业人员的需求。基于此，会计教材应着眼于国际，及时调整结构，不断更新和充实内容，以帮助新背景下的会计专业学生和会计从业人员更好地掌握会计专业英语知识。本教材以国际会计准则委员会(IASB)颁布的国际财务报告准则(International Financial Reporting Standards，IFRS)和国际会计准则(International Accounting Standards，IAS)为蓝本，介绍财务会计的有关内容。

本教材具有如下特点：

1. 内容新颖

本教材的编写建立在最新的国际会计准则基础之上，采用英汉对照的模式编写，全书一共十四章，章节内容均融合了新准则中的新规定，如第二章理论框架的知识点是根据国际会计准则理事会(IASB)2018 年 3 月 29 日修订后的最新规定编写的。本教材是新准则颁布后时间较早、内容较为新颖的一本双语教学用书。

2. 体系完整

本教材在编写上力求系统全面、通俗易读，特别注重基础方法与应用相结合；其基础部分针对性地回顾了基础会计的内容，包括理论框架、会计等式、会计循环等；应用部分以会计核算为主进行分析，着重介绍了现金、应收项目、存货、固定资产、无形资产、负债、所有者权益、收入等账户的实务应用，同时配有大量的实例，多为日常经济活动中遇到的典型会计问题。

3. 实用性强

为了方便教师教学和学生理解，每章均配有重要的会计概念、理论、实务练习、案例分析以及专业词汇，每章后面根据章节内容设置有一定的练习题，其中包括单选题、多选题、计算题、业务处理题等。此安排有助于提升学生对知识点的阅读理解能力、实务操作中综合分析和解决问题的能力。

本教材由张倩、黄雨曦担任主编。张倩负责全书知识体系和教学内容的设置，以及全书的整理、统稿工作。具体编写分工如下：张倩编写第一章至第四章、第十二章至第十四章，黄雨曦编写第五章至第十一章。本教材编写过程中，承蒙学院领导的大力支持，感谢欧阳歆教授、李菲副教授、张敏副教授、殷菲菲副教授、李艳老师、雷艳丽老师、胡迪老师提供了相关资料并提出了宝贵意见。

本教材可供高等院校会计、财务管理等相关专业作为教学用书，也可供财务管理人员、审计人员、法律工作者等国际财务会计相关人员作为自学参考书。

本教材牵涉的内容较多、范围较广，由于编者水平有限，难免存在遗漏和不妥之处，恳请读者批评指正。

本教材 PPT 教学课件可通过 http://www.tupwk.com.cn 下载。

服务邮箱：476371891@qq.com

编　者

2022 年 2 月

目 录

Chapter 1　An Introduction to Accounting···· 1
　1.1　The Objective of Accounting ············ 1
　1.2　Accounting Information ················ 1
　　　1.2.1　The Users of Accounting
　　　　　　Information ··················· 2
　　　1.2.2　Financial Accounting and
　　　　　　Management Accounting ······ 2
　1.3　Profession Fields of Accounting········ 3
　1.4　Ethics of Accounting ···················· 4
　Key Words and Expressions ················ 5
　Exercises··································· 6

第1章　会计概述············ 8
　1.1　会计目标 ············ 8
　1.2　会计信息 ············ 8
　　　1.2.1　会计信息的使用者··········· 8
　　　1.2.2　财务会计和管理会计········ 9
　1.3　会计的职业领域····················· 9
　1.4　会计职业道德······················· 10

Chapter 2　Financial Accounting Conceptual
　　　　　Framework······················· 12
　2.1　Definition of Conceptual
　　　Framework ························· 12
　2.2　Basic Objectives ····················· 13
　2.3　Qualitative Characteristics ············· 13
　　　2.3.1　Fundamental Qualitative
　　　　　　Characteristics··············· 14
　　　2.3.2　Enhancing Qualitative
　　　　　　Characteristics··············· 14

　　　2.3.3　Cost constraints for financial
　　　　　　information ··················· 15
　2.4　The Elements of Financial
　　　Statements························· 15
　　　2.4.1　Statement of Financial Position ····· 15
　　　2.4.2　Statement of Profit or Loss and
　　　　　　Other Comprehensive Income······ 16
　2.5　Recognition and Derecognition ········ 16
　　　2.5.1　Recognition Criteria ················ 16
　　　2.5.2　Derecognition ······················ 17
　2.6　Measurement Concepts ················ 18
　　　2.6.1　Accounting Assumptions ············ 18
　　　2.6.2　Principles of Accounting ············ 19
　　　2.6.3　Measurement Bases ················ 20
　2.7　Presentation and Disclosure ············ 22
　2.8　Concepts of Capital and Capital
　　　Maintenance ························· 23
　　　2.8.1　Capital ···························· 23
　　　2.8.2　Capital Maintenance and the
　　　　　　Determination of Profits ········ 23
　Key Words and Expressions ··············· 24
　Exercises································· 25

第2章　财务会计概念框架················ 28
　2.1　概念框架的定义···················· 28
　2.2　基本目标··························· 29
　2.3　会计信息质量特征················· 29
　　　2.3.1　基本质量特征················· 29
　　　2.3.2　增强质量特征················· 30
　　　2.3.3　财务信息的成本约束·········· 30
　2.4　财务报表要素······················ 30

	2.4.1	资产负债表 ········· 31
	2.4.2	利润表 ············· 31
2.5	确认和终止确认 ············· 31
	2.5.1	确认标准 ········· 31
	2.5.2	终止确认 ········· 32
2.6	计量概念 ··················· 32
	2.6.1	会计假设 ········· 32
	2.6.2	会计原则 ········· 33
	2.6.3	计量基础 ········· 34
2.7	列报和披露 ··················· 35
2.8	资本和资本保全的概念 ········ 36
	2.8.1	资本 ············· 36
	2.8.2	资本保全和利润的确定 ··· 36

Chapter 3 The Accounting Equation and Double Entry Rules ········· 37

3.1 Accounting Equation ············ 37
    3.1.1 Accounting Equation ······ 37
    3.1.2 The Effect of Business Transaction Types on The Accounting Equation ···················· 38
3.2 Double Entry Rules ············ 42
    3.2.1 The Account ············ 42
    3.2.2 The Rules of Debit and Credit ··· 42
    3.2.3 Double Entry ············ 43
Key Words and Expressions ········ 45
Exercises ························ 46

第3章 会计等式和复式记账 ········ 48

3.1 会计等式 ··················· 48
    3.1.1 会计等式 ············ 48
    3.1.2 业务交易类型对会计等式的影响 ·············· 48
3.2 复式记账原理 ··············· 52
    3.2.1 账户 ··············· 52
    3.2.2 借贷记账原理 ········ 52
    3.2.3 复式记账 ············ 53

Chapter 4 Accounting Cycle ········ 54

4.1 Journalizing and Posting ········ 54
    4.1.1 Journalizing ··········· 54
    4.1.2 Posting ················ 56
4.2 Preparing a Trial Balance ········ 61
4.3 Adjusting Accounts ··············· 62
    4.3.1 Accrued Revenues ········ 63
    4.3.2 Accrued Expenses ········ 63
    4.3.3 Unearned Revenues ······ 65
    4.3.4 Prepaid Expenses ········ 66
    4.3.5 Depreciation ············ 66
4.4 Adjusting Trial Balance ·········· 67
4.5 Preparing Financial Reporting ···· 68
4.6 The Worksheet ··················· 70
4.7 Closing Entries ················· 71
4.8 The Post-Closing Trial Balance ··· 72
Key Words and Expressions ········ 73
Exercises ························ 74

第4章 会计循环 ················· 76

4.1 日记账和过账 ··············· 76
    4.1.1 日记账 ·············· 76
    4.1.2 过账 ················ 78
4.2 试算平衡表 ················· 82
4.3 调整账户 ··················· 83
    4.3.1 应计收入 ············ 84
    4.3.2 应计费用 ············ 84
    4.3.3 预收收入 ············ 86
    4.3.4 预付费用 ············ 86
    4.3.5 折旧 ················ 87
4.4 调整后试算平衡表 ··········· 87
4.5 编制财务报表 ··············· 88
4.6 工作表 ····················· 90
4.7 结账分录 ··················· 91
4.8 结账后的试算平衡表 ········· 92

Chapter 5 Cash ···················· 93

5.1 Cash and Cash Equivalents ······ 93
    5.1.1 Definition ············· 93
    5.1.2 Cash on Hand ·········· 94
5.2 Internal Control over Cash ······ 95
    5.2.1 Separate from Record-keeping ···· 96
    5.2.2 Internal Control over Cash Receipts ················ 96

　　　　5.2.3　Internal Control over Cash
　　　　　　　Disbursements·················96
　5.3　The Petty Cash Funds ················97
　5.4　Bank Reconciliation ················98
　Key Words and Expressions················100
　Exercises··101

第5章　现金···103
　5.1　现金及现金等价物··························103
　　　　5.1.1　定义································103
　　　　5.1.2　库存现金························104
　5.2　现金的内部控制···························105
　　　　5.2.1　现金的保管应与记录分开···105
　　　　5.2.2　现金收入的内部控制········105
　　　　5.2.3　现金支出的内部控制········105
　5.3　备用金···106
　5.4　银行存款余额调节表··················106

Chapter 6　Receivables···························109
　6.1　Classification of Receivables ·········109
　　　　6.1.1　Accounts Receivable ·········109
　　　　6.1.2　Notes Receivable ·············109
　　　　6.1.3　Other Receivables ···········110
　6.2　Accounting for Accounts
　　　　Receivables································110
　6.3　Uncollectible Accounts··············110
　　　　6.3.1　Direct Write-off Method ·····111
　　　　6.3.2　Allowance Method·········111
　6.4　Notes Receivables······················112
　　　　6.4.1　Accounting for Notes
　　　　　　　Receivables·····················112
　　　　6.4.2　Discounting Notes Receivables ···113
　Key Words and Expressions················113
　Exercises··114

第6章　应收款项································116
　6.1　应收款的分类·····························116
　　　　6.1.1　应收账款························116
　　　　6.1.2　应收票据························116
　　　　6.1.3　其他应收款····················116
　6.2　应收账款的计量···························116

　6.3　坏账··117
　　　　6.3.1　直接转销法····················117
　　　　6.3.2　备抵法····························117
　6.4　应收票据···118
　　　　6.4.1　应收票据的会计处理······118
　　　　6.4.2　应收票据贴现··················119

Chapter 7　Inventory·····························120
　7.1　Measurement of Inventory upon Initial
　　　　Recognition·································120
　　　　7.1.1　Costs of purchase ···········121
　　　　7.1.2　Costs of Conversion ·······122
　　　　7.1.3　Other Costs ···················122
　　　　7.1.4　Lower of Cost and Net Realizable
　　　　　　　Value·······························122
　7.2　Inventory Systems·······················124
　　　　7.2.1　Perpetual Inventory System ·····124
　　　　7.2.2　Periodic Inventory System ·······124
　7.3　Inventory Measures ·····················124
　　　　7.3.1　Specific Identification ·······125
　　　　7.3.2　Average-cost Method·······125
　　　　7.3.3　First-in, First-out Method
　　　　　　　(FIFO) ····························125
　7.4　Inventory Estimation Method·········126
　　　　7.4.1　Gross Profit Method·········126
　　　　7.4.2　Retail Inventory Method ·····127
　Key Words and Expressions················127
　Exercises··129

第7章　存货···130
　7.1　存货的初始计量···························130
　　　　7.1.1　采购成本························130
　　　　7.1.2　加工成本························131
　　　　7.1.3　其他成本························131
　　　　7.1.4　成本与可变现净值孰低···131
　7.2　存货盘存制度······························133
　　　　7.2.1　永续盘存制····················133
　　　　7.2.2　定期盘存制····················133
　7.3　存货计价方法······························133
　　　　7.3.1　个别计价法····················133

  7.3.2 平均成本法 ·················· 134
  7.3.3 先进先出法 ·················· 134
 7.4 存货估价方法 ······················· 134
  7.4.1 毛利法 ························· 135
  7.4.2 零售价格法 ·················· 135

Chapter 8 Plant Assets ················ 136
 8.1 Acquisition of Plant Assets ·········· 136
  8.1.1 Acquisition by Cash ············· 137
  8.1.2 Acquisition through Non-cash Exchange ········ 137
  8.1.3 Acquisition through Self-construction ········ 138
 8.2 Accounting for Depreciation ········· 138
  8.2.1 Straight-line Method ············ 139
  8.2.2 Unit-of-production Method ······ 139
  8.2.3 Double-declining-balance Method ····· 140
  8.2.4 Sum-of-the-years'-digits Method ····· 140
 8.3 Plant Assets Disposals ·············· 141
 Key Words and Expressions ·············· 142
 Exercises ······························ 142

第 8 章 固定资产 ························· 145
 8.1 固定资产的取得 ···················· 145
  8.1.1 购入固定资产 ················ 146
  8.1.2 资产置换 ····················· 146
  8.1.3 自建 ·························· 146
 8.2 折旧 ······························ 147
  8.2.1 直线法 ························ 147
  8.2.2 产量法 ························ 147
  8.2.3 双倍余额递减法 ············· 148
  8.2.4 年数总和法 ·················· 148
 8.3 固定资产的处置 ···················· 148

Chapter 9 Intangible Assets and Natural Resource ·············· 150
 9.1 Intangible Assets ··················· 150
  9.1.1 Types of Intangible Assets ······ 151
  9.1.2 Initial Measurement of Intangible Assets ······· 152
  9.1.3 Amortization of Intangible Assets ······· 153
  9.1.4 Disposal of Intangible Assets ···· 155
 9.2 Natural Resource ··················· 155
 Key Words and Expressions ·············· 156
 Exercises ······························ 157

第 9 章 无形资产和自然资源 ··············· 159
 9.1 无形资产 ·························· 159
  9.1.1 无形资产的种类 ············· 159
  9.1.2 无形资产的初始计量 ········ 160
  9.1.3 无形资产的摊销 ············· 161
  9.1.4 无形资产的处置 ············· 163
 9.2 自然资源 ·························· 163

Chapter 10 Liability ······················ 164
 10.1 Current Liability ·················· 165
  10.1.1 Accounts Payable ············· 166
  10.1.2 Notes Payable ················ 167
  10.1.3 Unearned Revenue ············ 167
  10.1.4 Cash Dividends Payable ······ 168
  10.1.5 Current Maturities of Long-term Debt ·········· 168
  10.1.6 Wages Payable ················ 169
  10.1.7 Income Taxes Payable ········ 169
  10.1.8 Interest Payable ·············· 170
 10.2 Non-Current Liability ··············· 170
  10.2.1 Long-term Loans Payable ······ 171
  10.2.2 Long-term Accounts Payable ········ 172
  10.2.3 Bonds Payable ················ 172
  10.2.4 Deferred Income Taxes ········ 173
 10.3 Provision ·························· 173
  10.3.1 Definition ···················· 173
  10.3.2 Distinguishing from Other Liabilities ·········· 174
 10.4 Contingent Liabilities ··············· 174
  10.4.1 Definition ···················· 174
  10.4.2 Contingent Liabilities VS Provisions ··············· 175

Key Words and Expressions ········· 176
Exercises ································ 178

第 10 章　负债 ······················· 179
 10.1　流动负债 ························· 179
  10.1.1　应付账款 ················· 180
  10.1.2　应付票据 ················· 181
  10.1.3　预收收入 ················· 181
  10.1.4　应付股利 ················· 182
  10.1.5　一年内到期的长期负债 ······· 182
  10.1.6　应付职工薪酬 ············ 182
  10.1.7　应交所得税费用 ·········· 182
  10.1.8　应付利息 ················· 183
 10.2　非流动负债 ······················ 183
  10.2.1　长期借款 ················· 184
  10.2.2　长期应付款 ··············· 184
  10.2.3　应付债券 ················· 185
  10.2.4　递延所得税 ··············· 185
 10.3　预计负债 ························· 185
  10.3.1　定义 ····················· 185
  10.3.2　预计负债与其他负债的区别 ··· 186
 10.4　或有负债 ························· 186
  10.4.1　定义 ····················· 186
  10.4.2　或有负债 VS 预计负债 ······· 187

Chapter 11　Owners' Equity ············· 188
 11.1　Share ····························· 189
  11.1.1　Common Share ············ 190
  11.1.2　Preferred Share ············ 192
 11.2　Dividends and Retained Earnings ··· 194
  11.2.1　Dividends ················· 194
  11.2.2　Retained Earnings ·········· 195
 11.3　Treasury Stock ···················· 195
 Key Words and Expressions ··········· 198
 Exercises ···························· 199

第 11 章　所有者权益 ················· 201
 11.1　股票 ······························ 202
  11.1.1　普通股 ···················· 202
  11.1.2　优先股 ···················· 204

 11.2　股利和留存收益 ··················· 205
  11.2.1　股利 ······················ 205
  11.2.2　留存收益 ·················· 206
 11.3　库存股 ···························· 206

Chapter 12　Revenues ················· 209
 12.1　Accounting for Revenue ·········· 209
  12.1.1　Definition of Revenue ········ 209
  12.1.2　Recognition and Measurement of Revenue ················ 209
  12.1.3　Accounting for special transactions ················ 215
  12.1.4　Presentation in financial statements ················ 216
 12.2　Contract cost ····················· 216
 Key Words and Expressions ··········· 217
 Exercises ···························· 217

第 12 章　收入 ······················· 220
 12.1　收入的核算 ······················· 220
  12.1.1　收入的定义 ················· 220
  12.1.2　收入的确认和计量 ·········· 220
  12.1.3　特殊交易的会计处理 ········ 225
  12.1.4　财务报表的披露 ············ 226
 12.2　合同成本 ························· 226

Chapter 13　Financial Statement ········· 227
 13.1　Components of Financial Statements ······················ 227
 13.2　Statement of Profit or Loss and Other Comprehensive Income ············· 227
  13.2.1　The Objective of the Statement of Profit and Loss ·············· 228
  13.2.2　Statement of Profit and Loss ··· 228
  13.2.3　Statement of Comprehensive Income ···················· 230
 13.3　Statement of Changes in Equity ····· 231
  13.3.1　The Objective of the Statement of Changes in Equity ··············· 231

	13.3.2	Presentation of the Statement of Changes in Equity ············ 232
	13.3.3	The Link Within the Financial Statement ············ 233
13.4	Balance Sheet ·················· 234	
	13.4.1	The Objective of the Balance Sheet ············ 234
	13.4.2	Presentation of Balance Sheet ············ 234
13.5	Statement of Cash Flows ············ 235	
	13.5.1	The Definition of Cash and Cash Equivalents ············ 236
	13.5.2	Business Activities of Statement of Cash Flows ······ 236
	13.5.3	Preparation of Statement of Cash Flows ············ 237
13.6	Notes ············ 242	
Key Words and Expressions ············ 243		
Exercises ············ 243		

第 13 章 财务报表 ············ 247
  13.1 财务报表的构成 ············ 247
  13.2 损益表和其他综合收益表 ········ 247
    13.2.1 损益表的作用 ············ 247
    13.2.2 损益表的列报 ············ 248
    13.2.3 其他综合收益表 ············ 250
  13.3 权益变动表 ············ 251
    13.3.1 权益变动表的目的 ············ 251
    13.3.2 权益变动表的列报 ············ 251
    13.3.3 所有者权益变动表与财务报表之间的联系 ············ 252
  13.4 资产负债表 ············ 252
    13.4.1 资产负债表的作用 ············ 252
    13.4.2 资产负债表的列报 ············ 253
  13.5 现金流量表 ············ 254
    13.5.1 现金及现金等价物的概念 ······ 254
    13.5.2 现金流量表的商业活动 ········ 255
    13.5.3 现金流量表的编制 ············ 255
  13.6 附注 ············ 260

Chapter 14 Financial Statement Analysis ············ 261
  14.1 Purpose of Financial Statement Analysis ············ 261
  14.2 Basic Analytical Procedures ········ 262
    14.2.1 Horizontal Analysis ············ 262
    14.2.2 Vertical Analysis ············ 263
  14.3 Current Analysis ············ 265
    14.3.1 Working Capital ············ 265
    14.3.2 Current Ratio ············ 265
    14.3.3 Acid-Test Ratio ············ 266
  14.4 Solvency ············ 267
    14.4.1 Debt Ratio ············ 267
    14.4.2 Times Interest Earned (TIE) ···· 268
  14.5 Assets Efficiency ············ 268
    14.5.1 Accounts Receivable ············ 268
    14.5.2 Inventory Turnover ············ 269
    14.5.3 Total Assets Turnover ············ 271
  14.6 Profitability ············ 272
    14.6.1 Profit Margin ············ 272
    14.6.2 Return on Total Assets (ROA) ············ 272
    14.6.3 Return on Capital Employed (ROCE) ············ 273
    14.6.4 Return on Equity (Rate Earned on Total Assets) ······ 273
    14.6.5 Earnings Per Share on Common Stock ············ 274
    14.6.6 Price to Earnings Ratio ············ 275
  Key Words and Expressions ············ 275
  Exercises ············ 276

第 14 章 财务报表分析 ············ 280
  14.1 财务报表分析的目的 ············ 280
  14.2 基本分析程序 ············ 280
    14.2.1 水平分析 ············ 280
    14.2.2 垂直分析 ············ 282
  14.3 流动性分析 ············ 283
    14.3.1 营运资金 ············ 283
    14.3.2 流动比率 ············ 284

14.3.3	速动比率	284
14.4	偿债能力	285
14.4.1	资产负债率	285
14.4.2	利息保障倍数	285
14.5	资产效率	286
14.5.1	应收账款	286
14.5.2	存货	287
14.5.3	总资产周转率	288
14.6	盈利能力	289

14.6.1	利润率	289
14.6.2	资产回报率	290
14.6.3	资本使用回报率	290
14.6.4	股东权益收益率(净资产收益率)	291
14.6.5	每股收益	291
14.6.6	市盈率	292

参考文献 ……………………………………… 293

Chapter 1

An Introduction to Accounting

Accounting is a measurement system used to identify, record, and communicate relevant, reliable, and comparable information about an organization's business activities. Identifying business activities requires selecting transactions and events that are relevant to the organization. Recording business activities requires recording transactions and events in chronological order, measured in monetary units, and classified and summarized in a useful format. Communication of business activities requires the preparation of accounting reports, such as financial statements. It also needs to analyze and interpret such reports.

1.1 The Objective of Accounting

The ultimate goal of accounting is to provide useful financial information to users. Quality information can help users make more informed decisions.

These decisions involve buying and selling, providing or settling loans and other forms of credit, or holding equity and debt instruments. The decision of existing and potential investors to buy or sell stocks and debt instruments depends on the expected return on their investment in these instruments, such as dividends, principal and interest payments, or rising market prices. Similarly, existing and potential lenders and other creditors' decisions regarding the provision or settlement of loans and other forms of credit depend on their expected principal and interest payments or other returns.

1.2 Accounting Information

Accounting information is an important part of a company's daily decision-making process and is designed to meet users' needs. The users of accounting information can be divided into external users and internal users. This means that accounting can also be divided into two categories: financial accounting and management accounting. Financial accounting is an accounting area that aims to serve external users by providing financial statements, while management accounting is an accounting area that provides information to internal users to meet their decision-making needs.

1.2.1 The Users of Accounting Information

1. Internal users of accounting information

Internal users of accounting information are those who are directly involved in the management and operation of the organization, and they use this information to help improve the efficiency and effectiveness of the organization. Examples of internal users are managers, senior managers, directors, internal auditors, sales staff, budget officers and controllers. Business owners and senior managers need accounting information to assist them in the initial management planning process and make business-related decisions. Budget personnel needs accounting information to evaluate the performance and budget of an enterpris and judge its degree of achievement in achieving the set goals.

2. External users of accounting information

External users of accounting information are not directly involved in the operation of the organization. Examples of external users include shareholders, investors, potential investors, creditors, governments, external auditors, and the general public. Investors need accounting information to assist in making decisions or capital investment decisions. Customers need to understand the quality of the product and the company's ability to fulfill its obligations through accounting information. The government needs to check accounting information to see if the business complies with government regulations. The public needs to know whether the company has a sense of social responsibility through accounting information.

1.2.2 Financial Accounting and Management Accounting

With the different internal and external requirements for accounting information, accounting is divided into two subsystems: financial accounting and management accounting.

1. Financial accounting

Financial accounting, also known as external reporting accounting, refers to the economic management activities carried out through the comprehensive and systematic accounting and supervision of the capital movement completed by the enterprise, so as to provide economic information such as the financial status and profitability of the enterprise to investors, creditors and relevant government departments with economic interests. Financial accounting is an important basic work of modern enterprises. Through a series of accounting procedures, it provides useful information for decision-making, and actively participates in business management decisions to improve the economic efficiency of enterprises and serve the healthy and orderly development of the market economy.

2. Management accounting

Management accounting, also known as internal analysis report accounting, is a branch of corporate accounting that is separated from the traditional accounting system and parallel to financial accounting, focusing on making optimal decisions for enterprises, improving business management and improving economic benefits. To this end, management accounting needs to meet the demands of enterprise management departments in preparing plans, making decisions, controlling economic activities, recording and analyzing economic operations, "capturing" and reporting management information, and directly participating in the decision-making process. The goal of management accounting is to realize the optimal allocation of resources on the basis of reflecting the entrusted management of resources to resource providers, thereby improving the production efficiency, economic effects and economic benefits of enterprises.

Tax accounting is a natural extension of financial accounting and management accounting. The prerequisite for this natural extension is the increasing complexity of tax regulations. Tax accounting is a management activity that reflects and supervises the formation, declaration, and payment of tax payables of taxpayers, using the legal system of tax laws as the criterion and as the unit of measurement, and applying the principles and methods of financial accounting.

1.3 Profession Fields of Accounting

The profession of accounting is divided into three areas: public accounting, private accounting, and government and nonprofit accounting.

1. Public accounting

Public accounting is the field of accounting in which various accounting services are provided to the public in accordance with prescribed fees. Public accountants work mainly in public accounting firms. Most people engaged in public accounting are licensed certified public accountants. Almost all countries in the world have laws on certified public accountants. Britain is the birthplace of professional accountants worldwide. There are five groups of accountants recognized by the United Kingdom Department of Commerce: The Institute of Certified Public Accountants of England and Wales, the Institute of Certified Public Accountants of Scotland, the Institute of Certified Public Accountants of Ireland, the Institute of Certified Public Accountants, and the Association of Chartered Certified Accountants. In the United States, certification exams are prepared and administered by the American Institute of Certified Public Accountants (AICPA), and in China, the Chinese Institute of Certified Public Accountants (CICPA) is responsible for management. The basic services provided by public accountants are auditing and preparing tax reports, assisting in solving various tax issues and advising on business decisions.

The main responsibility of a certified public accountant is auditing, which refers to an activity performed by an accountant by analyzing the company's accounting books and investigating and collecting evidence related to each item in the financial report.

Management accountants help track product costs, prepare budgets and serve as a consultant to managers.

The field of taxation includes everything from the preparation of tax returns to consulting with clients about estate and gift planning.

2. Private accounting

Private accounting happens when an accountant provides services to a single organization. A private accountant maintains accounting records and provides management with the financial data needed for business decisions. Accountants serve all types of business organizations. A business is normally organized in one of three different forms: proprietorship, partnership, or corporation.

One individual owns a proprietorship. The popularity of this form is due to the ease and low cost of organizing. The primary disadvantage of proprietorship is that the financial resources available to the business are limited to the individual owners' resources. Small local businesses such as hardware stores, repair shops, laundries and restaurants are often organized as proprietorship.

As a business grows and requires more financial and managerial resources, it may become a partnership. A partnership is owned by two or more individuals. Like proprietorship, small local businesses such as automotive repair shops, music stores, beauty shops, and men's and women's clothing stores can be organized as partnerships.

Like proprietorship, a partnership can outgrow its ability to finance its operations. As a result, it can become a corporation. A corporation is organized under state or federal statutes as a separate legal entity. The ownership of a corporation is divided into shares of stocks. A corporation issues stocks to individuals or other businesses who then become owners, or stockholders, of the corporation. A primary advantage of the corporate form is the ability to obtain large amounts of resources by issuing stocks. For this reason, most companies that require large investments in equipment and facilities are organized as corporations.

3. Government and nonprofit accounting

Some accountants undertake work in government departments or nonprofit organizations. These two areas are commonly referred to as government accounting and nonprofit accounting. According to the International Accounting Standards Board, government and non-profit accounting refers to the accounting system which is used to confirm, measure, record and report the financial revenues and expenditure activities of the government and public institutions and the performance of their fiduciary duties.

1.4 Ethics of Accounting

The professional ethics of accounting refers to the ethics of accounting and ethics formed on the basis of common professional interests, hobbies, habits, and psychology of people engaged in accounting, such as professional responsibilities and professional disciplines in accounting. Ethics is the basis for developing professional ethical behavior. They also provide a framework for ethical practice.

Ethical behavior is the cornerstone of the accounting profession. Recently, we have seen many corporate scandals involving individuals who acted in an unethical, and oftentimes illegal way. Ethics are beliefs that distinguish right from wrong. They are accepted standards of good and bad behavior.

You have faced ethical situations in school and will face similar situations at work. We should be capable of identifying ethical concerns and analyzing our options, that is, what is the right or wrong thing to do. Making an ethical decision means we choose the best option available under the circumstances.

Whether the accounting work can provide objective and fair accounting information, and whether it can monitor the legality, compliance, and authenticity of the economic activities of the unit, depends largely on whether the accounting staff complies with the professional ethics of accounting in the accounting work. In accordance with the requirements of accounting laws and accounting standards, the professional ethics of accounting runs through all areas and the entire process of accounting. The emphasis is on adjusting the relationship between people and society in the field of accounting. Its realization depends on people's internal concepts, practices, traditions, and social education.

The basic ethical standards set out the obligations placed on all accountants, whether or not they are in practice. Five ethical standards are set out below:

1. Integrity

Accountants shall be "straightforward and honest in all professional and business relationships".

2. Objectivity

Accountants shall not allow bias, conflicts of interest or the undue influence of others to compromise their professional or business judgments.

3. Professional competence and due care

Accountants have a continuing duty "to maintain professional knowledge and skill at a level required to ensure that clients or employers receive competent professional services". Accountants shall "act diligently in accordance with applicable technical and professional standards when providing professional services".

4. Confidentiality

Accountants shall respect the confidentiality of information "acquired as a result of professional and business relationships", and shall not disclose any such information to third parties "without proper and specific authority or unless there is a legal or professional right or duty to disclose". Similarly, confidential information acquired as a result of professional and business relationships shall not be used for the personal advantage of accountants or third parties.

5. Professional behavior

Accountants shall comply with relevant laws and regulations and shall avoid any action that may discredit the profession.

Key Words and Expressions

conceptual framework	概念框架
accounting objective	会计目标
accounting	会计，会计学
accountant	会计人员，会计师
enterprise	企业
entity	主体，实体
decision making	决策
budget	预算
tax returns	纳税申报表

external user	外部信息使用者
internal user	内部信息使用者
certified public accountant (CPA)	注册会计师
auditing	审计
owner	所有者
executive senior manager	高级管理人员
creditor	债权人
stakeholder	利益相关者
financial accounting	财务会计
management accounting	管理会计
taxation accounting	税务会计
public accounting	公共会计
private accounting	私人会计(企业会计)
governmental accounting	政府会计
nonprofit organizations	非营利组织
professional ethics	职业道德
integrity	诚信，正直
objectivity	客观性
professional competence and due care	专业能力和应有的注意
confidentiality	机密性
professional behavior	职业行为

Exercises

Please select the best answer for the following questions or uncompleted sentences.

1. What is the objective of accounting? (   )
   A. To realize the optimal allocation of resources on the basis of reflecting the entrusted management of resources to resource providers.
   B. To provide useful information to users of financial accounting information that can help users make more informed decisions.
   C. To improve the production efficiency, economic effects and economic benefits of enterprises.
   D. To provide a company's financial status.
2. Which are the external users of accounting information? (   )
   A. Owners.
   B. Executives senior manager.
   C. Creditors.
   D. Managers.

3. Which is the accounting area that provides information to internal users to meet their decision-making needs? (   )

   A. Financial accounting.
   B. Management accounting.
   C. Taxation accounting.
   D. Cost accounting.

4. Which are the professional areas of accounting? (   )

   A. Public accounting.
   B. Private accounting.
   C. Government accounting.
   D. Non-profit accounting.

5. Which are the basic professional ethics that accountants should have? (   )

   A. Integrity.
   B. Objectivity.
   C. Professional competence and due care.
   D. Confidentiality.
   E. Professional behavior.

第1章　会计概述

会计是一种信息和度量系统，用于识别、记录和传达有关组织业务活动的相关、可靠和可比较的信息。识别业务活动需要选择与组织相关的交易和事件。记录业务活动需要按时间顺序记录交易和事件，以货币单位计量，并以有效的格式进行分类和汇总。交流业务活动需要准备会计报告，例如财务报表。它还需要分析和解释此类报告。

1.1　会计目标

会计的最终目标是向财务信息的使用者提供有用的信息。优质信息可以帮助使用者做出更明智的决定。

这些决定涉及买卖、提供或结算贷款和其他形式的信贷，以及持有股本和债务工具。现有和潜在投资者对买卖或出售股票和债务工具的决定取决于他们对这些工具的投资所期望的回报，例如股息、本金和利息支付或市场价格上涨。同样，现有的和潜在的贷方及其他债权人关于提供或结清贷款和其他形式的信贷的决定取决于他们期望的本金和利息支付或其他回报。

1.2　会计信息

会计信息是企业日常决策过程中的重要组成部分，旨在满足使用者对会计信息的需求。会计信息的使用者可分为外部使用者和内部使用者。这意味着会计也可分为财务会计和管理会计两大类。财务会计是通过向外部使用者提供财务报表来为其服务的会计领域，而管理会计则是为内部使用者提供信息，以此来满足其决策需求的会计领域。

1.2.1　会计信息的使用者

1. 会计信息的内部使用者

会计信息的内部使用者是直接参与组织管理和运营的人员，他们使用这些信息来帮助提高组织的效率和效力。内部使用者包括经理、高级管理人员、主管、内部审计师、销售人员、预算官员和控制人员。企业的所有者和高级管理人员需要会计信息以协助他们进行初始管理规划过程，做出与企业经营相关的决策。预算人员需要会计信息评估企业的绩效与预算，评判其在实现既定目标方面的完成程度。

2. 会计信息的外部使用者

会计信息的外部使用者并不直接参与组织的运行。外部使用者包括股东、投资者、潜在的投资者、债权人、政府、外部审计师和普通大众。投资者需要会计信息辅助做出决策或者资本投资决策。顾客需要通过会计信息了解产品的质量以及公司履行义务的能力。政府需要查阅会计信息了解该企业是否遵守政府法规。公众需要通过会计信息了解公司是否具有社会责任感等。

1.2.2 财务会计和管理会计

根据企业内部和外部对会计信息的要求不同,将会计划分为两个子系统:财务会计和管理会计。

1. 财务会计

财务会计,亦被称为对外报告会计,是指通过对企业已经完成的资金流动全面系统的核算与监督,以为外部与企业有经济利害关系的投资人、债权人和政府有关部门提供企业的财务状况与盈利能力等经济信息为主要目标而进行的经济管理活动。财务会计是现代企业的一项重要的基础性工作,通过一系列会计程序,提供决策有用的信息,并积极参与经营管理决策,提高企业经济效益,服务于市场经济健康有序的发展。

2. 管理会计

管理会计,又称对内分析报告会计,是从传统的会计系统中分离出来,与财务会计并列,着重为企业进行最优决策,改善经营管理,提高经济效益服务的一个企业会计分支。为此,管理会计需要针对企业管理部门编制计划、做出决策、控制经济活动的要求,记录和分析经济业务,"捕捉"和呈报管理信息,并直接参与决策控制过程。管理会计的目标是在向资源提供者反映资源受托管理情况的基础上,实现资源的优化配置,进而提高企业的生产效率、生产经济效果和经济效益。

税务会计是财务会计和管理会计的自然延伸,这种自然延伸的先决条件是税收法规的日益复杂化。税务会计是以税法法律制度为准绳,以货币为计量单位,运用财务会计的原理和方法,对纳税人应纳税款的形成、申报、缴纳进行反映和监督的一种管理活动。

1.3 会计的职业领域

会计的职业领域主要分为三个方面:公共会计、私人会计和政府与非营利组织会计。

1. 公共会计

公共会计属于会计领域,在该领域中,按照规定的收费标准为公众提供各种会计服务。公共会计师主要在公共会计师事务所工作。从事公共会计的大多数人都是有执照的注册会计师。世界上几乎所有国家都有关于注册会计师的法律。英国是全世界职业会计师的发源地。英国商务部承认的会计师团体有五个:英格兰与威尔士注册会计师协会、苏格兰注册会计师协会、爱尔兰注册会计师协会、公司注册会计师协会和特许公认会计师公会。在美国,认证考试由美国注册会计师协会(AICPA)进行准备和管理。在中国,中国注册会计师协会(CICPA)负责管理。公共会计师提供的基本服务是审计和准备税务报告,协助解决各种税务问题以及为业务决策提供建议。

注册会计师的主要职责是审计,是指会计师通过研究公司的会计账簿,并调查、收集与财务报告中每个项目相关的证据来进行分析的一项活动。

管理会计师帮助跟踪产品成本,准备预算并担任经理顾问。

征税领域包括准备关于客户房地产和赠与计划的咨询等所有方面的纳税申报表。

2. 私人会计

私人会计是指会计师向单个组织提供服务的情况。私人会计师维护会计记录并向管理层提供商业决策所需的财务数据。会计师为所有类型的企业组织服务。企业通常有三种组织形式：独资、合伙企业和公司。

一个人拥有所有权。这种形式的流行是由于组织的简便性和低成本。独资经营的主要缺点是企业可用的财务资源仅限于个人所有者资源。诸如五金店、维修店、洗衣店和餐馆之类的小型本地企业通常被组织为独资企业。

随着企业的发展并需要更多的财务和管理资源，它可能会成为合伙企业。合伙企业由两个或更多个人拥有。像独资经营一样，当地的小型企业，例如汽车修理厂、音乐商店、美容店以及男女服装店等也可以组织为合伙企业。

就像独资经营一样，合伙企业可以超越其为运营筹集资金的能力。结果，它可以成为一家公司。公司根据州或联邦法规组织为独立的法人实体。公司的所有权分为股份。公司向个人或其他企业发行股票，然后这些个人或其他企业成为公司的所有者或股东。公司形式的主要优势是能够通过发行股票获得大量资源。因此，大多数需要在设备和设施上进行大量投资的公司都是由公司组成的。

3. 政府和非营利组织会计

部分会计师在政府部门或者非营利组织工作。这两个领域通常合称为政府会计和非营利组织会计。根据国际会计准则委员会的规定，政府和非营利组织会计是指用于确认、计量、记录和报告政府和事业单位财务收支活动及其受托责任的履行情况的会计体系。

1.4 会计职业道德

会计职业道德是指行为道德规范和以从事会计工作的人员的共同职业兴趣、爱好、习惯和心理为基础而形成的道德规范，例如会计专业责任和职业纪律。道德是发展职业道德行为的基础，它们还提供了道德实践的框架。

道德行为是会计界的基石。最近，我们看到了许多公司丑闻，涉及以不道德且常常是非法行为行事的个人。道德是一种区分是非的信念。它们是良好和不良行为的公认标准。

您在学校里曾遇到过道德问题，在工作中也会遇到类似情况。我们应该能够识别道德问题并分析我们的选择，即做什么是对还是错。做出道德决策意味着我们在这种情况下做出最佳选择。

会计工作能否提供客观公正的会计信息，是否能够监测单位经济活动的合法性、合规性和真实性，在很大程度上取决于会计人员在会计工作中是否符合会计职业道德。按照会计法和会计准则的要求，会计职业道德贯穿于会计的各个领域和整个过程，重点是在会计领域调整人与社会之间的关系。它的实现取决于人们的内部观念、实践、传统和社会教育。

基本职业道德标准规定了所有会计师的义务，无论它们是否在实践中。五项基本职业道德标准如下：

1. 诚实正直

会计师应"在所有专业和业务关系中坦率而诚实"。

2. 客观性

会计师不得因偏见、利益冲突或他人的不当影响而损害其专业或业务判断。

3. 专业能力和应有的注意

会计师有持续的责任"将专业知识和技能维持在确保客户或雇主获得称职的专业服务所需的水平上"。会计师应"在提供专业服务时按照适用的技术和专业标准勤勉尽责"。

4. 机密性

会计师应尊重"由于专业和业务关系而获得的信息"的机密性，并且不得"在没有适当和特定权限的情况下或除非有合法或专业的披露权利或义务"向第三方披露任何此类信息。同样，由于专业和业务关系而获得的机密信息也不得用于会计师或第三方的个人利益。

5. 职业行为

会计师应遵守相关法律法规，并应避免做出任何可能使该专业声誉受损的行为。

Chapter 2

Financial Accounting Conceptual Framework

On March 29, 2018, the International Accounting Standards Board (IASB) issued the revised Conceptual Framework for Financial Reporting(referred to as the New Concept Framework). It is the largest comprehensive revision and improvement of the conceptual framework made by international accounting standards setting institutions. The IASB believes that the conceptual framework plays a key role in the development of accounting standards and the treatment of accounting practices. In particular, International Financial Reports Standards(IFRS)as a principle-oriented accounting standard requires a set of concepts system that can adapt to the development of the situation, with clear concepts and complete content. A logically consistent conceptual system provides theoretical support and conceptual basis. To this end, the Council has positioned the conceptual framework as a three-pronged role in the new conceptual framework:

The first is to help the Council develop IFRS based on a consistent concept.

The second is to help financial statement preparers adopt a consistent accounting policy.

The third is to help all stakeholders involved in financial reporting understand and interpret IFRS.

Based on this, the new conceptual framework mainly regulates the basic objectives of general financial reporting, what financial information is useful, how to define financial reporting elements and their financial accounting basic issues such as confirmation, measurement, presentation and disclosure requirements.

2.1 Definition of Conceptual Framework

The conceptual framework is composed of accounting objectives and a series of related basic concepts of accounting. It can guide the consistent accounting standards during the accounting period, and can explain the nature, function and limitations of financial accounting and financial statements.

The purpose of the conceptual framework system is to enable users of accounting information to increase their understanding and confidence in financial reporting. It will improve the comparability of financial statements between companies.

The conceptual framework of financing accounting consists of three main levels:

The first level is the accounting objective that points out the ultimate goal of accounting.

The second level consists of two elements, i.e., the qualitative characteristics that make the accounting information useful and the definition of the financial statement elements.

The third level is the concept of recognition and measurement of accounting applications, including basic assumptions, accounting principles and constraints that are affected by the current accounting reporting environment.

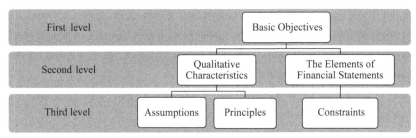

Figure 2-1　Conceptual Framework of Financing Accounting

2.2　Basic Objectives

The objective of general purpose financial reporting is to provide financial information about the reporting entity that is useful for existing and potential investors, lenders and other creditors to make decisions about providing resources to the entity.

2.3　Qualitative Characteristics

The conceptual framework states that qualitative characteristics are the attributes that make the information provided in financial statements useful to users. The two main groups of qualitative characteristics can be identified as follows:
- Fundamental qualitative characteristics include relevance and faithful representation.
- Enhancing qualitative characteristics include comparability, verifiability, timeliness and understandability.

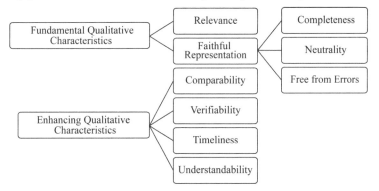

Figure 2-2　The Overview of Qualitative Characteristics

2.3.1 Fundamental Qualitative Characteristics

1. Relevance

The conceptual framework stipulates that relevant financial information should be able to make decisions made by users differently. In other words, information that has the ability to make users make different decisions is relevant. If the financial information has predictive value and confirmatory value, it indicates that the information has the ability to make the decision made by the user differently, indicating that the information is relevant. The new conceptual framework also emphasizes that materiality is based on the relevance and extent of the project at a particular level of the subject.

Information is material omitting it or misstating it could influence decisions that users make on the basis of financial information about a specific reporting entity.

2. Faithful representation

Faithful representation means that when a company publishes a formal financial report, it must fully and correctly reflect the company's financial status, operating results and cash flow information, as well as information on changes in equity, and must not intentionally ignore or conceal important financial data, resulting in misleading accounting information.

Three characteristics must be achieved:

(1) Completeness

A complete depiction includes all information necessary for users to understand the phenomenon being depicted, including all necessary descriptions and explanations.

(2) Neutrality

A neutral depiction is without bias in the selection or presentation of financial information.

(3) Free from error

Free from error indicates that there is no error or omission in the description of the phenomenon and no errors in the process by which the financial information was prepared.

However, being free from error does not mean perfectly accurate in all respects. In other words, it does not mean that no inaccuracies can arise, particularly where estimates have to be made.

Faithful representation of a transaction is only possible if it is accounted for according to its substance and economic reality. For example, a business may have entered into a leasing agreement for some equipment. However, the terms are such that the business is really buying the equipment. The equipment should be included in the statement of financial position and the leasing agreement should be treated as a financing arrangement. (IAS1)

2.3.2 Enhancing Qualitative Characteristics

1. Comparability

Information about a reporting entity is more useful if it can be compared with similar information about other entities and with similar information about the same entity for another period or another date.

Consistency, although related to comparability, is not the same. It refers to the use of the same methods for the same items, either from period to period within a reporting entity or in a single period across entities. Comparability is the goal, and consistency helps to achieve that goal.

2. Verifiability

Verifiability means that different knowledgeable and independent observers could reach consensus, although not necessarily complete agreement, that a particular depiction is a faithful representation. Verification can be direct or indirect.

3. Timeliness

Timeliness means having information available to decision makers which is capable of influencing their decisions. Generally, the older the information is, the less useful it is. (Conceptual framework)

4. Understandability

Classifying, characterizing and presenting information clearly and concisely makes it understandable. Understandability does not mean excluding information about inherently complex phenomena.

2.3.3 Cost constraints for financial information

Cost has always been a constraint on the information that financial reporting can provide. The cost of providing financial information includes the costs associated with collecting, processing, validating, disseminating, and storing it. When considering cost constraints, the information provided by the entity should be evaluated. Can the benefits of this information outweigh the cost of compiling and using it? When developing guidelines to consider cost constraints, the cost and benefit information for the new criteria should be obtained from a wide range of providers, users, auditors, academics and others, and this cost-benefit consideration but should not be limited to a single reporting body, but should be considered from the broad scope of the financial report.

2.4 The Elements of Financial Statements

A complete set of financial statements include: a statement of financial position as at the end of the period; a statement of profit or loss and other comprehensive income for the period; a statement of changes in equity for the period; a statement of cash flows for the period and notes which include significant accounting policies and other explanatory information.

2.4.1 Statement of Financial Position

It is simply a list of all the assets and liabilities owed by a business at a particular date. It is a snapshot of the financial position of the business. The particular monetary amounts are attributed to each of the assets and liabilities.

1. Assets

An asset is a resource controlled by the entity as a result of past events. Economic resources refer to the right to generate economic benefits.

2. Liabilities

A liability is a present obligation that results in the transfer of economic resources by companies due to past events. An obligation is a duty or responsibility that the entity has no practical ability to avoid.

3. Equity

Equity is the residual interest in the assets of the entity after deducting all its liabilities.

2.4.2 Statement of Profit or Loss and Other Comprehensive Income

A record of income generated and expenditure incurred over a given period. The statement shows whether the business has had more revenue than expenditure (a profit) or vice versa (loss). It is to provide information about the financial performance of entity.

1. Income

Income increases in economic benefits during the accounting period in the form of inflows or enhancements of assets or decreases of liabilities that result in increases in equity, other than those contributions from equity participants.

2. Expenses

Expenses are decreases in economic benefits during the accounting period in the form of outflows or depletions of assets or incurrences of liabilities that result in decreases in equity, other than those relating to distributions to equity participants.

2.5 Recognition and Derecognition

2.5.1 Recognition Criteria

Recognition is the process of capturing, for inclusion in the statement of financial position or the statement(s) of financial performance, an item that meets the definition of an element.

An entity recognizes an asset or a liability (and any related income, expenses or changes in equity) if such recognition provides users of financial statements with:

- Relevant information about the asset or the liability and any income, expenses or changes in equity.
- A faithful representation of the asset or the liability and any income, expenses or changes in equity; and.
- Information that results in benefits exceeding the cost of providing that information.

Under the premise of requiring the relevant project to meet the definition of the elements of the financial statements, the new concept framework proposes two criteria: one is that the relevant assets or liabilities and the corresponding changes in income, expenses or equity are relevant; the second is to faithfully reflect the relevant changes in assets or liabilities and corresponding gains, expenses or equity. The relevant items can only be confirmed if they meet the two criteria for confirmation.

Regarding the "relevance" criteria in the above-mentioned validation criteria, the new conceptual framework emphasizes that the standard may be affected by two factors:

- If it is uncertain whether an asset exists, or is separable from goodwill, or whether a liability exists.
- If an asset or a liability exists, but there is only a low probability that an inflow or outflow of economic benefits will result.

Regarding the "faithful representation" criteria in the above-mentioned validation criteria, the new conceptual framework emphasizes that the standard may be affected by three factors:

1. Measurement uncertainty

In many cases, there is measurement uncertainty, and sometimes even a high degree of measurement uncertainty does not prevent relevant accounting estimates from providing useful information. Of course, in limited circumstances, if there is a very high measurement uncertainty for all relevant measures available for the asset or liability, no measure can provide useful information about the asset or liability (including the corresponding benefit or expense). In this case, the relevant assets or liabilities do not meet the recognition criteria and should not be confirmed.

2. Accounting mismatch

In some cases, the recognition of an asset or liability should be considered whether the relevant asset or liability should also be recognized. If the relevant asset or liability is not recognized, it may result in inherent inconsistency in the recognition of assets and liabilities (accounting mismatch), unable to faithfully reflect the full of a transaction or matter.

3. The requirement for presentation and disclosure

Confirmation is only a part of providing useful information to users, considering the presentation and disclosure requirements of relevant information, and helping to better reflect the amount of assets, liabilities, equity, income or expenses, etc. Consideration of the conditions should be combined with the relevant presentation and disclosure requirements.

2.5.2 Derecognition

Derecognition is the removal of all or part of a previously recognized asset or liability from an entity's statement of financial position. For an asset, this normally occurs when the entity loses control of all or part of the previously recognized asset; for a liability, this normally occurs when the entity no longer has a present obligation for all or part of the previously recognized liability.

The new concept framework stipulates the specific objectives of the derecognition accounting treatment, that is, the derecognition accounting treatment should aim to accurately reflect the two aspects of information: one is to terminate the confirmation of the assets or liabilities retained by the entity after the transaction has occurred; the second is to terminate the confirmation transaction. All these lead to changes in the principal assets or liabilities.

Based on the above specific objectives, the new concept framework specifies the specific treatment principles for termination confirmation based on different trading scenarios.

If an entity transfers a previously recognized asset or liability to another party that is acting as its agent, then the asset is still controlled by the transferor (the liability is still an obligation of the transferor) and derecognition would not faithfully represent the transferor's assets, liabilities, income and expenses.

If an entity retains exposure to positive or negative variations in the amount of economic benefits produced by an economic resource, this may indicate that the entity retains control of that economic resource, in which case derecognition is not appropriate.

2.6 Measurement Concepts

The accounting profession continues to use concepts such as basic assumptions and principles as guidelines, which serve as both a guideline and a reasonable response to controversial financial reporting issues.

2.6.1 Accounting Assumptions

There are four basic assumptions in financial accounting structure:

1. Accounting entity

One of the main assumptions of accounting is that economic activity can be identified with specific accountability units. In other words, the activities of a business enterprise can be independent and different from its owner and any other business unit. If there is no meaningful way to separate all economic events that occur, then there is no accounting basis.

According to this concept, for accounting purposes, all types of business problems are treated as a single entity, separate and distinct from their owners and other concerns. Most economic activities can be directly or indirectly attributed to a business enterprise called an economic entity. Financial accounting focuses on the economic activity of each entity, regardless of its size, and involves recording and reporting its transactions and events. A transaction involves transferring something of value between the entity and the other party. In some cases, the financial records of relevant but independent legal entities may be combined to more realistically report the resources, obligations and operating performance of the entire economic entity.

Because the entity assumes that each organization is distinguished from its owner, the independent entity prepares its financial records and reports. Therefore, all accounting records and reports will be treated as an independent entity.

2. Going concern

The entity is normally viewed as a going concern, that is, as continuing operation for the foreseeable future. It assumes that the entity has neither the intention nor the necessity of liquidation or of curtailing materially the scale of its operations. Experience has shown that although the company has a large number of data that have been suspended due to failure, it still maintains a relatively high continuance rate. Although the accountants do not believe that the company will last forever, they expect the company to continue to meet its goals and obligations.

The enterprise's preparation of the balance sheet is also based on such a going concern assumption. Therefore, in order to maintain the business, the assets of the enterprise are used for the operation of the enterprise rather than for sale, so the market price of the assets has nothing to do with it, and need not be listed; and if not for sale, the market price lacks the basis of objective existence and violates the principle of objectivity.

3. Period of time

The most accurate method of the results of a company's economic activities may be at the time of final liquidation of the company. However, companies, governments, investors, and various users of accounting information cannot wait until the end. Accountants should provide financial information on a regular basis so that users can make various decisions.

The period-of-time assumptions implies that the enterprise's economic activities can be divided into several equidistant periods, and the periods can vary, but the most common periods are monthly, quarterly, and yearly. In accordance with the period-of-time assumptions, a company prepares financial statements at the end of a year and includes them in its annual report.

4. Monetary unit

Accounting is based on the assumption that money is a common measure of econometric activity, and monetary units provide an appropriate basis for accounting measurement and analysis. It means that the monetary unit is the most effective means of expression: It reflects the changes in the exchange of capital and goods and the provision of labor services among various interest groups of the enterprise. Monetary measurement is relevant, concise, universally available, understandable, and useful. The use of this hypothesis relies on more basic quantitative data that is useful for communicating economic information and making rational economic decisions.

2.6.2 Principles of Accounting

Based on the basic assumptions of accounting, the accounting profession has developed principles that explain how economic events should be recorded and reported.

1. Accrual basis

Entities should prepare their financial statements on the basis that transactions are recorded in them, not as the cash is paid or received, but as the revenues or expenses are earned or incurred in the accounting period to which they relate.

According to the accrual's assumption, profit computing, revenue earned must be matched against the expenditure incurred in earning it. This is also known as the matching convention.

2. Matching principle

The matching principle requires that the revenue and its costs and expenses should be matched with each other. The expenses are reported in the same accounting period as the revenues generated by the expenses. The matching of expenses with revenues will sometimes require a company to predict future events.

3. Cost principle

Both the preparer and the user of the financial statements have always considered the historical cost to be the most useful basis for accounting measurement and reporting. According to the cost principle, all business transactions will be recorded at cost or actual payment and reported on the financial statements at cost. These costs will remain in the accounting records until the asset is sold or consumed. Costs provide a reliable measure of the value of an asset at the time of acquisition, eliminating the possibility of underestimation or overestimation of an undervalued asset.

4. Revenue recognition principle

The revenue recognition principle requires that all revenue be measured to the accounting period in which it occurs, rather than the accounting period actually received. The following three points are essential for understanding the revenue recognition principle:
- Revenue-related asset inflows are not necessarily in the form of cash.
- Revenue is recorded in the accounting period in which goods and services are provided or when the ownership of the merchandise is transferred.
- The amount of income is equal to the cash received plus the cash equivalent of other assets received.

5. Full disclosure principle

The full disclosure principle requires the company to fully and completely disclose all the relevant information and data related to its financial position, operating results, cash flow, etc. in the financial statements (including its notes). In other words, accountants should fully consider the information in the economic business of the enterprise that can affect the decision-making judgment of users of accounting information, and should not conceal important information.

2.6.3 Measurement Bases

1. Historical cost

The property acquired by the enterprise should be accounted for at the actual cost incurred at the time of purchase or construction and used as the basis for the cost of the apportionment and conversion costs. Under the historical cost measurement, the assets are measured according to the amount of cash or cash equivalents paid at the time of purchase, or the fair value of the consideration paid at the time of purchase of the assets; the liabilities are actually received according to the amount of money or assets due to the present obligations, or the amount of the contract that bears the present obligation, or the amount of cash or cash equivalents that are expected to be paid for the repayment of liabilities in daily activities. When the price changes, the book value should not be adjusted unless otherwise stipulated by the state. Valuation based on actual purchase cost can prevent randomness and make accounting information true and reliable, easy to understand and compare.

With regard to the historical cost measurement basis, the new conceptual framework defines the following:

First, the historical cost should provide at least the price information of the transaction related to the measured items, but in principle does not reflect the value change information.

Second, the use of historical cost measurement does not mean that the historical cost of the relevant assets and liabilities is constant, and sometimes it needs to be updated as time goes by and the situation changes. For example, the loss of assets needs to be depreciated or amortized, and the assets need to be reduced. The increase in the value of the economic resources required to perform the liability obligation results in a deficit in the performance of the liabilities, which in turn requires an increase in the historical cost of the liabilities.

Third, the use of amortized cost measurement for related financial assets or financial liabilities is the specific application of historical cost measurement basis in the accounting field of financial assets and financial liabilities. Amortized cost belongs to the historical cost measurement basis.

2. Current value (Present value)

The current value is the value of converting the future cash flow into the benchmark time to reflect the intrinsic value of the investment. The process of using the discount rate to convert future cash flows into present value is called "discounting". The discount rate is the ratio used to convert future cash flows into present value. The discount rate is the necessary or minimum rate of return required by the investor.

With regard to the current value measurement basis, the new conceptual framework defines the following:

First, the current value should provide information on the status update of the measurement date, that is, the current value of the relevant assets or liabilities should reflect the changes in cash flows included in the current value from the previous measurement date and other factors.

Second, the current value measurement basis includes fair value, value in use (for assets) and performance value (for liabilities) and current costs, where fair value reflects the amount, time and uncertainty of market participants' future cash flows on assets or liabilities. The current value of the amount, time and uncertainty of the future cash flow of the asset or liability is reflected in the value of the use and the value of the performance; the current cost reflects the current need to pay for the same asset or the same liability should receive the amount.

3. Fair value

A price determined by a buyer and seller who is familiar with the market conditions under conditions of fair transaction and voluntary, or the transaction price at which an asset can be sold or a liability can be paid off by the unrelated parties under the conditions of fair transaction. Under fair value measurement, assets and liabilities are measured at the amount of voluntary exchange of assets or debt settlement by both parties to the transaction in an arm's length transaction. In practice, the asset assessment agency usually evaluates the net assets of the acquired company.

In one of the following three situations, the fair value of the assets exchanged is considered to be reliably measurable:

(1) There is an active market in which assets are exchanged for assets, and fair value is determined based

on the market price.

(2) There is no active market for the exchange of assets, but there are active markets for similar assets, and the fair value is determined based on the market price of similar assets.

(3) There is no comparable market for similar assets, and valuation techniques are used to determine fair value. When the valuation method is used to determine the fair value, the variation range of the fair value estimate determined by the valuation technique is required to be small, or the probability of determining the fair value estimate can be reasonable within the range of the fair value estimate.

4. Net realizable value

Net realizable value refers to the net value of the estimated selling price minus the further processing cost and estimated selling expenses and related taxes and fees in daily activities. Under the net realizable value measurement, the amount of cash or cash equivalents that an asset can receive in accordance with its normal external sales are deducted from the asset's estimated cost, estimated selling expense and related taxes.

2.7 Presentation and Disclosure

The new concept framework has increased the relevant content of financial statement presentation and disclosure, and has clearly defined the objectives, principles and classification, offset, and summary of financial statement presentation and disclosure, especially for profit and loss statements. The other comprehensive income and its reversal and principles of presentation and disclosure have been clearly defined and highly targeted. Its core content mainly includes:

1. The statement of profit or loss

The statement of profit or loss as a basic statement reflects the financial performance of the entity during the reporting period.

2. Profit or loss

It can be a separate part of a financial performance statement (for example, profit and loss is a component of the comprehensive income statement), or it can be the content of a separate statement (such as a separate income statement).

3. Profit or loss and other comprehensive income

It is clear that all income or expense items should in principle be included in the income statement. In exceptional circumstances, the Board may decide to exclude certain income or expense items from the income statement and include other comprehensive income, thereby more accurately reflecting the subject's financial performance, providing users with more relevant information. However, all income and expense items included in other comprehensive income can be transferred back to profit or loss in principle in the future, as long as the reversal can provide more relevant information or more accurately reflect the financial performance of the entity, if it is to be reversed. If it is not possible to provide more relevant information or to reflect the financial performance of the entity more faithfully, the Board may decide that the income and expense items included in other comprehensive income will not be reversed in the future.

2.8 Concepts of Capital and Capital Maintenance

2.8.1 Capital

Most companies use the financial concept of capital when preparing financial statements. According to the financial concept of capital, capital is like the purchasing power of invested money or input, which is synonymous with the net assets or equity of the enterprise. According to the physical concept of capital, capital is like the operational capability, and is regarded as a company based on daily output or production capacity.

Companies should choose the appropriate capital concept based on the needs of users of financial statements. Therefore, if the users of the financial statements are mainly concerned with preserving the nominal investment capital or the purchasing power of the invested capital, the financial concept of capital should be adopted. However, if the user is mainly concerned with the operational capacity of the enterprise, the physical concept of capital should be adopted. The concept chosen by the firm points out the goals to be achieved in determining the profit, although there may be some measurement difficulties in effectively applying the concept.

2.8.2 Capital Maintenance and the Determination of Profits

1. Capital maintenance

Capital maintenance can be divided into two concepts: financial capital maintenance and physical capital maintenance.

(1) Financial capital maintenance

When the financial (or monetary) amount of the net assets at the end of the period exceeds the financial (or monetary) amount of the net assets at the beginning of the period after deducting the allocation to the owner and the investment of the owner during the period, the profit is earned. Financial capital preservation can be measured either in nominal currency units or in constant purchasing power units.

(2) Physical capital maintenance

Profit is only earned when the physical production capacity (or operation capacity) at the end of the period exceeds the physical production capacity at the beginning of the period after deducting the allocation to the owner and the input from the owner during this period.

The concept of physical capital maintenance requires the use of the current cost measurement basis. However, the concept of financial capital maintenance does not require the use of a specific measurement basis. Accordingly, the choice of the measurement basis depends on the type of financial capital the company is trying to maintain.

2. The impact of capital maintenance on profits

The concept of capital maintenance relates to how companies define the capital they are trying to maintain. Since it provides a reference point for measuring profits, a link is established between the concept of capital and the concept of profit. This is a prerequisite for distinguishing between corporate capital remuneration and capital recovery. Only when the inflow of assets exceeds the amount required to maintain capital can it be regarded as profit and capital remuneration. Therefore, the profit is the remaining amount retained after deducting the fee from the income. If the fee exceeds the income, the remaining amount is a net loss.

According to the concept of financial capital maintenance, when capital is defined in nominal currency units, the profit represents an increase in nominal currency capital during the period. The increase in the price of assets held during this period, usually called holding profits, is conceptually a profit. So, this profit can only be confirmed when the exchange business occurs and the assets are disposed of. When a constant purchasing power unit defines the concept of financial capital maintenance, the profit represents an increase in the purchasing power during this period. Therefore, in the increase in asset prices, only the portion that exceeds the general price level can be regarded as the rest of the profit as capital. The maintenance adjustment is handled as part of the equity.

However, when capital is defined by physical production capacity, profit represents an increase in physical capital during this period. All price changes affecting corporate assets and liabilities are considered to be changes in the measurement of physical production capacity of the enterprise. Therefore, they are treated as capital maintenance adjustments as part of the equity rather than as profits.

The choice of the measurement basis and the concept of capital maintenance will determine the use of the accounting model in the preparation of the financial statements. Different accounting models show varying degrees of relevance and reliability, and as in other respects, management must balance trade-offs between relevance and reliability.

Key Words and Expressions

conceptual framework	概念框架
accounting objective	会计目标
qualitative characteristics	质量特征
relevance	相关性
materiality	重要性
realization principle	实现原则
completeness	完整性
neutrality	中立性
free from error	无差错
substance over form	实质重于形式
comparability	可比性
consistency	一致性

Chapter 2 Financial Accounting Conceptual Framework

verifiability	可验证性
timeliness	及时性
understandability	可理解性
full disclosure	充分反映
constraint	约束
conservatism	稳健性
accounting elements	会计要素
measurement and recognition	确认与计量
accounting entity	会计主体
money measurement	货币计量
going concern	持续经营
accruals basis	权责发生制
statement of financial position	财务状况表
statement of changes in equity	权益变动表
statement of profit or loss	利润表
statement of cash flows	现金流量表
historical cost	历史成本
current value	现值
fair value	公允价值
net realization value	可变现净值
capital	资本
capital maintenance	资本保全
financial capital maintenance	财务资本保全
physical capital maintenance	实物资本保全

Exercises

Please select the best answer for the following questions or uncompleted sentences.

1. How does the conceptual framework define an asset? (   )

   A. A present economic resource, which is a right that has the potential to produce economic benefits, owned by an entity as a result of past events.

   B. A present economic resource over which an entity has legal rights and from which the economic resource is a right that has the potential to produce economic benefits.

   C. A present economic resource controlled by an entity as a result of past events and from which the economic resource is a right that has the potential to produce economic benefits.

   D. A present economic resource to which an entity has a future commitment as a result of the past.

2. Which of the following would be classified as a liability? (   )

   A. Vince's business manufactures a product under license. In twelve months, time the license expires and Vince will have to pay $50,000 for it to be renewed.

   B. Nick purchased an investment nine months ago for $120,000. The market for these investments has now fallen and Nick's investment is valued at $90,000.

   C. Carter has estimated the tax charge on its profits for the year just ended as $165,000.

   D. Tom is planning to invest in new machinery which has been quoted at a price of $570,000.

3. What are appropriate qualitative characteristics of financial information given by the IASB's conceptual framework for Financial Reporting? (   )

   A. Relevance, faithful representation, comparability, verifiability, timeliness and understandability

   B. Accuracy, faithful representation, comparability, verifiability, timeliness and understandability

   C. Relevance, faithful representation, consistency, verifiability, timeliness and understandability

   D. Relevance, comparability, consistency, verifiability, timeliness and understandability

4. Reliability means that (   ).

   A. the information is a faithful representation of what it purports to be

   B. a company uses the same accounting principles from year to year

   C. accounting information can be compared with that of other enterprises in the industry

   D. the information has feedback value

5. The conceptual framework identifies an underlying assumption in preparing financial statements. This is (   ).

   A. going concern

   B. materiality

   C. substance over form

   D. accruals

6. The conceptual framework identifies four enhancing qualitative characteristics of financial information. Which one of the following is NOT an enhancing qualitative characteristic? (   )

   A. Verifiability.

   B. Timeliness.

   C. Consistency.

   D. Understandability.

7. Under current value accounting, what is the definition of value in using measurement method? (   )

   A. Costs incurred at the time of acquisition.

   B. Present value of future cash flows, fewer costs of disposal.

   C. Open market value of the asset.

   D. Open market value of the asset, less than the present value of the future cash outflows.

8. All of the following are objectives of financial reporting except (   ).

   A. To provide information that is helpful in making investment decisions

   B. To provide information that is helpful in assessing future cash flows

   C. To provide information that identifies economic resources

   D. To maximize social welfare

Chapter 2 Financial Accounting Conceptual Framework

9. The basic principles of accounting include each of the following except the (   ).
   A. cost principle
   B. full disclosure principle
   C. going concern principle
   D. matching principle

第2章 财务会计概念框架

2018年3月29日,国际会计准则理事会(IASB)发布了修订后的财务报告概念框架(简称新概念框架)。这是国际会计准则制定机构对概念框架最大的一次全面修订和完善。国际会计准则理事会认为,概念框架在会计准则制定和会计实务处理中发挥着关键作用。特别是,《国际财务报告准则》(IFRS)作为原则导向的会计准则,需要一套能够适应形势发展、概念清晰、内容完整的概念体系,以此来提供理论支持和概念基础。因而,理事会认为概念框架在新概念框架中有以下三个作用:

第一,帮助理事会在一致的概念基础上制定《国际财务报告准则》。

第二,帮助财务报表编制者采用一致的会计政策。

第三,帮助参与财务报告的所有利益相关者理解和解释《国际财务报告准则》。

在此基础上,新概念框架主要规范了一般财务报告的基本目标,财务信息的有用性,如何定义财务报告要素及其财务会计基本问题,如确认、计量、列报和披露要求。

2.1 概念框架的定义

概念框架由会计目标和一系列相关的会计基本概念组成。它可以指导会计期间的一致会计准则,并可以解释财务会计和财务报表的性质、功能和局限性。

概念框架系统的目的是使会计信息的用户能够增加他们对财务报告的理解和信心。它将提高公司之间财务报表的可比性。

财务会计的概念框架包括三个主要层次:

第一个层次是目标,指出了会计的基本目标。

第二个层次包括两个要素,即会计信息有用的质量特征和财务报表要素。

第三个层次是会计应用的识别和计量的概念,包括受当前会计报告环境影响的基本假设、会计原则和限制。

图2-1 财务会计概念框架

2.2 基本目标

通用财务报告的目的是提供有关报告实体的财务信息,这对于现有和潜在投资者、贷款人和其他债权人在决定向实体提供资源方面非常有用。

2.3 会计信息质量特征

概念框架指出,会计信息质量特征是使财务报表中提供的信息对用户有用的属性。两个主要的质量特征组如下:
- 基本质量特征包括相关性和充分反映。
- 增强质量特征包括可比性、可验证性、及时性和可理解性。

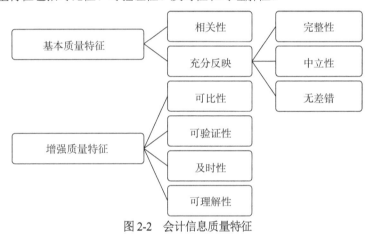

图 2-2 会计信息质量特征

2.3.1 基本质量特征

1. 相关性

概念框架规定,相关的财务信息应该能够使使用者做出不同的决策。换句话说,能够使使用者做出不同决策的信息是相关的。如果财务信息具有预测价值和确认价值,则表明该信息具有使信息使用者做出不同决策的能力,表明该信息是相关的。新的概念框架还强调,重要性是基于项目在特定主题层面的相关性和范围。

如果省略信息或信息错误可能会影响用户根据特定报告实体的财务信息做出的决策,则说明信息是重要的。

2. 充分反映

充分反映是指企业在发布正式的财务报告时,必须全面正确地反映企业的财务状况、经营成果和现金流量信息,以及权益变动的信息,不得有意忽略或者隐瞒重要的财务数据,以免使会计信息的使用者产生误解。

充分反映是指以下三个特征：

(1) 完整性

完整的描述包括用户理解所描述现象必需的所有信息，包括所有必要的描述和解释。

(2) 中立性

中立性描述是指在选择或呈现财务信息时没有偏见。

(3) 无差错

无差错表示对该现象的描述中没有错误或遗漏，并且在准备财务信息的过程中没有错误。

但是，没有错误并不意味着在所有方面都完全准确。换句话说，这并不意味着不会出现任何不准确之处，尤其是在必须进行估算时。

只有在根据其实质和经济现实对其进行核算时，才可能对交易进行正确的陈述。例如，企业可能已经签订了某些设备的租赁协议。但是，这些条款其实是企业购买设备的条款。设备应包括在财务状况表中，租赁协议应视为融资安排(IAS1)。

2.3.2 增强质量特征

1. 可比性

如果可以将报告实体的信息与其他实体的类似信息进行比较，并与另一个期间或另一个日期的同一实体的类似信息进行比较，则该信息更有用。

一致性虽然与可比性相关，但并不相同。一致性是指对报告实体内的一个时期或一个时期内的相同项目使用相同的方法。可比性是目标，一致性则有助于实现该目标。

2. 可验证性

可验证性意味着不同的知识渊博的和独立的观察者可以达成共识，尽管不一定完全一致。验证可以是直接的，也可以是间接的。

3. 及时性

及时性意味着为决策者提供可以影响其决策的信息。通常，信息越旧，就越不实用。

4. 可理解性

指清晰简明地分类、表征和呈现信息使其易于理解。可理解性并不意味着排除固有的复杂信息。

2.3.3 财务信息的成本约束

成本一直是提供财务报告信息的必选。提供财务信息的成本包括与收集、处理、验证、传播和存储财务信息相关的成本。在考虑成本限制时，应评估实体提供的具体信息，这些信息的好处是否可以超过编译和使用此信息的成本。在制定考虑成本限制的指导原则时，新标准的成本和收益信息应该从广泛的提供者、用户、审核员、学者和其他人那里获得，这种成本效益的考虑因素不应局限于单一报告机构，应从广泛的财务报告的范围考虑。

2.4 财务报表要素

一套完整的财务报表包括：资产负债、利润表、所有者权益变动表及现金流量表和附注，附注又包括重要的会计政策和其他解释性信息。

2.4.1 资产负债表

资产负债表列出了所有资产以及企业在特定日期所欠的所有负债。它反映了一个企业的财务状况，具体的货币数额归属于每项资产和负债。

1. 资产
资产是指由于过去事项所导致的、由主体控制的现时经济资源。经济资源是指产生经济利益的权利。

2. 负债
负债是由于过去事项所导致的、会导致企业转移经济资源的现时义务。义务是指主体没有实际能力可予避免的一项职责或者责任。

3. 权益
权益是指主体资产扣除主体全部负债以后的剩余利益。

2.4.2 利润表

指在特定时期内产生的收入和支出的记录。该表格显示了企业是否有比支出(利润)更多的收入还是反之亦然(亏损)，提供了有关实体的财务业绩的信息。

1. 收入
收入是指在会计期间经济利益的增加，其表现形式是资产的流入或增加及负债的减少，这些增加导致资产增加，但不包括来自权益持有者的贡献。

2. 费用
费用是指在会计期间经济利益的减少，其表现形式是资产的流出或耗竭及劳动力的减少导致权益的下降，但与分配给权益参与者相关的费用除外。

2.5 确认和终止确认

2.5.1 确认标准

确认是将符合要素定义的项目纳入到财务状况表或财务执行情况表中的过程。

实体确认一项资产或负债(以及任何相关的收入、费用或权益变动)，需要该确认为财务报表的使用者提供：

- 有关资产或负债以及任何收入、支出或权益变动的有关信息。
- 资产或负债以及任何收入、支出或权益变动的真实表示。
- 产生的收益超过提供该信息的成本的信息。

在要求相关项目符合财务报表要素定义的前提下，新概念框架提出了两个标准：一是相关资产或负债与相应的收入、支出或权益变化相关；二是如实反映资产或负债的有关变动以及相应的收益、费用或权益。只有满足两个确认标准的相关项目才能被确认。

关于上述验证标准中的"相关性"标准，新概念框架强调该标准可能受到两个因素的影响：

- 不确定资产是否存在，是否可以与商誉分离，或负债是否存在。
- 如果存在资产或负债，但经济利益流入或流出的可能性很小。

关于上述验证标准中的"如实反映"标准，新概念框架强调该标准可能受到三个因素的影响：

1. 计量不确定

在许多情况下，存在计量不确定性，有时甚至高度的计量不确定性也不会阻止相关会计估计提供有用的信息。当然，在有限的情况下，如果可用于资产或负债的所有相关计量存在高度的不确定性，并且没有任何计量可提供有关资产或负债的有用信息(包括相应的收益或费用)。在这种情况下，相关资产或负债不符合确认条件，因此不予确认。

2. 会计不匹配

在某些情况下，无论是否还应确认相关资产或负债，都应考虑资产或负债的确认。如果未确认相关资产或负债，则可能导致资产和负债的确认存在内在矛盾(会计错配)，无法准确地反映交易或事项的全部内容。

3. 列报和披露的要求

确认仅是向用户提供部门有用信息，需要考虑相关信息的列报和披露要求，有助于更好地反映资产、负债、权益、收入或支出等金额。对条件的考虑应与相关列报和披露要求相结合。

2.5.2 终止确认

终止确认是指从实体的财务状况表中删除先前确认的全部或部分资产或负债。对于资产，通常会在实体失去对全部或部分先前确认资产的控制权时发生；对于负债，通常在实体不再承担全部或部分先前确认的负债的现时义务时发生。

新概念框架规定了终止确认会计处理的特定目标，即终止确认会计处理应旨在准确反映信息的两个方面：一是终止交易后主体对所保留的资产或负债的确认已经发生了；二是终止确认交易，导致主要资产或负债发生变化。

基于上述特定目标，新概念框架为基于不同交易场景的终止确认指定了特定的处理原则。

如果某实体将先前确认的资产或负债转移给充当其代理人的另一方，则该资产仍受转让方控制(该负债仍然是转让方的义务)，终止确认将不会准确反映转让方的资产、负债、收入和支出。

如果实体继续承受某项经济资源产生的经济利益的正变动或负变动的风险，则可能表明该实体保留了对经济资源的控制，在这种情况下，终止确认就不合适。

2.6 计量概念

会计行业使用基本假设和原则等概念作为指导方针，既作为指导，也是对有争议的财务报告问题进行合理回应。

2.6.1 会计假设

财务会计结构有四个基本假设：

1. 会计实体

会计的主要假设之一是可以用特定的单位来确定经济活动。换句话说，企业的活动可以是独立的，与其所有者和任何其他业务单位不同。如果没有有意义的方法将所有发生的经济事件分开，那么就没有会计基础。

根据这一概念，出于会计目的，所有类型的业务问题都被视为单个实体，与其所有者和其他关注点分开且不同。大多数经济活动可以直接或间接归因于称为经济实体的企业。财务会计侧重于每个实体的经济活动，无论其规模如何，均涉及记录和报告其交易和事件。交易涉及在实体和另一方之间转移有价值的东西。在某些情况下，相关但独立的法律实体的财务记录可以合并，以更真实地报告整个经济实体的资源、义务和经营业绩。

由于该实体假定每个组织与其所有者不同，因此独立主体编制自己的财务记录和报告。因此，所有会计记录和报告将被视为一个独立的实体。

2. 持续经营

该实体通常被视为持续经营，即在可预见的未来继续经营。它假定该实体既不计划清算也没有清算的必要，或实质性地削减其业务规模。经验表明，虽然公司有大量数据因故障而被暂停，但仍保持较高的持续率。虽然会计师不相信公司会永远存在下去，但他们希望公司继续履行其目标和义务。

企业资产负债表的编制也是基于这种持续经营假设。为了维持企业的业务，企业的资产用于企业的经营而非销售，因此资产的市场价格与其无关，不需要上市；如果不出售，市场价格缺乏客观存在的基础，违反了客观性原则。

3. 会计分期

衡量公司经济活动结果的最准确方法可能是在公司最终清算时。但是，对公司、政府、投资者和各种会计信息，用户不能等到最后。会计师应定期提供财务信息，以便用户做出各种决策。

会计分期假设意味着企业的经济活动可以分为几个等距的时期，时期可以变化，最常见的时期是月度、季度和年度。根据时间段假设，公司在年末编制财务报表将其包含在年度报告中。

4. 货币单位

基于货币是会计计量经济活动的常用衡量标准，货币单位为会计计量和分析提供了恰当的基础。这意味着货币单位是最有效的表达方式：它反映了资本和货物交换的变化以及企业各利益集团之间劳务服务的提供。货币计量具有相关、简明、普遍可用、可理解和有用等特性。这种假设依赖于更基本的定量数据，这些数据对于传达经济信息和做出合理的经济决策很有用。

2.6.2 会计原则

根据会计的基本假设，会计行业制定了解释记录和报告经济事件的原则。

1. 权责发生制

会计实体应以交易为基础编制财务报表，不是以支付或收到现金为基础，而是以相关会计期间的收入或费用为基础。

根据权责发生制假设，在计算利润时，收入必须与支出相匹配。这也称为配比原则。

2. 匹配原则

匹配原则要求收入及其成本和费用相互匹配。费用在与费用产生的收入相同的会计期间报告。费用与收入的匹配有时需要公司预测未来事件。

3. 成本原则

财务报表编制者和使用者一直认为历史成本对会计计量和报告最有用。根据成本原则,所有业务交易将按成本或实际支付记录,并在财务报表中按成本报告。在出售或消耗资产之前,这些成本将保留在会计记录中。成本提供了收购时资产价值的可靠衡量标准,消除了被低估或高估资产的可能性。

4. 收入确认原则

收入确认原则要求所有收入按其发生的会计期间而非实际收到的会计期间计量。以下三点对于理解收入确认原则至关重要:

- 与收入相关的资产流入不一定是现金形式。
- 收入在提供商品和服务的会计期间或商品的所有权转移时被记录。
- 收入金额等于收到的现金加上收到的其他资产的现金等价物。

5. 完全披露原则

完全披露原则要求公司在财务报表(包括其附注)中全面、完整地披露与其财务状况、经营成果、现金流量等相关的所有相关信息和数据。换句话说,会计师应充分考虑企业经济业务中可能影响会计信息使用者做出决策判断的信息,不应隐瞒重要信息。

2.6.3 计量基础

1. 历史成本

企业获得的财产应按购买或建造时产生的实际成本入账,并作为分摊成本和转换成本的依据。根据历史成本计量,资产按购买时支付的现金或现金等价物的金额或购买资产时支付的对价的公允价值计量;负债实际上是根据现时义务的资金或资产金额收取的,或是承担当前义务的合同金额,或预期为日常活动中偿还负债而支付的现金或现金等价物的金额。价格变动时,除非国家另有规定,否则不得调整账面价值。基于实际购买成本的估值可以防止随机性,并使会计信息真实可靠、易于理解和比较。

关于历史成本计量基础,新的概念框架定义了以下内容:

首先,历史成本应至少提供与测量项目相关的交易的价格信息,但原则上不反映价值变化信息。

其次,使用历史成本计量并不意味着相关资产和负债的历史成本是不变的,有时需要随着时间的推移和情况的变化而更新。例如,资产损失需要折旧或摊销,资产需要减少。履行责任义务所需的经济资源价值的增加导致负债履行的赤字,这反过来又要求增加负债的历史成本。

第三,对相关金融资产或金融负债的摊余成本计量的使用是历史成本计量基础在金融资产和金融负债会计领域的具体应用。摊余成本属于历史成本计量基础。

2. 现值

现值是将未来现金流量转换为以基准时间反映投资内在价值的价值。使用贴现率将未来现金流转换为现值的过程称为"贴现"。贴现率是用于将未来现金流量转换为现值的比率。贴现率是投资者要求的必要或最低回报率。

关于现值的计量基础,新的概念框架定义了以下内容:

首先,现值应提供有关计量日状态更新的信息,即相关资产或负债的当前价值应反映当前价值中包含的现金流量与前一计量日的变化等因素;

其次,现值的计量基础包括公允价值,使用价值(资产)和业绩价值(负债)和当前成本,公允价值反映市场参与者未来资产或负债现金流量的金额、时间和不确定性。资产或负债未来现金流量的金额、时间和不确定性的现值，反映在使用价值和性能价值中；现时成本反映了当前支付同一资产需要或应收到的相同负债金额。

3. 公允价值

指熟悉市场条件的买方和卖方在公平交易和自愿条件下所确定的价格，或者无关联的双方在公平交易条件下可以买卖资产或清偿债务的成交价格。根据公允价值计量，资产和负债按公平交易中交易双方自愿交换资产或债务清偿金额计量。在实践中，资产评估机构通常评估被收购公司的净资产。

在以下三种情况之一中，资产交换的公允价值被认为是可衡量的：

(1) 存在资产交换的活跃市场，公允价值根据市场价格确定。

(2) 资产交换没有活跃市场，但类似或类似资产存在活跃市场，公允价值根据类似或类似资产的市场价格确定。

(3) 类似资产没有可比市场，可用估值技术确定公允价值。当估值方法用于确定公允价值时，估值技术确定的公允价值估计的变动范围要求较小，或者确定公允价值估计的概率在公允价值范围内是合理的估计。

4. 可变现净值

可变现净值是指估计售价减去进一步处理成本和预计销售费用以及日常活动相关税费的净值。根据可变现净值计量，资产按其正常对外销售收取的现金或现金等价物的金额从资产的估计成本、估计销售费用和相关税费中扣除。

2.7 列报和披露

新概念框架增加了财务报表列报和披露的相关内容，并明确定义了财务报表列报和披露的目标、原则和分类、抵销和摘要，尤其是损益表。其他综合收益及其冲销以及呈报和披露的原则已经明确定义并且具有很高的针对性。其核心内容主要包括：

1. 损益表

损益表作为基本报表，反映了该实体在报告期内的财务业绩。

2. 损益

它可以是财务执行情况表的单独部分(例如损益是综合收益表的组成部分)，也可以是单独的表(例如单独的收益表)的内容。

3. 损益及其他综合收益

显然，所有收入或支出项目原则上都应包括在损益表中。在特殊情况下，董事会可能会决定从损益表中排除某些收入或支出项目，并包括其他综合收益，从而更准确地反映主题的财务状况，为用户提供更多相关信息；但是，只要转回可以提供更多相关信息或更准确地反映主体的财务状况，则可以将其他综合收益中包括的所有收入和支出项目原则上转回损益。如果无法提供更多相关信息或更准确地反映被审计单位的财务状况，董事会可能会决定其他综合收益中包含的收入和支出项目将不会转回。

2.8 资本和资本保全的概念

2.8.1 资本

大多数公司在编制财务报表时都使用资本这一财务概念。根据资本的财务概念，资本就像投入资金或投入的购买力一样，与企业的净资产或股权同义；根据资本的实物概念，资本就像运营能力一样，被视为以日产量为基础的公司生产能力。

公司应根据财务报表使用者的需求选择合适的资本概念。因此，如果财务报表使用者主要关注的是保留名义投资资本或投资资本的购买力，则应采用资本财务概念。但是，如果用户主要关注企业的运营能力，则应采用资本的实物概念。公司选择的概念表明了在确定利润时要实现的目标，即使在有效应用概念方面可能存在一些测量困难。

2.8.2 资本保全和利润的确定

1. 资本保全

资本保全可分为两个概念：财务资本保全和实物资本保全。

(1) 财务资本保全

当期末净资产的金融(或货币)金额超过扣除对所有者的分配后的期初净资产的金融(或货币)金额，即为利润。财务资本保全可以用名义货币单位或恒定购买力单位来衡量。

(2) 实物资本保全

只有当期末的实际生产能力(或运营能力)超过在扣除对所有者的分配和所有者的投入之后的期初的实际生产能力时才能获得利润。

实物资本保全的概念需要使用当前的成本计量基础。但是，财务资本保全的概念不需要使用特定的计量基础。因此，计量基础的选择取决于公司试图保全的资本类型。

2. 资本保全对利润的影响

资本保全的概念涉及公司如何定义它们试图保全的资本。由于它提供了衡量利润的参考点，因此在资本概念和利润概念之间建立了联系。这是区分公司资本报酬和资本回收的先决条件。只有当资产流入超过维持资本所需的金额时，才能将其视为利润，也可以视为资本报酬。因此，利润是从收入中扣除费用后保留的剩余金额。如果费用超过收入，剩余金额为净损失。

根据财务资本保全的概念，当资本以名义货币单位定义时，利润代表期内名义货币资本的增加。因此，在此期间持有的资产价格(通常称为持有利润)的增加在概念上是一种利润。只有在交易所业务发生且资产处置时才能确认该利润。当恒定购买力单位定义实物资本保全的概念时，利润代表在此期间购买力的增加。因此，在资产价格上涨的情况下，只有超过一般价格水平的部分才能被视为其余的利润作为资本。资本保全调整作为权益的一部分处理。当资本由实际生产能力定义时，利润代表在此期间实物资本的增加。影响公司资产和负债的所有价格变动均被视为企业实际生产能力计量的变化。因此，它们被视为财务资本保全调整，作为权益的一部分而不是利润。

计量基准和资本保全概念的选择将决定会计模型在编制财务报表中的使用。不同的会计模型显示出不同程度的相关性和可靠性，并且在其他方面，管理层必须平衡相关性和可靠性之间的权衡。

Chapter 3

The Accounting Equation and Double Entry Rules

3.1 Accounting Equation

3.1.1 Accounting Equation

1. Basic Accounting Equation

In order to carry out normal business activities, any enterprise must have a certain amount of funds as the basis for engaging in economic activities. These funds show different forms of occupation in the production and operation process, such as houses, buildings, machinery and equipment, inventory and currency funds, etc. The funds occupied by these different forms are collectively referred to as assets. There is a certain source of funds for any asset of the enterprise. There are two channels for its source: investor input. When investors invest economic resources, on the one hand, corporate assets will increase, on the other hand, owner's equity will increase. Obtaining part of the loan, this economic business will lead to an increase in corporate assets on the one hand, and also increase corporate liabilities on the other. In accounting, the former is called owner's equity, the latter is called creditor's equity, collectively called equity. Assets and liabilities and owner's equity are two aspects of capital. From any point in time, there is a balanced relationship between property and equity. That is, if there is a certain amount of assets, there must be an equal amount of liabilities and owner's equity; conversely, if there is a certain amount of liabilities and owner's equity, there must also be an equal amount of assets. This balanced relationship is expressed by a formula called an accounting equation, that is:

Assets = Equity

Assets = Liabilities + Owners' Equity

The accounting equation reflects the quantitative relationship among the basic elements of accounting (assets, liabilities, and owner's equity). It is the theoretical basis for accounting methods such as setting up accounts, double-entry accounting, and preparing financial statements.

2. Expanded Accounting Equation

At the beginning of the accounting period, the accounting elements only represented three static elements: assets, liabilities, and owner's equity, and it maintained a balanced relationship. In the accounting period, the three dynamic elements of income, expenses and profit must also maintain a balanced relationship. The income obtained increases the profit and the owner's equity, which leads to the increase of assets or the decrease of liabilities; the expenditure reduces the profit and the owner's equity, resulting in the decrease of assets or the increase of liabilities. Therefore, before the company closes the accounting period, the accounting identity will evolve into an expanded accounting equation, that is,

Assets = Liabilities + Owner's Equity + (Revenue − Expenses)

Assets = Liabilities + Owners' Equity + Profit (Loss)

At the end of the accounting period, after the company distributes (or makes up for) its net profit, the owner's equity is increased or decreased, and the expanded accounting equation is restored to the beginning of the accounting period, that is, assets = liabilities + owner's equity.

3.1.2　The Effect of Business Transaction Types on The Accounting Equation

In an accounting entity, various economic activities will inevitably occur. All economic activities that occur in accounting entities must be recorded and reflected through accounting, which is called business transaction. Taking an enterprise as an example, there are two major types of business transactions that occur in a company within a certain period of time. One type of business transactions involves only changes in the number of assets, liabilities, and owner's equity; the other such business transactions involve changes in income, expenses and profits.

[Example 3-1] The following transaction for December 2019:

Dec. 1. Z. Daisy invested $36,000 cash to D.Z. Co.'s consulting business.

1. Borrowed $8,000 from National Bank. The note bears interest at the annual rate of 6% and is due to be repaid in one year.

1. Paid $3,600 to cover its insurance for 36-months.

2. Purchased general office supplies by paying $2,500 cash.

3. Purchased equipment for $10,000 cash.

11. Provided consulting services to a customer receiving $6,000 cash in full payment.

11. Employees earn $90 a day and pay every two weeks on Wednesday. The payday is Wednesday, December 11, 2019.

13. Paid cash for office rent, $4,000.

15. Completed accounting work for Elle Company on credit, $5,200.

23. Paid the monthly utility bills of the accounting office, $600.

25. Employees earn $90 a day and pay every two weeks on Wednesday. The last payday of 2019 is Wednesday, December 25, 2019.

26. Z. Daisy withdrew $300 to pay for personal use.

28. Agrees to provide consulting services to a client for a fixed fee of $3,000 for 30 days.

These transactions might be analyzed and recorded as followed:

Chapter 3 The Accounting Equation and Double Entry Rules

Transaction (1): Invested $36,000 cash to start a consulting business.

There are two accounts that are affected: The increase in the asset account, cash, and the increase in the equity account, Z. Daisy Capital, by $36,000. Our basic accounting equation is in balance. Assets have a total balance of $36,000 and liabilities plus equity have a total balance of $36,000.

Asset	=	Liability	+	Owner's Equity
Cash				Z. Daisy, Capital
$36,000	=			$36,000

Transaction (2): Borrowed the short-term loan.

In this transaction, the company borrowed $8,000 from National Bank. The note bears interest at the annual rate of 6% and is due to be repaid in one year. Cash in the asset account increased and short-term loan in the liability account increased by $8,000.

Asset	=	Liability	+	Owner's Equity
Cash		Short-term loan		Z. Daisy, Capital
$36,000				$36,000
+$8,000		+$8,000		
$44,000	=	$8,000	+	$36,000

Transaction (3): Paid $3,600 to cover its insurance for 36-months.

The company paid the insurance for $3,600 and its cover 36-months. On the day of payment, the asset account, cash, will decrease by $3,600. The insurance expense will increase by the same amount, which will affect the owners' equity account decreased.

Asset	=	Liability	+	Owner's Equity
Cash		Short-term loan		Z. Daisy, Capital
$44,000		$8,000		$36,000
−$3,600				−$3,600 (expense)
$40,400	=	$8,000	+	$32,400

Transaction (4): Purchased general office supplies by paying $2,500 cash.

In this transaction, the company purchases general office supplies by paying $2,500 cash. The asset account, cash, will decrease by the $2,500 paid. The asset account, supplies, will increase by $2,500, the cost of the supplies. In this transaction we are giving up one asset, cash, and receiving another asset, supplies.

Asset		=	Liability	+	Owner's Equity
Cash	Supplies		Short-term loan		Z. Daisy, Capital
$40,400			$8,000		$32,400
−$2,500	+$2,500				
$37,900	$2,500	=	$8,000	+	$32,400

Transaction (5): Purchased equipment of $10,000 for cash.

In this transaction, the company purchases equipment of $10,000. The asset account, equipment, increases by $10,000 and cash, decreases by $10,000.

	Asset		=	Liability	+	Owner's Equity
Cash	Supplies	Equipment		Short-term loan		Z. Daisy, Capital
$37,900	$2,500			$8,000		$32,400
- $10,000		+ $10,000				
$27,900	$2,500	$10,000	=	$8,000	+	$32,400

Transaction (6): Provided consulting services to a customer receiving $6,000 cash in full payment.

The company rendered consulting services to a customer receiving $6,000 cash in full payment. The asset account, cash, will increase by $,6000. The service revenue will also increase by the same amount.

	Asset		=	Liability	+	Owner's Equity
Cash	Supplies	Equipment		Short-term loan		Z. Daisy, Capital
$27,900	$2,500	$10,000		$8,000		$32,400
+ $6,000						+ $6,000 (revenue)
$33,900	$2,500	$10,000	=	$8,000	+	$38,400

Transaction (7): Paid every two weeks salaries.

In this transaction, the company paid every two weeks, salaries on Wednesday. The asset account, cash, decreases by $900 and the salaries expense increases by $900 will affect the owners' equity account decreased.

	Asset		=	Liability	+	Owner's Equity
Cash	Supplies	Equipment		Short-term loan		Z. Daisy, Capital
$33,900	$2,500	$10,000		$8,000		$38,400
- $900						- $900 (expense)
$33,000	$2,500	$10,000	=	$8,000	+	$37,500

Transaction (8): Paid cash for office rent, $4,000.

In this transaction, the company paid office rent of $4,000. The asset account, cash, decreases by $8,000 and the rent expense increases by $8,000 will affect the owners' equity account decreased.

	Asset		=	Liability	+	Owner's Equity
Cash	Supplies	Equipment		Short-term loan		Z. Daisy, Capital
$33,000	$2,500	$10,000		$8,000		$37,500
- $4,000						- $4,000 (expense)
$29,000	$2,500	$10,000	=	$8,000	+	$33,500

Transaction (9): Completed accounting work for Elle Company on credit, $5,200.

In this transaction, the company completed accounting work of $5,200 on credit. We do not receive cash, but agree to receive the account at some point in the future. The asset account, accounts receivables, increases by $5,200 and the service revenue, increases by $5,200.

	Asset			=	Liability	+	Owner's Equity
Cash	Supplies	Equipment	Accounts receivable		Short-term loan		Z. Daisy, Capital
$29,000	$2,500	$10,000			$8,000		$33,500
			+$ 5,200				+ $5,200 (revenue)
$29,000	$2,500	$10,000	$5,200	=	$8,000	+	$38,700

Chapter 3 The Accounting Equation and Double Entry Rules

Transaction (10): Paid the monthly utility bills of the accounting office, $600.

In this transaction, the company paid monthly utility bills of $600. The asset account, cash, decreases by $600 and the utility expense increases by $600 will affect the owners' equity account decreased.

Asset				=	Liability	+	Owner's Equity
Cash	Supplies	Equipment	Accounts receivable		Short-term loan		Z. Daisy, Capital
$29,000	$2,500	$10,000	$5,200		$8,000		$38,700
- $600							- $600 (expense)
$28,400	$2,500	$10,000	$5,200	=	$8,000	+	$38,100

Transaction (11): Paid every two weeks salaries.

In this transaction, the company paid every two weeks salaries on Wednesday. The asset account, cash, decreases by $900 and the salaries expense increases by $900 will affect the owners' equity account decreased.

Asset				=	Liability	+	Owner's Equity
Cash	Supplies	Equipment	Accounts receivable		Short-term loan		Z. Daisy, Capital
$28,400	$2,500	$10,000	$5,200		$8,000		$38,100
- $900							- $900 (expense)
$27,500	$2,500	$10,000	$5,200	=	$8,000	+	$37,200

Transaction (12): Withdrew $300 for personal use.

In this transaction, the withdrawal of $300 cash for her personal use. The asset account, Cash, will decrease by the $300 paid. The equity account, Z. Daisy personal, will decrease by $300. Withdrawal accounts are not salary or business expenses. Owner's income withdrawal or expected income includes withdrawal of cash (or other assets) to cover personal expenses. Withdrawals are a distribution of benefits, not expenses. It should be deducted directly from the owner's equity. For companies, a dividend account is used and deducted from retained earnings (undistributed profits).

Asset				=	Liability	+	Owner's Equity
					Short-term		
Cash	Supplies	Equipment	Accounts receivable		loan		Z. Daisy, Capital
$27,500	$2,500	$10,000	$5,200		$8,000		$37,200
- $300							- $300 (drawing)
$27,200	$2,500	$10,000	$5,200	=	$8,000	+	$36,900

Transaction (13): Provided consulting services to a client for a fixed fee of $3,000 for 30 days.

On December 28, 2019, DZ Co. makes an entry to debit, or increase, to the cash account and a credit, or increase, to a liability account called unearned revenue.

Asset				=	Liability		+ Owner's Equity
Cash	Supplies	Equipment	Accounts receivable		Short-term loan	Unearned Revenue	Z. Daisy, Capital
$27,200	$2,500	$10,000	$5,200		$8,000		$36,900
+ $3,000						+ $3,000	
$30,200	$2,500	$10,000	$5,200	=	$8,000	$3,000	+ $36,900

To sum up, there is an identity relationship among the major accounting elements: assets, liabilities, owner's equity, income and expenses. The occurrence of any business transaction will not destroy this balanced relationship.

3.2 Double Entry Rules

Accounting information is an important part of a company's daily decision-making process, and is designed to meet users' needs for accounting information. The users of accounting information can be divided into external users and internal users. This means that accounting can also be divided into two categories: financial accounting and management accounting. Financial accounting is an accounting area that aims to serve external users by providing financial statements, while management accounting is an accounting area that provides information to internal users to meet their decision-making needs.

3.2.1 The Account

In business transactions, enterprises need to record the content of what the economic business occurs, which is to set up an account to complete. The account is set up according to the accounting subjects, has a certain structure, and is the carrier for recording accounting information.

An account generally has a complete account format and a basic account structure. A complete account format is generally an accounting book used in actual work. Its contents mainly include account name (accounting title) the date when the economic business occurred, voucher number, summary, debit amount, credit amount and balance, and the direction of the balance debit or credit. Exhibit 3-1 shows a complete account format.

Exhibit 3-1

Account Title   Acct. No. XX

Date	Description	P.R.	Debit	Credit	Balance
20XX					
Mar. 1			XXX		XXX

The basic structure of the account is a T-accounts. The account is divided into two sides, the left is the debit and the right is the credit. One of them is used to register the increase and balance, and the other is used to register the decrease. Exhibit 3-2 shows the basic structure of the account — T-accounts.

Exhibit 3-2

Title
Left side	Right side
Debit	Credit

3.2.2 The Rules of Debit and Credit

Whether an increase or decrease in an account is recorded on the debit or credit side depends on the nature of the account. According to the convention, increases in asset and expense accounts are recorded on the debit side, decreases are recorded on the credit side, while increases in liabilities, owner's equity, and income are recorded on the credit side, and decreases are recorded on the debit side. Debit and credit are abbreviated as Dr.

and Cr. The rules of debit and credit are depicted with T-accounts, as follows:

Asset and Expense		Liability, Owners' equity and Revenue	
Debit for increases	Credit for decreases	Debit for decreases	Credit for increases

3.2.3 Double Entry

Double entry bookkeeping refers to a kind of bookkeeping method in which any business transactions must be registered with two or more related accounts in an equivalent amount to reflect changes in the specific content of the accounting object.

The theoretical basis of the double entry bookkeeping method is the principle of balance of funds reflected in the accounting identities of "Assets = Liabilities + Owners' equity". It takes the balanced relationship between the accounting contents as the basis of the accounting method. The occurrence of any business transactions will inevitably cause the absolute amount changes in one or two of the assets, liabilities, and owner's equity related to each other. When only one side of assets, liabilities and owner's equity is involved, changes in the opposite direction (one increases and another decreases) will inevitably occur. Therefore, the balance between assets, liabilities and owner's equity will never be destroyed by the increase and decrease. The double entry bookkeeping method is to record the inevitable phenomenon of the objectively existing increase and decrease of funds, to record it through two or more interconnected accounts, and then to check whether the recorded result is correct methods with this identified relationship.

[**Example 3-2**] Take the transaction given in Example 3-1 to learn how to record transactions using double entry bookkeeping.

Transaction (1): Invested $36,000 cash to start a consulting business.

Cash		Capital	
Dr. (+)	Cr. (-)	Dr. (-)	Cr. (+)
$36,000			$36,000

Transaction (2): Borrowed the short-term loan.

Cash		Short-term Loan	
Dr. (+)	Cr. (-)	Dr. (-)	Cr. (+)
$8,000			$8,000

Transaction (3): Paid $3,600 to cover its insurance for 36-months.

Cash		Prepaid Insurance	
Dr. (+)	Cr. (-)	Dr. (+)	Cr. (-)
	$3,600	$3,600	

Transaction (4): Purchased general office supplies by paying $2,500 cash.

Cash		Supplies	
Dr. (+)	Cr. (−)	Dr. (+)	Cr. (−)
	$2,500	$2,500	

Transaction (5): Purchased equipment of $10,000 for cash.

Cash		Equipment	
Dr. (+)	Cr. (−)	Dr. (+)	Cr. (−)
	$10,000	$10,000	

Transaction (6): Provided consulting services to a customer receiving $6,000 cash in full payment.

Cash		Service Revenue	
Dr. (+)	Cr. (−)	Dr. (−)	Cr. (+)
$6,000			$6,000

Transaction (7): Paid every two weeks salaries.

Cash		Salaries Expense	
Dr. (+)	Cr. (−)	Dr. (+)	Cr. (−)
	$900	$900	

Transaction (8): Paid cash for office rent, $4,000.

Cash		Rent Expense	
Dr. (+)	Cr. (−)	Dr. (+)	Cr. (−)
	$4,000	$4,000	

Transaction (9): Completed accounting work for Elle Company on credit, $5,200.

Accounts Receivable		Service Expense	
Dr. (+)	Cr. (−)	Dr. (+)	Cr. (−)
$5,200			$5,200

Transaction (10): Paid the monthly utility bills of the accounting office, $600.

Cash		Utility Expense	
Dr. (+)	Cr. (−)	Dr. (+)	Cr. (−)
	$600	$600	

Chapter 3 The Accounting Equation and Double Entry Rules

Transaction (11): Paid every two weeks salaries.

Cash		Salaries Expense	
Dr. (+)	Cr. (-)	Dr. (+)	Cr. (-)
	$900	$900	

Transaction (12): Withdrew $30 for personal use.

Cash		Drawing	
Dr. (+)	Cr. (-)	Dr. (-)	Cr. (+)
$300			$300

Transaction (13): Provided consulting services to a client for a fixed fee of $3,000 for 30 days.

Cash		Unearned Revenue	
Dr. (+)	Cr. (-)	Dr. (-)	Cr. (+)
$3,000			$3,000

Key Words and Expressions

accounting equation	会计等式
expanded accounting equation	扩展会计等式
business transaction	经济业务
accounts receivables	应收账款
capital	资本
accounts payable	应付账款
utility expense	公共费用
rent expense	租金费用
supplies	物料用品
equipment	设备
in advance	预先，提前
on account/credit	赊账
installment payment	分期付款
withdraw	提款
retained earning	留存收益
double entry	复式记账
debit (dr.)	借方
credit (cr.)	贷方
balance (bal.)	余额，平衡
trial balance	试算平衡
account title	会计科目

Exercises

Ⅰ. **Please select the best answer for the following questions or uncompleted sentences.**

1. What changes may result from the increase in owner's equity? (   )

    A. Decreases expense.

    B. Increases liability.

    C. Increases expense.

    D. Increases asset.

2. Which of the accounting elements does the company equipment? (   )

    A. Asset.

    B. Liability.

    C. Expense.

    D. Revenue.

3. Which of the following business transactions caused the reduction in assets and liabilities at the same time? (   )

    A. Deposit cash in a bank.

    B. Paid employees in cash.

    C. Purchases outstanding.

    D. Use bank deposits to pay for purchases in advance.

4. A company's short-term loan from a bank directly returns the purchase payment due. Which of the following types of business transaction? (   )

    A. Increase and decrease between income and expenses.

    B. Increase and decrease between assets.

    C. Increase and decrease between owners' equity.

    D. Increase and decrease between liabilities.

5. After the following business transactions occur, which of the two sides of the accounting equation will not change? (   )

    A. Bank deposits to repay purchases.

    B. Withdrawing cash from the bank.

    C. Unpaid purchase materials.

    D. Deposits received in advance for sales.

Ⅱ. **Finish the following tasks based on the information given.**

6. Identify changes in the following accounts that affect debits or credits.

    A. Accounts receivables are increased.

    B. Capital is decreased.

    C. Accounts payable is increased.

    D. Utility expense is decreased.

    E. Rent expense is increased.

    F. Supplies are increased.

G. Equipment is decreased.
H. Cash is decreased.
I. Withdrawals is increased.
J. Prepaid issuance is increased.
K. Unearned revenue is decreased.

第3章 会计等式和复式记账

3.1 会计等式

3.1.1 会计等式

1. 基本会计等式

为了进行正常的商业活动,任何企业必须有一定数量的资金作为从事经济活动的基础。这些资金在生产和经营过程中显示出不同的占用形式,例如房屋、建筑物、机械设备、存货和货币资金等。这些不同形式占用的资金统称为资产。企业的任何资产都有一定的资金来源。其来源有两种渠道:第一,投资者投入。当投资者投入经济资源时,一方面,公司资产将增加,另一方面,所有者权益也将增加。第二,获得一部分贷款,这一经济业务一方面将导致公司资产增加,另一方面也将导致公司负债增加。在会计中,前者称为所有者权益,后者称为债权人权益,统称为权益。资产和负债及所有者权益是资金的两个方面。任何时候,企业的资产与权益之间存在平衡的关系。也就是说,如果有一定数量的资产,负债和所有者权益必须与资产相等。相反,如果存在一定数量的负债和所有者权益,那么必须与资产相等。这种平衡关系又称为会计恒等式,即:

资产=权益

资产=负债+所有者权益

会计等式反映了会计基本要素(资产、负债和所有者权益)之间的定量关系。它是建立账户、复式记账和编制财务报表等会计方法的理论基础。

2. 扩展会计等式

在会计期初,会计要素仅表现为三个静态要素:资产、负债和所有者权益,并保持平衡的关系。在会计期间内,收入、支出和利润这三个动态要素也必须保持平衡的关系。获得的收入使得利润和所有者权益增加,从而导致资产增加或负债减少;发生的支出使得利润和所有者权益减少,从而导致资产减少或负债增加。因此,在会计期末结账之前,会计恒等式将演变为一个扩展的会计等式,即

资产=负债+所有者权益+(收入)

资产=负债+所有者权益+利润(损失)

在会计期末,公司分配(或弥补)其净利润后,所有者权益增加或减少,并且扩展的会计等式恢复到会计期初,即资产=负债+所有者权益。

3.1.2 业务交易类型对会计等式的影响

在会计实体中,不可避免地会发生各种经济活动。会计实体中发生的所有经济活动必须通过会计进行记录和反映,这称为业务交易。以企业为例,在一定时间内公司中发生两种主要的业务交易。一种商业交易只涉及资产、负债和所有者权益数量的变化;另外一种业务交易则涉及收入、费用和利润的变化。

【例3-1】该企业的一般日记账记录了以下2019年12月的交易：

12月1日，Z. Daisy 向 D.Z. Co.的咨询业务投资了36,000美元。

1日，从国家银行借款8,000美元。该票据的年利率为6%，将在一年内偿还。

1日，支付3,600美元的36个月保险。

2日，支付2,500美元现金购买一般办公用品。

3日，以10,000美元现金购置设备。

11日，为客户提供咨询服务，收到现金6,000美元。

11日，员工每天的工资为90美元，每两周的星期三支付。发薪日是2019年12月11日，星期三。

13日，以现金支付办公室租金的4,000美元。

15日，为Elle公司赊账完成会计工作，5,200美元。

23日，支付会计处的每月水电费600美元。

25日，员工每天的工资为90美元，每两周的星期三支付。2019年的最后一个发薪日是2019年12月25日，星期三。

26日，Z. Daisy 提取了300美元用于个人使用。

28日，同意向客户提供30天的咨询服务费用为3,000美元。

按以下方式分析和记录这些事务：

交易(1)：投资36,000美元现金开始咨询业务。

有两个受影响的账户：资产账户现金增加，以及权益账户 Z. Daisy Capital 增加36,000美元。基本会计等式处于平衡状态。资产的总余额为36,000美元，负债加所有者权益的总余额为36,000美元。

资产	=	负债	+	所有者权益
现金				Z. Daisy, 资本
$36,000	=			$36,000

交易(2)：借入短期贷款。

在这笔交易中，该公司从国家银行借了8,000美元。该票据的年利率为6%，将在一年内偿还。资产账户的现金增加，负债账户的短期贷款增加8,000美元。

资产	=	负债	+	所有者权益
现金		短期贷款		Z. Daisy, 资本
$36,000				$36,000
+$8,000		+$8,000		
$44,000	=	$8,000	+	$36,000

交易(3)：支付3,600美元，以支付其36个月的保险。

该公司支付3,600美元的保险费，保险期为36个月。在付款当天，资产账户的现金将减少3,600美元。保险费用将增加相同数额，这将使得所有者权益账户减少。

资产	=	负债	+	所有者权益
现金		短期贷款		Z. Daisy, 资本
$44,000		$8,000		$36,000
−$3,600				−$3,600(费用)
$40,400	=	$8,000	+	$32,400

交易(4)：以 2,500 美元现金购买了办公用品。

在此交易中，公司通过支付 2,500 美元现金来购买办公用品。资产账户现金将减少 2,500 美元。资产账户将增加耗材 2,500 美元。在此交易中，我们放弃一项资产现金，而接受另一项资产供应。

资产		=	负债	+	所有者权益
现金	办公用品		短期贷款		Z. Daisy, 资本
$40,400			$8,000		$32,400
- $2,500	+ $2,500				
$37,900	$2,500	=	$8,000	+	$32,400

交易(5)：以现金购买了 10,000 美元的设备。

在此交易中，公司购买了 10,000 美元的设备。资产账户设备增加 10,000 美元，现金减少 10,000 美元。

资产			=	负债	+	所有者权益
现金	办公用品	设备		短期贷款		Z. Daisy, 资本
$37,900	$2,500			$8,000		$32,400
- $10,000		+ $10,000				
$27,900	$2,500	$10,000	=	$8,000	+	$32,400

交易(6)：向客户提供咨询服务收到现金 6,000 美元。

该公司向客户提供咨询服务，收到现金 6,000 美元。资产账户现金将增加 6,000 美元，权益账户收入也将增加相同的金额。

资产			=	负债	+	所有者权益
现金	办公用品	设备		短期贷款		Z. Daisy, 资本
$27,900	$2,500	$10,000		$8,000		$32,400
+ $6,000						+ $6,000(revenue)
$33,900	$2,500	$10,000	=	$8,000	+	$38,400

交易(7)：每两周支付一次工资。

在这项交易中，每两周的星期三支付一次工资。资产账户现金减少 900 美元，而薪金费用增加 900 美元，将使得所有者权益账户减少。

资产			=	负债	+	所有者权益
现金	办公用品	设备		短期贷款		Z. Daisy, 资本
$33,900	$2,500	$10,000		$8,000		$38,400
- $900						- $900(费用)
$33,000	$2,500	$10,000	=	$8,000	+	$37,500

交易(8)：办公室租金的现金 4,000 美元。

在这笔交易中，公司支付了 4,000 美元的办公室租金。资产账户现金减少 4,000 美元，费用发生增加 4,000 美元。

资产			=	负债	+	所有者权益
现金	办公用品	设备		短期贷款		Z. Daisy, 资本

$33,000	$2,500	$10,000		$8,000		$37,500
- $4,000						- $4,000(expense)
$29,000	$2,500	$10,000	=	$8,000	+	$33,500

交易(9)：为 Elle 公司完成会计工作，该公司支付报酬 5,200 美元。

在这笔交易中，公司完成了会计核算工作。我们不会收到现金，但是同意在将来的某个时候接收该笔款项。资产账户应收账款增加 5,200 美元，收入增加 5,200 美元。

		资产		=	负债	+	所有者权益
现金	办公用品	设备	应收账款		短期贷款		Z. Daisy, 资本
$29,000	$2,500	$10,000			$8,000		$33,500
			+$ 5,200				+$5,200(收入)
$29,000	$2,500	$10,000	$5,200	=	$8,000	+	$38,700

交易(10)：支付会计处的每月水电费 600 美元。

在此笔交易中，公司支付 600 美元的水电费。资产账户现金减少 600 美元，公用事业费用发生增加 600 美元。

		资产		=	负债	+	所有者权益
现金	办公用品	设备	应收账款		短期贷款		Z. Daisy, 资本
$29,000	$2,500	$10,000	$5,200		$8,000		$38,700
- $600							- $600(费用)
$28,400	$2,500	$10,000	$5,200	=	$8,000	+	$38,100

交易(11)：每两周支付一次工资。

在这项交易中，公司每两周的星期三支付一次工资。资产账户现金减少 900 美元，而薪金费用增加 900 美元，将使得所有者权益账户减少。

		资产		=	负债	+	所有者权益
现金	办公用品	设备	应收账款		短期贷款		Z. Daisy, 资本
$28,400	$2,500	$10,000	$5,200		$8,000		$38,100
- $900							- $900(费用)
$27,500	$2,500	$10,000	$5,200	=	$8,000	+	$37,200

交易(12)：提款 300 美元供个人使用。

在这笔交易中，公司为她的个人使用支付了 300 美元现金。资产账户现金将减少 300 美元。权益账户将减少 300 美元。提款账户不是薪金或业务费用。所有者的收益提取或预期收益包括提取现金(或其他资产)以支付个人开支。提款是收益的分配，而不是费用，应直接从所有者权益中扣除。对于公司，使用股息账户并从留存收益(未分配利润)中扣除。

		资产		=	负债	+	所有者权益
现金	办公用品	设备	应收账款		短期贷款		Z. Daisy, 资本
$27,500	$2,500	$10,000	$5,200		$8,000		$37,200
- $300							- $300(drawing)
$27,200	$2,500	$10,000	$5,200	=	$8,000	+	$36,900

交易(13)：为客户提供 30 天的咨询服务，费用为 3,000 美元。

在 2019 年 12 月 28 日，DZ 公司输入现金账户的借方或增加项，以及称为未赚收入的负债账户的贷方或增加项。

		资产		=	负债		+	所有者权益
现金	办公用品	设备	应收账款		短期贷款	未实现收入		Z. Daisy, 资本
$27,200	$2,500	$10,000	$5,200		$8,000			$36,900
+$3,000						+$3,000		
$30,200	$2,500	$10,000	$5,200	=	$8,000	$3,000	+	$36,900

综上所述，主要会计要素之间存在恒等关系：资产、负债、所有者权益、收入和支出。任何业务交易的发生都不会破坏这种平衡的关系。

3.2 复式记账原理

会计信息是企业日常决策过程的重要组成部分，是为满足用户对会计信息的需求而设计的。会计信息的使用者可以分为外部使用者和内部使用者。这意味着会计也可以分为两大类：财务会计和管理会计。财务会计是以提供财务报表为目的的会计领域，而管理会计是向内部用户提供信息以满足其决策需要的会计领域。

3.2.1 账户

在经济业务交易中，企业需要记录发生的经济业务的内容，即建立一个完整的账户。账户是根据会计科目设置的，具有一定的结构，是记录会计信息的载体。

账户通常具有完整的账户格式和基本的账户结构。完整的账户格式通常是实际工作中使用的会计账簿。其内容主要包括：账户名称(会计科目)、开展经济业务的日期、凭证编号、摘要、借方金额、贷方金额和余额以及余额借方或贷方的方向。表 3-1 列示了完整的账户格式：

表 3-1

账户名称					字号××
日期	摘要	过账索引	借方	贷方	余额
20×× 3月1日			×××		×××

账户的基本结构是 T 型账户。账户分为两个部分，左边是借方，右边是贷方。其中一个用于记录增加额和余额，另一个用于记录减少额。表 3-2 列示了账户的基本结构——T 型账户：

表 3-2

账户名称(会计科目)	
左侧	右侧
借方	贷方

3.2.2 借贷记账原理

账户的增加或减少是记录在借方还是贷方取决于账户的性质。按照惯例，资产和费用账户的增加记在借方，减少的记在贷方；而负债、所有者权益和收入的增加记在贷方，减少的记为借方。借方和贷方缩写为 Dr.和 Cr.，借记和贷记规则用 T 型账户描述，如下所示：

资产和费用账户		负债、所有者权益和收入账户	
借方表示增加	贷方表示减少	借方表示减少	贷方表示增加

3.2.3 复式记账

复式记账是指任何业务交易都必须在两个或两个以上的相关账户中登记，以反映会计对象特定内容的变化。

复式记账法的理论基础是资金平衡原则，反映在"资产＝负债＋所有者权益"的会计恒等式中。它以记账内容之间的平衡关系作为记账方法的基础。任何业务交易的发生都不可避免地导致资产、负债和所有者权益中的相互关联一方或两方的数额变化。当仅涉及资产、负债和所有者权益的一方时，将不可避免地发生相反方向的变化(一增一减)。因此，增加或减少不会破坏资产、负债和所有者权益之间的平衡。复式记账法记录客观上所发生的资金增减的现象，通过两个或两个以上相互关联的账户进行记录，然后使用恒等关系检查记录的结果是否正确。

Chapter 4

Accounting Cycle

The accounting cycle is the process of the complete accounting work of an accounting period from the start of obtaining the source documents and the registration of books when economic business events occur, to the preparation of financial accounting statements.

The enterprise will record, classify and summarize all economic transactions that occurred in a certain period of time, according to certain steps and methods, until the entire accounting process of preparing accounting statements. These work cycles are repeated over and over again in successive accounting periods. The main processes of the accounting cycle are as follows:

1. Analyze business transactions and prepare accounting entries based on the original documents obtained using the double-entry rules.
2. Record accounts in the journal, including debits and credits.
3. Post debits and credits from the journal to the corresponding ledger accounts.
4. Prepare the unadjusted trial balance sheet and summarize the unadjusted ledger accounts and amounts.
5. At the end of the accounting period, adjust entries, journalizing, and postings on an accrual basis.
6. Prepare the adjusted trial balance sheet and summarize the adjusted ledger accounts and amounts.
7. Prepare financial statements which based on the adjusted trial balance.
8. Journalize and post entries to close temporary accounts.
9. Prepare a post-closing trial balance.

4.1 Journalizing and Posting

4.1.1 Journalizing

According to double entry accounting, an accountant first records business transactions in a journal. The journal is an accounting entry prepared by the economic business that occurs every day, and all are registered one by one in chronological order. The business transactions are recorded as debit and credit in the journal, as follows:

1. Date column: The date on which the registered economic business occurred. The year is entered at the top of the date column, and the month and day are registered in two small columns.

2. Description column: briefly explain the content of the economic business and the title of the account.

3. P.R. (Posting Reference): After registering to the classified account according to the debit and credit accounts and their amounts in the journal daily, indicate in the posting column that it has been posted.

4. Amount column: Register the economic business amount in the debit and credit columns.

5. General ledger pages: Enter the number of ledger pages in this column.

In double entry bookkeeping accounting, the nature of business transactions and how to analyze and classify them are discussed. Entering accounting information in the "T" account shows the effect of the transaction. However, these items do not provide the necessary data for business transactions, nor do these items provide a chronological record of transactions. Next, according to the previous accounting information, use the journal to clearly record business transactions in the books in chronological order.

[**Example 4-1**] The following transaction for the month of December 2019 were recorded in the business's general journal:

Dec. 1. Z. Daisy invested $36,000 cash in D.Z. Co.'s consulting business.

1. Borrowed $8,000 from National Bank. The note bears interest at the annual rate of 6% and is due to be repaid in one year.

1. Paid $3,600 to cover its insurance for 36-months.

2. Purchased general office supplies by paying $2,500 cash.

3. Purchased equipment for $10,000 cash.

11. Provided consulting services to a customer receiving $6,000 cash in full payment.

11. Employees earn $90 a day and pay every two weeks on Wednesday. The payday is Wednesday, December 11, 2019.

13. Paid cash for office rent, $4,000.

15. Completed accounting work for Elle Company on credit, $5,200.

23. Paid the monthly utility bills of the accounting office, $600.

25. Employees earn $90 a day and pay every two weeks on Wednesday. The last payday of 2019 is Wednesday, December 25, 2019.

26. Z. Daisy withdrew $300 to pay for personal use.

28. Agrees to provide consulting services to a client for a fixed fee of $3,000 for 30 days.

The journal entries are shown in Exhibit 4-1.

Exhibit 4-1

General Journal Page G1

Date		Description	P.R.	Debit	Credit
Dec.	1	Cash		$36,000	
		Z. Daisy, Capital			$36,000
		Investment of consulting business			
	1	Cash		$8,000	
		Short-term loan			$8,000

(Continued)

Date	Description	P.R.	Debit	Credit
	To borrow the loan.			
1	Insurance Expense		$3,600	
	Cash			$3,600
	To pay the insurance expense in advance.			
2	Supplies			$2,500
	Cash		$2,500	
	The Purchase of office supplies			
3	Equipment		$10,000	
	Cash			$10,000
	The Purchase of Equipment			
11	Cash		$6,000	
	Service Revenue			$6,000
	The revenue of consulting services			
11	Salaries Expense		$900	
	Cash			$900
	To pay ten workdays' salary.			
13	Rent Expense		$4,000	
	Cash			$4,000
	Paid cash for office rent			
15	Accounts Receivables		$5,200	
	Service Revenue			$5,200
	The credit revenue of accounting work			
23	Utility Expense		$600	
	Cash			$600
	The payment of monthly utility bills			
25	Salaries Expense		$900	
	Cash			$900
	To pay ten workdays' salary.			
26	Drawing		$300	
	Cash			$300
	Withdrawal of personal use			
28	Cash		$3,000	
	Unearned Revenue			$3,000
	Consulting fees received in.			
	Total		$85,000	$85,000

4.1.2 Posting

Posting is the process of entering information from a journal to a ledger. To avoid omissions and duplications, please quote account numbers and journal page numbers in the Posting Reference (PR) column.

Specific steps are as follows:
1. Record dates and amounts in accounting account.
2. Register the number of the journal page in the PR column of the accounting account.
3. Record the ledger account number in the PR column of the journal.

Step1: Record dates and amounts in accounting account.

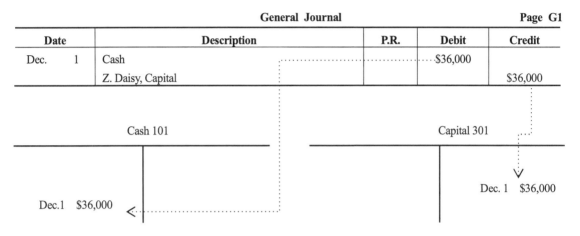

Step2: Register the number of the journal page in the PR column of the accounting account.

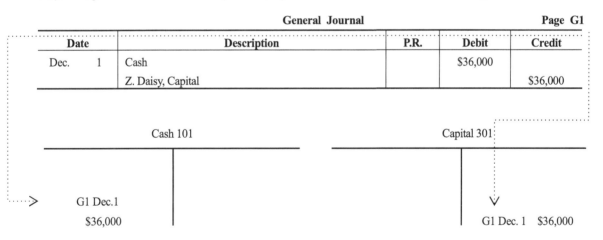

Step3: Record the ledger account number in the PR column of the journal.

General Journal   Page G1

Date	Description	P.R.	Debit	Credit
Dec. 1	Cash	→101	$36,000	
	Z. Daisy, Capital	301 ←		$36,000

Cash 101   Capital 301

G1 Dec.1   G1 Dec. 1 $36,000
$36,000

[**Example 4-2**] Demonstrate the posting process based on the chart of accounts for DZ Co. consulting business and the journal entries in Example 4-1.

The Charts of Accounts

Acct No.	Account Title
	Asset
101	Cash
102	Bank Deposit
121	Notes Receivable
122	Accounts Receivable
126	Prepaid Insurance
134	Allowance for Bad Debts
141	Supplies
142	Equipment
149	Accumulated Depreciation
171	Intangible Assets
172	Accumulated Amortization
176	Goodwill
	Liability
201	Short-term Loan
221	Notes Payable
222	Accounts Payable
228	Salaries Payable
229	Interest payable
231	Unearned Revenue
261	Long-term Loan

(Continued)

Owners' Equity

301	Capital	
321	Common Stock	
331	Drawing	

Revenues

401	Sales	
402	Service Revenue	

Expenses

501	Cost of Goods Sold	
502	General and Administrative Expense	
503	Selling Expense	
504	Advertising Expense	
505	Rent Expense	
506	Insurance Expense	
507	Utility Expense	
508	Salaries Expense	
509	Interest Expense	
510	Depreciation Expense	

Cash — Acct. No. 101

Date		Description	P.R.	Debit	Credit	Balance
2019						
Dec.	1	Cash	G1	$36,000		$36,000
	1		G1	$8,000		$44,000
	1		G1		$3,600	$40,400
	2		G1		$2,500	$37,900
	3		G1		$10,000	$27,900
	11		G1	$6,000		$33,900
	11		G1		$900	$33,000
	13		G1		$4,000	$29,000
	23		G1		$600	$28,400
	25		G1		$900	$27,500
	26		G1		$300	$27,200
	28		G1	$3,000		$30,200

Accounts receivable — Acct. No. 122

Date		Description	P.R.	Debit	Credit	Balance
2019						
Dec.	15		G1	$5,200		$5,200

Supplies   Acct. No. 141

Date	Description	P.R.	Debit	Credit	Balance
2019					
Dec.2		G1	$2,500		$2,500

Equipment   Acct. No. 142

Date	Description	P.R.	Debit	Credit	Balance
2019					
Dec.3		G1	$10,000		$10,000

Short-term Loan   Acct. No. 201

Date	Description	P.R.	Debit	Credit	Balance
2019					
Dec.1		G1		$8,000	$8,000

Unearned Revenue   Acct. No. 231

Date	Description	P.R.	Debit	Credit	Balance
2019					
Dec.28		G1		$3,000	$3,000

Capital-Daisy   Acct. No. 301

Date	Description	P.R.	Debit	Credit	Balance
2019					
Dec.1		G1		$36,000	$36,000

Drawing   Acct. No. 331

Date	Description	P.R.	Debit	Credit	Balance
2019					
Dec.26		G1	$300		$300

Service Revenue   Acct. No. 402

Date	Description	P.R.	Debit	Credit	Balance
2019					
Dec.11		G1		$6,000	$6,000
Dec.15				$5,200	$11,200

Rent Expense   Acct. No. 505

Date	Description	P.R.	Debit	Credit	Balance
2019					
Dec.13		G1	$4,000		$4,000

Insurance Expense   Acct. No. 506

Date	Description	P.R.	Debit	Credit	Balance
2019					
Dec.1		G1	$3,600		$3,600

Utility Expense   Acct. No. 507

Date	Description	P.R.	Debit	Credit	Balance
2019					
Dec.26		G1	$600		$600

Salaries Expense   Acct. No. 508

Date	Description	P.R.	Debit	Credit	Balance
2019					
Dec.11		G1	$900		$900
Dec.25		G1	$900		$1,800

4.2 Preparing a Trial Balance

After all transactions recorded in the current period are posted to the ledger, the balance of each account can be determined. Each account will have a debit, credit or zero balance. In order to determine whether the sum of the debit amounts of all subordinate accounts is equal to the sum of the debit amounts of all subordinate accounts, a trial balance should be prepared. The trial balance consists of two columns, listing the names and balances of all accounts in the order in which they appear in the ledger. Debit balances are listed in the left column and credit balances are listed in the right column. The sum of the two columns should be equal. If the trial balance is unbalanced, it means that the accountants cannot prepare further financial statements. Before proceeding, the accountants must find the error and correct it. Therefore, the trial balance can check the correctness of our records and postings, and can also serve as a tool to remind us of errors. However, it is not absolute to check whether the book records are correct through trial balance. In a sense, if the debit and credit are unbalanced, you can be sure that the account records or calculations are wrong. It is not certain that there are no errors in the account records, as some errors do not affect the balance between the borrower and the lender. If an economic business is re-recorded or missed in the relevant account, or the direction of the debit and credit of the economic business is reversed, the error may not be found through trial balance.

[Example 4-3] Based on Example 4-2 the general ledger accounts to verify whether the debit is equal to the lender.

D.Z. Co.

Trial Balance

December 31, 2019

	Debit	Credit
Cash	$53,000	$22,800
Accounts Receivable	$5,200	
Supplies	$2,500	
Equipment	$10,000	
Prepaid Insurance	$3,600	
Short-term Loan		$8,000

		(Continued)
Unearned Revenue		$3,000
Capital		$36,000
Drawing	$300	
Service Revenue		$11,200
Rent Expense	$4,000	
Utility Expense	$600	
Salaries Expense	$1,800	
Total	$81,000	$81,000

4.3 Adjusting Accounts

Adjustment accounts are to determine the accrued income and expenses for the current period and prepare necessary adjustment entries for related accounts at the end of the accounting period in accordance with the accrual basis. The purpose of the account adjustment is to correctly calculate the profit and loss, so that the revenue and expense due in the reporting period are matched so that the profit and loss of each period and the financial performance of each accounting period is correctly evaluated.

According to the accrual principle and matching principle, adjustments fall into two categories. The first is when cash is paid or received before expense or revenue is recognized. This category includes prepaid or deferred expenses (including depreciation) and unearned or deferred revenues. The second major category of adjustment is when cash is paid or received after expense or revenue is recognized. This category includes accrued expenses and accrued revenues.

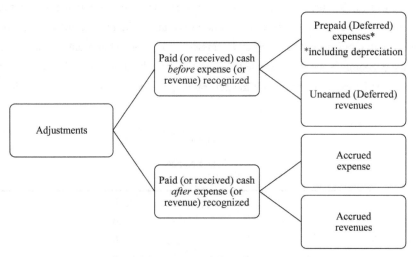

Figure 4-1　Framework for Adjustments

4.3.1 Accrued Revenues

Accrued revenue refers to various incomes that have been realized in the accounting period but have not yet received the payment, such as interest receivables and rent receivables. Adjustment entries that record accrued revenue will always be debited or added to the asset account, and credited or added to the revenue account. After the revenue is confirmed, it needs to be settled, and the assets are retained for the next period and will be written off when the cash is received.

[Example 4-4] At the end of the year, DZ Co. realized consulting revenue for $2,640 should be recorded. On December 10, 2019, DZ Co. agreed to render consulting services under a 60-day fixed fee contract for $7,200 ($120 per day). All services are to be completed by February 7, 2020, when the client will pay in full.

Date	Description	P.R.	Debit	Credit
Dec.31	Accounts Receivable		$2,640	
	Service Revenue			$2,640
	To accrue revenue (22days*120=2,640).			

Accounts Receivable 122		Service Revenue 402	
Dec.31 $2,640			Dec.31 $2,640

The company will debit or increase the asset, accounts receivable, and credit or increase the revenue account, consulting revenue for $2,640. Twenty days have passed since the contract was signed and no payment is due or received from the client. So, D.Z. Co. will recognize $2,640 in revenue ($120 per day times 22-days).

Notice that the accounts receivable and service revenue accounts have been updated to include the earned but unbilled amount of services provided. The subsequent completion of the consulting work and the collection of cash are recorded.

Date	Description	P.R.	Debit	Credit
Feb.7	Cash		$7,200	
	Service Revenue			$4,560
	Accounts Receivable			$2,640
	To record completion of contract and cash collection.			

On February 7, 2020, D.Z. Co. completed its obligation under the consulting contract. The client was billed $7,200 and D.Z. Co. received $7,200 in cash. D.Z. Co. will debit the cash account for $7,200, eliminate the account receivable of $2,640 and recognize the revenue earned in February of $4,560.

4.3.2 Accrued Expenses

Accrued expenses being called payable expenses refer to various expenses that have occurred but have not been paid in the current period, such as rents payable, interest payable and wages payable. For all accrued expense adjustment entries, it debits or increases expense accounts, and credits or increases liability accounts. Accrued expenses must be reported in the income statement of the current period.

[Example 4-5] D.Z. Co.'s employees earn $90 a day and pay every two weeks on Wednesday. The year-end, December 31, 2019 is Tuesday. The last payday of 2019 is Wednesday, December 25, 2019. It is four working days from 12/26 to 12/31 of the year. The employee has a salary of $360 from Thursday to Tuesday. Employees will not be paid until the next Wednesday.

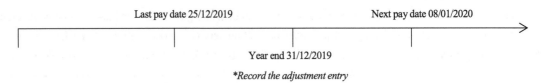

*Record the adjustment entry

It needs to record an adjusting entry on December 31, 2019, to recognize the salaries earned by employees but not paid. In adjusting journal entry it will debit, or increase, salaries expense and credit, or increase, salaries payable for $360. After the adjustment, salaries expense for 2019 is stated properly.

Date		Description	P.R.	Debit	Credit
Dec.	31	Salaries Expense		$360	
		Salaries Payable			$360
		To accrue 4days' salary (4*90=360).			

Salaries Expense 508			Salaries Payable 228	
Dec.11	$900		Dec.31	$360
Dec.25	$900			
Dec.31	$360			
Bal.	$2160			

Salaries expense recorded during the year amounted to $1,800. After posting our adjusting entry, the new balance at the end of the year is $2,160. The salaries payable account will be eliminated when the employee is paid on January 8, 2020.

Date		Description	P.R.	Debit	Credit
Jan.	8	Salaries Payable *(4*90=360)*		$360	
		Salaries Expense *(6*90=540)*		$540	
		Cash			$900
		Paid two-week salary.			

D.Z. Co. will pay the payroll for the two weeks from December 25, 2019 through January 8, 2020. The journal entry for this payroll involves a debit to the liability account, salaries payable, for $360, the amount we accrued on December 31, 2019. A debit to salaries expense for $540 (6 work days times $90 per day), and a credit to cash for $900. It must be careful to remove the accrued payable when actually pay the employee for all amounts previously owed.

[Example 4-6] D.Z. Co. borrowed $8,000 from National Bank on December 1, 2019. The note bears interest at the annual rate of 6% and is due to be repaid in one year. It does accrue interest for the month ended 12/31/19.

Date	Description	P.R.	Debit	Credit
Dec.31	Interest Expense		$40	
	Interest Payable			$40
	*To accrue interest. ($8,000*6%*30/360)*			

Interest Expense 509		Interest Payable 229	
Dec.31 $40			Dec.31 $40

The adjusting journal entry will debit or increase interest expense, and credit or increase interest payable for $40 ($8,000 times 6% for one month or 30/360). After the adjustment, interest expense for 2019 is accurately reported. Interest Expense accrued at the end of the year is $40. The interest payable account will be eliminated when the bank is repaid the principal of $8,000 and the annual interest of $480 on December 1, 2020.

4.3.3 Unearned Revenues

Unearned revenues refer to cash received before products and services are provided. Unearned revenue, also known as deferred income, is a liability. When considering deferred revenue, it faces a transaction that collects cash before offering a product or service. In other words, the business has received cash, but has not done anything to earn cash.

[Example 4-7] On December 28, 2019, D.Z. Co. agrees to provide consulting services to a client for a fixed fee of $3,000 in 30 days. On this date, D.Z. Co. makes an entry to debit, or increase, to the cash account and a credit, or increase, to a liability account called unearned revenue. And the adjusting entry D.Z. Co. will make on December 31, 2019, the end of the accounting period.

Date	Description	P.R.	Debit	Credit
Dec.31	Unearned Revenue		$300	
	Service Revenue			$300
	To recognize 3-days of consulting fees.			

As of December 31, 2019, D.Z. Co. has earned $300 of consulting fees as a result of the passage of time. Three days have gone by since the company entered into the 30-day contract. The adjusting entry is to debit or decrease the liability account, unearned revenue, and credit or increase the revenue account, consulting revenue for $300 (three days at the rate of $100 per day).

Unearned Revenue 231				Service Revenue 402		
Dec.31	$300	Dec.28	$3,000		Dec.31	$300
		Bal.	$2,700			

The unearned revenue account has a credit balance of $2,700. This balance will be recognized as more time passes. The consulting revenue account has a credit balance of $300. The revenue account will appear on the income statement and be closed at the end of the accounting period. The liability account, unearned revenue, will appear on the balance sheet on December 31, 2019.

4.3.4 Prepaid Expenses

Prepaid expenses refer to a claim that occurs when a business transaction agrees that one party pays part of the expense in advance to another party. Prepaid accounts generally include prepaid insurance, supplies, prepaid rent and so on. Other prepaid expenses, are accounted for exactly as insurance and supplies. It should note that some prepaid expenses are both paid for and fully used up within a single period. For example, a company may pay monthly rent on the first day of each month. This payment creates a prepaid expense on the first day of the month that fully expires by the end of the month. In these special cases, the cash paid with a debit can be recorded into the expense account instead of an asset account.

[Example 4-8] On December 1, 2019, D.Z. Co. paid $3,600 to cover its insurance for 36-months, December 2019 through November 2022. When D.Z. Co. made the payment, it debited prepaid insurance and credited cash. The adjusting entry would make on December 31, 2019.

Date		Description	P.R.	Debit	Credit
Dec.	31	Insurance Expense		$100	
		Prepaid Insurance			$100
		To record the first month's expired insurance.			

Insurance Expense 506				Prepaid Insurance 126			
Dec.31	$100			Dec.1	$3,600	Dec.31	$100
				Bal.	$3,500		

The prepaid insurance account is reduced to $3,500, representing $100 per month for the remaining 35 months of the policy. The insurance expense account now has a $100 balance, the amount of the insurance for December 2019.

4.3.5 Depreciation

Plant assets, with the exception of land, are depreciated over their useful life. Depreciation is the process of systematically and rationally allocating the cost of an enterprise's assets over its useful life. So far, a depreciation method called straight-line depreciation is introduced in the accounting process. Depreciation on a straight line is the most common method used by companies. They determine the annual depreciation amount by calculating the cost of the company's assets, subtracting the estimated residual value, and dividing that amount by the useful life of the asset. Residual value refers to the amount expected to be obtained when an enterprise disposes of the asset at the end of its useful life. In the following sections, other depreciation methods will be discussed further.

[**Example 4-9**] On December 3, 2019, D.Z. Co. purchased equipment for $10,000 cash. The equipment has an estimated useful life of five years or 60-months, and an estimated salvage value of $1000 at the end of the five-year period. Can you determine the depreciation expense for the month of December 2019?

Date	Description	P.R.	Debit	Credit
Dec.31	Depreciation Expense		$150	
	Accumulated Depreciation - Equipment			$150
	To record monthly equipment.			

Depreciation Expense510		Accumulated Depreciation 149	
Dec.31 $150			Dec.31 $150

On December 31, 2019, it's will debit, or increase, depreciation expense for $150 and credit a new account called accumulated depreciation. Accumulated depreciation is a contra asset account. A contra-account means that the amount in the account reduces the related asset account. In this case, accumulated depreciation will reduce the asset account and equipment. The adjusting entry has been posted to record depreciation expenses. It's also shown that the balance in the equipment account. The depreciation expense account will appear on income statement for the year ended December 31, 2019. The contra-account, accumulated depreciation, will be shown as a reduction in the cost of the asset and equipment. Cost of a plant asset less accumulated depreciation is known as book value. So the asset equipment, will be shown on the balance sheet at its net amount, or book value, of $9,850. Because the contra account appears on the balance sheet it will not be closed at the end of the period. It will be carried forward to 2020 and used to accumulate the depreciation related to the equipment.

4.4 Adjusting Trial Balance

After the adjustment entries are posted at the end of the period, the "adjusted trial balance sheet" is prepared, the purpose of which is to check whether the adjustment account processing is correct and complete. The compilation of the "adjusted trial balance sheet" should add two columns beside the original trial balance sheet, adjust the debit, adjust the lender, and then use the original trial balance to adjust the debit and credit balance by adding or subtracting to get the amount of the adjusted balance.

An adjusted trial balance for D.Z. Co. is shown in Exhibit 4-2.

Exhibit 4-2

D.Z. Co.
Adjusted Trial Balance
December 31, 2019

Account	Unadjusted Trial Balance		Adjustments		Adjusted Trial Balance	
	Debit	Credit	Debit	Credit	Debit	Credit
Cash	$53,000	$22,800			$30200	
Accounts Receivable	$5,200		$2,640		$7,840	
Prepaid Insurance	$3,600			$100	$3,500	
Supplies	$2,500				$2,500	
Equipment	$10,000				$10,000	
Accumulated Depreciation				$150		$150
Short-term Loan		$8,000				$8,000
Salaries Payable				$360		$360
Interest Payable				$40		$40
Unearned Revenue		$3,000	$300			$2,700
Capital		$36,000				$36,000
Drawing	$300				$300	
Service Revenue		$11,200		$2,940		$14,140
Rent Expense	$4,000				$4,000	
Insurance Expense			$100		$100	
Utility Expense	$600				$600	
Salaries Expense	$1,800		$360		$2,160	
Interest Expense			$40		$40	
Depreciation Expense			$150		$150	
Total	$81,000	$81,000	$3,590	$3,590	$61.390	$61,390

The results show that the occurrence of adjustment items did not affect the balance of the trial balance.

4.5 Preparing Financial Reporting

According to the process of the accounting cycle, financial statements can be prepared based on the adjusted trial balance. First, prepare the income statement. The two columns of the income statement contain expense and income. Net income is the difference between these two amounts, and it increases the owner's equity account. D.Z. Co. Income Statement for the year-end Dec. 31, 2019 is shown in Exhibit 4-3.

Exhibit 4-3

D.Z. Co.

Income Statement

For the Year End December 31, 2019

Revenue (Income):		
Service Revenue		$14,140
Expense:		
Rent Expense	$4,000	
Insurance Expense	$100	
Utility Expense	$600	
Salaries Expense	$2,160	
Interest Expense	$40	
Depreciation Expense	$150	$7,050
Net Profit		**$7,090**

*Suppose income tax is ignored.

After the income statement is completed, preparation of the owner's equity statement begins. Once again, adding up the net profit and investment amount and subtracting all withdrawals yields a closing capital balance of $42,790. After the preparation of the owner's equity income statement, the balance sheet can be prepared. Once the income statement of owner's equity is prepared, the balance sheet can be prepared. D.Z. Co. Statement of Changes in Owner's Equity for the year-end Dec. 31, 2019 is shown in Exhibit 4-4.

Exhibit 4-4

D.Z. Co.

Statement of Changes in Owners' Equity

For the Month Ended December 31, 2019

D.Z. Co. Capital Dec.1, 2019	
Investment during the month	$36,000
Plus: Net Profit	$7,090
Minus: Withdrawals	($300)
D.Z. Co. Capital Dec. 31, 2019	**$42,790**

The balance in D.Z. Co.'s capital account is shown in the owner's equity of the balance sheet. The adjusted balance sheet of assets and liabilities is taken directly. Total assets are equal to total liabilities plus total equity. D.Z. Co.'s Balance statement on Dec. 31, 2019 is shown in Exhibit 4-5.

Exhibit 4-5

D.Z. Co.

Balance Statement

December 31, 2019

Assets		
Cash		$30,200
Accounts Receivable		$7,840
Prepaid Insurance		$3,500
Supplies		$2,500
Equipment	$10,000	
Minus: Accumulated Depreciation	($150)	$9,850
Total Assets		**$53,890**
Liability		
Short-term Loan		$8,000
Salaries Payable		$360
Interest Payable		$40
Unearned Revenue		$2,700
Total Liabilities		**$11,100**
Owners' Equity		
D.Z. Co. Capital		$42,790
Total Owners' Equity		**$42,790**
Total Liabilities and Owners' Equity		**$53,890**

4.6 The Worksheet

Although a worksheet is not a required report during the accounting cycle, but there are many potential benefits to using it. Specifically, the purpose of the worksheet is to:

1. Assist in the preparation of financial statements.

2. Reduce the possibility of errors.

3. Link accounts and their adjustments to financial statements.

4. Assist in planning and organizing audits of financial statements.

5. Help prepare interim financial statements.

6. Show the effect of the proposed transaction.

Generally speaking, a worksheet contains the unadjusted trial balance, adjustments, adjusting trial balance, income statement, and the statements of financial position.

The worksheet for D.Z. Co. is shown in Exhibit 4-6.

Exhibit 4-6

D.Z. Co.

The worksheet

December 31, 2019

Account	Unadjusted Trial Balance		Adjustments		Adjusted Trial Balance		Income Statement		Balance sheet	
	Debit	Credit	Debit	Credit	Debit	Credit	Debit	Credit	Debit	Credit
Cash	$53,000	$22,800			$30,200				$30,200	
Accounts Receivable	$5,200			$2,640	$7,840				$7,840	
Prepaid Insurance	$3,600			$100	$3,500				$3,500	
Supplies	$2,500				$2,500				$2,500	
Equipment	$10,000				$10,000				$10,000	
Accumulated Depreciation				$150		$150				$150
Short-term Loan		$8,000				$8,000				$8,000
Salaries Payable				$360		$360				$360
Interest Payable				$40		$40				$40
Unearned Revenue		$3,000	$300			$2,700				$2,700
Capital		$36,000				$36,000				$36,000
Drawing	$300				$300				$300	
Service Revenue		$11,200		$2,940		$14,140		$14,140		
Rent Expense	$4,000				$4,000		$4,000			
Insurance Expense			$100		$100		$100			
Utility Expense	$600				$600		$600			
Salaries Expense	$1,800		$360		$2,160		$2,160			
Interest Expense			$40		$40		$40			
Depreciation Expense			$150		$150		$150			
Total	$81,000	$81,000	$3,590	$3,590	$3,590	$61,390	$7,050	$14,140	$54,340	$47,250
Net profit							$7,090			$7,090
							$14,140	$14,140	$54,340	$54,340

4.7 Closing Entries

The closing process is an important step at the end of the accounting period following the completion of the financial statements. With the formal financial statements, you can start the checkout and prepare for the next accounting period. Income is earned over time. At the end of this period, it needs to start over and calculate the revenue for the next period. The goal of the settlement process is to reset all temporary accounts to a zero balance at the end of the period. All accounts to be closed are called temporary accounts. The temporary account includes income, expenses, withdrawals and income summary. At the end of the period, the balances of these accounts should all be zero. Permanent accounts include assets, liabilities, and owner's capital. These accounts are inherently permanent because they carry over from one accounting period to the next. Businesses will use a temporary account called "Profit/Loss Summary" to streamline the settlement process. The checkout process only applies to temporary accounts, income, expenses, withdrawals, and income summary.

1. Closing the Revenue accounts to the Profit/Loss Summary accounts

Date	Description	P.R.	Debit	Credit
Dec.31	Service Revenue		$14,140	
	Profit/Loss Summary (P/L)			$14,140
	Closing revenues account			

2. Closing the Expense accounts to the Profit/Loss Summary accounts

Date	Description	P.R.	Debit	Credit
Dec.31	Profit/Loss Summary (P/L)		$7,050	
	Rent Expense			$4,000
	Insurance Expense			$100
	Utility Expense			$600
	Salaries Expense			$2,160
	Interest Expense			$40
	Depreciation Expense			$150
	Closing expenses accounts			

3. Closing the Profit/Loss Summary accounts to the Retained Earning accounts

Date	Description	P.R.	Debit	Credit
Dec.31	Profit/Loss Summary (P/L)		$7,090	
	Retained Earning			$7,090
	Closing Profit/Loss Summary account			

4. Closing Withdrawals accounts to the Dividend/Retained Earning accounts

Date	Description	P.R.	Debit	Credit
Dec.31	Retained Earning		$300	
	Drawing			$300
	Closing withdrawals account			

4.8 The Post-Closing Trial Balance

The final step in the accounting cycle is to prepare a trial balance after checkout, which needs to ensure that the journaling and posting of the closing entries is completed. The balance of the temporary account is reset to zero. The permanent account still exists. A post-closing trial balance is shown in Exhibit 4-7.

Exhibit 4-7

D.Z. Co.

Trial Balance

December 31, 2019

	Debit	Credit
Cash	$30,200	
Accounts Receivable	$7,840	
Prepaid Insurance	$3,500	
Supplies	$2,500	
Equipment	$10,000	
Accumulated Depreciation		$150
Short-term Loan		$8,000
Salaries Payable		$360
Interest Payable		$40
Unearned Revenue		$2,700
Capital		$36,000
Retained Earning		$6,790
Total	$54,040	$54,040

Key Words and Expressions

accounting cycle	会计循环
ledger account	分类账
general ledger	总分类账
journal ledger	日记账
posting	过账
accrued revenue	应计收入
accrued expense	应计费用
unearned revenue	未实现收入
prepaid expense	预付费用
depreciation expense	折旧费用
contra account	备抵账户
net book value	账面净值
trial balance	试算平衡表
unadjusted trial balance	未调整试算平衡表
end-of-period adjusting entries	期末调整分录
adjusted trial balance	账项调整后试算平衡表
worksheet	工作表
closing	结账

income summary	收益汇总
nominal account	虚账户
permanent account	永久性账户
temporary account	临时性账户

Exercises

1. Which of the following would not be identified by extracting a trial balance? (   )

    A. Two credit entries and no debit.

    B. One-sided entry.

    C. Transaction omitted completely.

    D. Two debit entries and no credit.

2. Given the following information:

Receivables on 1 Jan. 2019	$20,000
Receivables on 31 Dec. 2019	$8,500
Total receipts during 2019(including cash sales of $3,600)	$73,600

What are sales on credit during 2019? (   )

   A. $28,500.

   B. $62,100.

   C. $41,500.

   D. $45,100.

3. ABC's draft financial statements for the year to 31 December 2019 report a loss of $2,365. When he prepared the financial statements, Buster did not include an accrual of $1,749 and a prepayment of $913.

What is Buster's profit or loss for the year to 31 December 2019 following the inclusion of the accrual and prepayment? (   )

   A. A loss of $1,529.

   B. A loss of $3,201.

   C. A loss of $5,027.

   D. A profit of $297.

4. ABC's trial balance on 31 December 2019 includes the following balances:

Trade receivables $32,695	
Receivables allowance $1,078	

How should these balances be reported in ABC's statement of financial position as on 31 December 2019? (   )

   A. An asset of $31,617.

   B. An asset of $32,695 and a liability of $1,078.

   C. A Liability of $31,617.

   D. A liability of $32,695 and an asset of $1,078.

5. A trial balance is made up of a list of debit balances and credit balances. Which of the following statements is correct? (   )

   A. Every debit balance represents an expense.
   B. Assets are represented by debit balances.
   C. Liabilities are represented by debit balances.
   D. Income is included in the list of debit balances.

6. As on 30 Oct. 2019, your business has the following balances on its ledger accounts.

Accounts	Balance $
Bank loan	14,800
Cash at bank	13,600
Capital	16,000
Business taxes	2,000
Accounts payable	14,700
Purchases	16,000
Sales	15,800
Sundry payables	2,130
Accounts receivable	14,100
Bank loan interest	3,900
Other expenses	11,020
Vehicles	2,810

On 31 Oct. 2019, the business made the following transactions.

(1) Bought materials for $1,200, half for cash and half on credit;

(2) Made $2,200 sales, $1,600 of which was for credit;

(3) Paid wages to shop assistants of $480 in cash.

Required: Drawing up a trial balance showing the balances as at the end of 31 Oct. 2019.

第4章 会计循环

会计循环是发生经济业务事件时,获取原始凭证、进行账簿记录直到编制财务会计报表(即完成一个会计期间的会计工作)的过程。

企业将按照一定的步骤和方法,记录、分类和汇总在一定时期内发生的所有经济交易,直至编制会计报表。这些工作在连续的会计期间一遍遍重复。会计循环的主要过程如下:

1. 分析经济业务,根据取得的原始凭证利用复式记账原理编写会计分录。
2. 在日记账中记录账户,包括借方和贷方。
3. 将借方和贷方从日记账过账到相应的分类账。
4. 编制未调整的试用平衡表,汇总未调整的分类账科目和金额。
5. 会计期末,根据权责发生制,调整分录、日记账和过账。
6. 编制调整后的试算平衡表,汇总调整后的分类账科目和金额。
7. 编制财务报表,根据调整后的试算平衡表编制财务报表。
8. 编制结账分录,结清收入、费用等临时性账户和利润账户。
9. 编制结账后的试算表。

4.1 日记账和过账

4.1.1 日记账

根据复式记账原理,会计人员首先在日记账中记录经济业务,日记账是根据每天发生的经济业务所编制的会计分录,全部按时间顺序逐笔登记。在日记账中按照借方和贷方记录业务交易,具体方法如下:

1. 日期:登记经济业务发生的日期。年度记入日期栏上端,月、日分两小栏登记。
2. 说明栏:简要说明经济业务的内容和账户名称。
3. P.R.(过账参考)过账:每天根据日记账中借方和贷方账户及其金额登记到分类账户后,在过账栏内注明表示已经过账。
4. 金额:将经济业务金额登记到借方、贷方栏内。
5. 页数:在此列中输入总账页面数。

在复式记账会计中,讨论了业务交易的性质以及如何对其进行分析和分类,通过在 T 型账户中输入来显示交易的效果。然而,这些项目不提供特定交易的必要数据,也不提供交易的时间顺序记录。接下来,根据前文的会计信息,运用日记账将业务交易按时间顺序清晰地记录在账簿中。

【例 4-1】该企业的一般日记账记录了以下 2019 年 12 月的交易:

12 月 1 日,Z. Daisy 向 D.Z.公司的咨询业务投资了 36,000 美元。

1 日,从国家银行借款 8,000 美元。该票据的年利率为 6%,将在一年内偿还。

1 日,支付 3,600 美元的 36 个月保险。

2 日,支付 2,500 美元现金购买一般办公用品。

3 日,以 10,000 美元现金购置设备。

11 日,为客户提供咨询服务,收到现金 6,000 美元。

11 日,员工每天的工资为 90 美元,每两个星期三支付一次。发薪日是 2019 年 12 月 11 日,星期三。

13 日,以现金支付办公室租金的 4,000 美元。

15 日,Elle 公司赊账完成会计工作,5,200 美元。

23 日,支付会计处的每月水电费 600 美元。

25 日,员工每天的工资为 90 美元,每两个星期三支付一次。2019 年的最后一个发薪日是 2019 年 12 月 25 日,星期三。

26 日,Z. Daisy 提取了 300 美元用于个人使用。

28 日,同意向客户提供 30 天的咨询服务,费用为 3,000 美元。

日记账分录显示在表 4-1 中。

表 4-1

普通日记账　　　　　　　　　　　　　页数 G1

日期		摘要	过账参考	借方	贷方
12 月	1	现金		$36,000	
		Z. Daisy,资本			$36,000
		投资咨询业务			
	1	现金		$8,000	
		短期贷款			$8,000
		借款			
	1	保险费用		$3,600	
		现金			$3,600
		提前支付保险费用			
	2	耗材			$2,500
		现金		$2,500	
		购买办公耗材			
	3	设备		$10,000	
		现金			$10,000
		购买设备			
	11	现金		$6,000	
		服务收入			$6,000
		提供咨询业务的收入			
	11	薪金费用		$900	
		现金			$900
		支付两周工作日的薪酬			
	13	租赁费用		$4,000	
		现金			$4,000
		支付租赁费用			
	15	应收账款		$5,200	
		服务收入			$5,200

(续表)

日期	摘要	过账参考	借方	贷方
23	提供会计工作的收入			
	水电费		$600	
	现金			$600
	支付月度水电费			
25	薪金费用		$900	
	现金			$900
	支付两周工作日的薪酬			
26	提款		$300	
	现金			$300
	提款供个人使用			
28	现金		$3,000	
	未实现收入			$3,000
	获得咨询费收入			
	合计		$85,000	$85,000

4.1.2 过账

过账是将会计信息从日记账输入到分类账的过程。为避免遗漏和重复，请在 P.R. 列中引用账号和日记账页码。具体步骤如下：

1. 在会计账户中记录日期和金额。
2. 在会计账户的 P.R. 列中注册日记账页的编号。
3. 在日记账的 P.R. 栏中记录分类账账号。

第1步：在会计账户中记录日期和金额

日记账　　　　　　　　　　　　　　　　　页面 G1

日期	摘要	过账参考	借方	贷方
12月1日	现金		$36,000	
	资本			$36,000

现金 101

12月1日
$36,000

资本 301

12月1日　$36,000

第 2 步：在会计账户的过账参考列中登记日记账页的编号

日记账　　　　　　　　　　　　　　　　　　　　　　　　页面 G1

日期	摘要	过账参考	借方	贷方
12月1日	现金		$36,000	
	资本			$36,000

现金 101　　　　　　　　　　　　　资本 301

G1
12月1日
$36,000

G1　12月1日
$36,000

第 3 步：在日记账的过账参考列中记录分类科目编号

日记账　　　　　　　　　　　　　　　　　　　　　　　　页面 G1

日期	摘要	过账参考	借方	贷方
12月1日	现金	101	$36,000	
	资本	301		$36,000

现金 101　　　　　　　　　　　　　资本 301

G1 12月1日
$36,000

G1 12月1日
$36,000

【例 4-2】 根据 D.Z.公司咨询业务的会计科目表和例 4-1 中的日记账分录演示过账过程。

会计科目表	
会计科目编号	账户名称
	资产
101	现金
102	银行存款
121	应收票据
122	应收账款
126	预付保险
134	坏账准备
141	耗材
142	设备

(续表)

会计科目表

会计科目编号	账户名称
149	累计折旧
171	无形资产
172	累计摊销
176	商誉

负债

会计科目编号	账户名称
201	短期贷款
221	应付票据
222	应付账款
228	应付职工薪酬
229	应付利息
231	未实现收入
261	长期贷款

所有者权益

会计科目编号	账户名称
301	资本
321	普通股
331	提款

收入

会计科目编号	账户名称
401	销售收入
402	服务收入

费用/成本

会计科目编号	账户名称
501	销货成本
502	管理费用
503	销售费用
504	广告费用
505	租赁费用
506	保险费用
507	水电费用
508	薪金费用
509	利息费用
510	折旧费用

现金　　　　　　　　　　　　　　会计科目编号：101

日期		摘要	过账参考	借方	贷方	余额
2019						
12.	1	现金	G1	$36,000		$36,000
	1		G1	$8,000		$44,000
	1		G1		$3,600	$40,400
	2		G1		$2,500	$37,900
	3		G1		$10,000	$27,900

(续表)

11		G1	$6,000		$33,900
11		G1		$900	$33,000
13		G1		$4,000	$29,000
23		G1		$600	$28,400
25		G1		$900	$27,500
26		G1		$300	$27,200
28		G1	$3,000		$30,200

应收账款 会计科目编号：122

日期	摘要	过账参考	借方	贷方	余额
2019 12月15日		G1	$5,200		$5,200

耗材 会计科目编号：141

日期	摘要	过账参考	借方	贷方	余额
2019 12月2日		G1	$2,500		$2,500

设备 会计科目编号：142

日期	摘要	过账参考	借方	贷方	余额
2019 12月3日		G1	$10,000		$10,000

短期贷款 会计科目编号：201

日期	摘要	过账参考	借方	贷方	余额
2019 12月1日		G1		$8,000	$8,000

未实现收入 会计科目编号：231

日期	摘要	过账参考	借方	贷方	余额
2019 12月28日		G1		$3,000	$3,000

资本——Daisy 会计科目编号：301

日期	摘要	过账参考	借方	贷方	余额
2019 12月1日		G1		$36,000	$36,000

提款 会计科目编号：331

日期	摘要	过账参考	借方	贷方	余额
2019 12月26日		G1	$300		$300

服务收入					会计科目编号：402
日期	摘要	过账参考	借方	贷方	余额
2019 12月11日		G1		$6,000	$6,000
12月15日				$5,200	$11,200

租赁费用					会计科目编号：505
日期	摘要	过账参考	借方	贷方	余额
2019 12月13日		G1	$4,000		$4,000

保险费用					会计科目编号：506
日期	摘要	过账参考	借方	贷方	余额
2019 12月1日		G1	$3,600		$3,600

水电费用					会计科目编号：507
日期	摘要	过账参考	借方	贷方	余额
2019 12月26日		G1	$600		$600

薪金费用					会计科目编号：508
日期	摘要	过账参考	借方	贷方	余额
2019 12月11日		G1	$900		$900
12月25日		G1	$900		$1,800

4.2　试算平衡表

　　当期记录的所有交易过账到分类账以后，就可以确定每一个账户的余额。每一个账户将有一个借方余额、贷方余额或者零余额。为了确定所有分类账户借方金额的和是否等于所有分类账户贷方金额的和，应该编制一个试算平衡表。试算平衡表由两个栏目组成，按账户在分类账中出现的次序列出所有账户的名称和余额。借方余额列示在左边栏上，贷方余额列示在右边栏上。两栏的总和应该相等。如果试算平衡表不平衡，则表明会计人员不能进一步编制财务报表。在继续工作之前，会计人员必须找出错误，并把它改正过来。因此，试算平衡表可以核查记录和过账的正确性，也可以告知会计人员是否出错。然而，通过试算平衡表来检查账簿记录是否正确并不是绝对的，从某种意义上讲，如果借贷方不平衡，就可以肯定账户的记录是计算有误，但是如果借贷方平衡，也不能肯定账户记录没有错误，因为有些错误并不影响借方和贷方的平衡关系。如果在有关账户中重记或漏记了某项经济业务，或者将经济业务的借贷方方向记反了，就不一定能通过试算平衡发现错误。

【例 4-3】 根据例 4-2，总分类账进行核算，以验证借方是否等于贷方。

D.Z.公司
试算平衡表
2019 年 12 月 31 日

	借方	贷方
现金	$53,000	$22,800
应收账款	$5,200	
耗材	$2,500	
设备	$10,000	
预付保险	$3,600	
短期贷款		$8,000
未实现收入		$3,000
资本		$36,000
提款	$300	
服务收入		$11,200
租赁费用	$4,000	
水电费用	$600	
薪金费用	$1,800	
总额	$81,000	$81,000

4.3 调整账户

调整账项，是在会计期末，按照权责发生制原则，确定当期的收入和支出，并对相关账户编制必要的调整分录。账户调整的目的是正确计算损益，使报告期间应有的收支相匹配，以便正确评估每个期间的损益和每个会计期间的财务结果。

根据应计原则和匹配原则，调整账项分为两类。第一类是在确认费用或收入之前支付或接收的现金。此类别包括预付或递延费用(包括折旧)以及未赚取或递延收入。调整账项的第二个主要类别是在确认费用或收入后支付或收取的现金。此类别包括应计费用和应计收入。

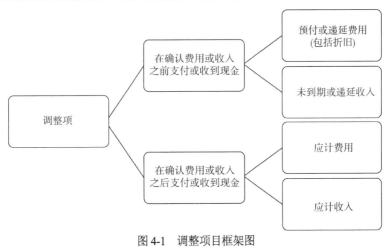

图 4-1 调整项目框架图

4.3.1 应计收入

应计收入指会计期内已实现但尚未收到款项的各项收入，如应收利息、应收租金等。记录应计收入的调整条目将始终借记或增加资产账户，贷记或增加收入账户。收入确认后需要结账，资产则留转到下期，待收到款项时再予冲销。

【例4-4】在年底，D.Z.公司实现了应记录的咨询收入2,640美元。在2019年12月10日，D.Z.公司同意根据60天固定费用合同提供咨询服务，费用为7,200美元(每天120美元)。所有服务将于2020年2月7日完成，届时客户将全额付款。

日期	摘要	过账参考	借方	贷方
12月31日	应收账款		$2,640	
	服务收入			$2,640
	计提收入(22×120=2,640)			

应收账款 122		服务收入 402	
12月31日 $2,640		12月31日 $2,640	

公司将借记或增加资产，应收账款，并贷记或增加收入账户，即咨询收入，为2,640美元。合同签订已经过去了二十二天，客户没有应收或未付款。因此，D.Z.公司将获得2,640美元的收入(每天120美元乘以22天)。

请注意，应收账款和服务收入账户已更新，包括所提供服务的已赚取但未开票的金额。记录咨询工作的后续完成和现金的收取。

日期	摘要	过账参考	借方	贷方
2月7日	现金		$7,200	
	服务收入			$4,560
	应收账款			$2,640
	记录合同完成情况和现金收款情况			

2020年2月7日，D.Z.公司完成了咨询合同下的业务。该客户的账单为7,200美元，D.Z.公司收到了7,200美元的现金。D.Z.公司将在现金账户中扣除7,200美元，从应收账款中扣除2,640美元，并确认二月份的收入4,560美元。

4.3.2 应计费用

应计费用也称应付费用，指本期已发生但尚未支付款项的各种费用，如应付租金、应付利息及应付工资等。对于所有应计费用调整分录，它借记或增加费用科目，贷记或增加负债科目。应计费用必须在发生当期的损益表中报告。

【例4-5】D.Z.公司员工的日薪为90美元，每两周的星期三支付。2019年12月31日是星期二。2019年的最后一个发薪日是2019年12月25日，星期三。从12月26日到12月31日共有四个工作日。员工从星期四到星期二的工资为360美元，下星期三才支付。

记录调整账户

2019 年 12 月 31 日记录一个调整分录，以确认员工还未领到的薪水。在调整日记账分录时，它将借记或增加薪金费用，贷记或增加薪金 360 美元。调整后，正确列出了 2019 年的薪金支出。

日期	摘要	过账参考	借方	贷方
12 月 31 日	薪酬费用		$360	
	应付职工薪酬			$360
	计提 4 天的工资 (4×90＝360)			

薪酬费用 508			应付职工薪酬 228	
12 月 11 日	$900		12 月 31 日	$360
12 月 25 日	$900			
12 月 31 日	$360			
余额	$2160			

年内的薪金开支为 1,800 元。过账调整分录后，年底的新余额为 2,160 美元。当员工于 2020 年 1 月 8 日支付工资时，应付薪金账户将被取消。

日期	摘要	过账参考	借方	贷方
1 月 8 日	应付职工薪酬*(4×90＝360)*		$360	
	薪酬费用*(6×90＝540)*		$540	
	现金			$900
	支付两周的工资			

D.Z. 公司将支付从 2019 年 12 月 25 日到 2020 年 1 月 8 日的两周的薪水。此薪金的日记账分录涉及负债账户——应付工资的借方，为 360 美元，即在 2019 年 12 月 31 日应计的金额，从薪金支出中扣除 540 美元(6 个工作日乘以每天 90 美元)，并从现金中扣除 900 美元。在实际向员工支付以前欠的所有款项时，必须小心结算应计应付款项。

【例 4-6】D.Z.公司于 2019 年 12 月 1 日从国家银行借款 8,000 美元。该票据的年利率为 6%，应于一年内偿还。截至 2019 年 12 月 31 日的一个月内累积了利息。

日期	摘要	过账参考	借方	贷方
12 月 31 日	利息费用		$40	
	应付利息			$40
	计提利息. ($8,000×6%×30/360)			

利息费用 509			应付利息 229	
12 月 31 日	$40		12 月 31 日	$40

调整日记账分录将借记或增加利息费用,贷记或增加利息 40 美元(8,000 美元乘以 6%的利率,再乘以 30/360)。调整后,2019 年的利息支出被准确记录。年末的利息费用为 40 美元。当银行于 2020 年 12 月 1 日偿还银行本金 8,000 美元和年度利息 480 美元时,应付利息账户将被去除。

4.3.3　预收收入

预收收入是指在提供产品和服务之前收到的现金。预收收入,也称为递延收入,是负债。在考虑递延收入时,它面临着一项交易,即在提供产品或服务之前先收取现金。换句话说,企业已收到现金,但还没有做事情。

【例 4-7】2019 年 12 月 28 日,D.Z.公司同意向客户提供 30 天固定费用为 3,000 美元的咨询服务。12 月 28 日这天 D.Z.公司记入借方或增加到现金账户,并贷记或增加到称为未实现收入的负债账户。调整分录 D.Z.公司将于 2019 年 12 月 31 日编制,即会计期结束。

日期	摘要	过账参考	借方	贷方
12 月 31 日	未实现收入		$300	
	服务收入			$300
	确认 3 天的咨询服务收入			

截至 2019 年 12 月 31 日,D.Z.公司已获得 3,000 美元的咨询费。自公司签订为期 30 天的合同以来,已经过去了三天。调整分录是借记或减少负债账户,未实现收入和贷记或增加收入账户——咨询收入,为 300 美元(三天,每天 100 美元)。

未实现收入 231				服务收入 402	
12 月 31 日　$300	12 月 28 日	$3,000		12 月 31 日	$300
	余额	$2,700			

未实现收入账户的贷方余额 2,700 美元。随着时间的流逝,这笔钱将被确认。咨询收入账户的贷方余额为 300 美元。收入科目将出现在损益表中,并在会计期末结转。负债科目,即未实现收入,将出现在 2019 年 12 月 31 日的资产负债表上。

4.3.4　预付费用

预付费用是指业务交易的一方将部分款项预先支付给另一方时发生的费用。预付费用通常包括预付保险、用品、租金等。其他预付费用,则与"保险和用品"完全一样。应该注意的是,一些预付费用在单个期间内已付清并已全部用完。例如,公司可以在每月的第一天支付月租金。这笔付款会在该月的第一天创建一个预付费用,并在该月底完全到期。在这些特殊情况下,可以将通过借方支付的现金记录到费用账户而不是资产账户中。

【例 4-8】2019 年 12 月 1 日,D.Z.公司为 2019 年 12 月至 2022 年 11 月的 36 个月保险支付了 3,600 美元。它从预付保险金和贷记现金中扣除。让我们看一下将在 2019 年 12 月 31 日进行的调整项。

日期	摘要	过账参考	借方	贷方
12 月 31 日	保险费用		$100	
	预付保险			$100
	记录第一个月到期的保费			

保险费用 506		预付保险 126			
12月31日 $100		12月1日	$3,600	12.31	$100
		余额	$3,500		

预付保险账户减少为 3,500 美元，代表剩余 35 个月每月支付 100 美元。保险费用账户现在余额为 100 美元，即 2019 年 12 月的保险金额。

4.3.5 折旧

除土地外，企业的资产在其使用寿命内都会折旧。折旧是系统地、合理地分配企业资产在其使用寿命内的成本的过程。至此，在会计过程中常用直线折旧的折旧方法。直线折旧是公司最常用的方法。通过计算企业资产的成本，减去估计的残值，然后将该金额除以资产的使用寿命来确定年折旧额。残值是指当企业在使用寿命结束时处置该资产时所期望获得的金额。在后面的章节中，将进一步讨论其他的折旧方法。

【例 4-9】2019 年 12 月 3 日，D.Z.公司以 10,000 美元的现金购买了设备。该设备的估计使用寿命为 5 年或 60 个月，在 5 年期限结束时的残值估计为 1,000 美元。可以确定 2019 年 12 月的折旧费用吗？

日期	摘要	过账参考	借方	贷方
12月31日	折旧费用		$150	
	累计折旧 – 设备			$150
	记录月折旧额			

折旧费用 510		累计折旧 149	
12月31日 $150		12月31日	$150

在 2019 年 12 月 31 日，它将借记 150 美元的折旧费用或增加折旧费用，并记入称为"累计折旧——设备"的新账户的贷方。累计折旧是对冲资产账户。对冲账户意味着账户中的金额减少了相关资产账户。在这种情况下，累计折旧将减少资产账户——设备。调整分录已过账以记录折旧费用，还显示了设备账户中的余额。折旧费用科目将出现在截至 2019 年 12 月 31 日的年度利润表中。对冲账户累计折旧将显示为资产——设备成本的减少。企业资产成本减去累计折旧的成本称为账面价值。因此，资产——设备将以其净额或账面价 9,850 美元显示在资产负债表上。由于该抵销账户显示在资产负债表上，因此期末将不会关闭该账户。它将结转到 2020 年，并用于累计与设备有关的折旧。

4.4 调整后试算平衡表

期末将各调整分录过账后再编制"调整后试算平衡表"，其目的是检查调整账务处理是否正确完整。"调整后试算平衡表"应在原试算平衡表旁增加两列——调整项借方及调整项贷方，然后用原试算平衡表余额通过加减调整项借方和调整项贷方余额得到调整后试算平衡表的金额(表 4-2)。

表 4-2

D.Z.公司调整后试算平衡表
2019 年 12 月 31 日

账户	未调整试算平衡表		调整项		调整后试算平衡表	
	借方	贷方	借方	贷方	借方	贷方
现金	$53,000	$22,800			$30200	
应收账款	$5,200		$2,640		$7,840	
预付保险	$3,600			$100	$3,500	
耗材	$2,500				$2,500	
设备	$10,000				$10,000	
累计折旧				$150		$150
短期贷款		$8,000				$8,000
应付职工薪酬				$360		$360
应付利息				$40		$40
未实现收入		$3,000	$300			$2,700
资本		$36,000				$36,000
提款	$300				$300	
服务收入		$11,200		$2,940		$14,140
租赁费用	$4,000				$4,000	
保险费用			$100		$100	
水电费	$600				$600	
薪酬费用	$1,800		$360		$2,160	
利息费用			$40		$40	
折旧费用			$150		$150	
总额	**$81,000**	**$81,000**	**$3,590**	**$3,590**	**$61,390**	**$61,390**

由结果可知，调整项目的发生并没有影响试算表的平衡。

4.5 编制财务报表

根据会计循环的过程，可以根据调整后的试算表编制财务报表。首先，编制损益表，损益表的两列分别包含支出和收入。净收入是这两个金额之间的差，它会增加所有者的权益账户。表 4-3 描述了 D.Z. 公司期末 2019 年 12 月 31 日的利润表。

表 4-3

D.Z.公司
利润表
截至年度 2019 年 12 月 31 日

收入(利润)：	
服务收入	$14,140
费用：	

(续表)

租赁费用	$4,000	
保险费用	$100	
水电费	$600	
薪酬费用	$2,160	
利息费用	$40	
折旧费用	$150	$7,050
净利润		**$7,090**

*假设此处忽略所得税费。

完成损益表后，开始准备所有者权益表的编制。再将净收入和投资额加在一起，减去所有取款，得出期末资本余额 42,790 美元。所有者权益的损益表编制完后就可以准备资产负债表了。D.Z.公司截至 2019 年 12 月 31 日的所有者权益变动表列示在表 4-4。

表 4-4

D.Z.公司所有者权益变动表
截至 2019 年 12 月 31 日

D.Z.公司 2019 年 12 月 1 日的资本	
本月投资	$36,000
加：净利润(利润表)	$7,090
减：提款	($300)
D.Z.公司 2019 年 12 月 31 日的资本	**$42,790**

D.Z.公司资本账户中的余额显示在资产负债表的所有者权益中上。资产和负债直接取调整后的试算平衡表。资产总额等于负债总额加上所有者权益总额。D.Z.公司 2019 年 12 月 31 日的资产负债表列示在表 4-5。

表 4-5

D.Z. Co.
资产负债表
2019 年 12 月 31 日

资产		
现金		$30,200
应收账款		$7,840
预付保险		$3,500
耗材		$2,500
设备	$10,000	
减：累计折旧	($150)	$9,850
资产总额		**$53,890**
负债		
短期贷款		$8,000
应付职工薪酬		$360

	(续表)
应付利息	$40
未实现收入	$2,700
负债总额	**$11,100**
所有者权益	
D.Z.公司资本	$42,790
所有者权益总额	$42,790
负债和所有者权益总额	$53,890

4.6 工作表

工作表在会计循环过程中并不是必需的，但是使用工作表具有许多潜在的好处。具体来说，工作表的作用有：

1. 协助编制财务报表。
2. 减少出错的可能性。
3. 将账户及其改动与财务报表连接。
4. 协助计划和组织财务报表审计。
5. 帮助准备中期财务报表。
6. 显示拟议交易的效果。

通常来说，工作表(表 4-6)中包含调整前的试算平衡表、调整账项、调整后的试算平衡表、利润表和资产负债表。

表 4-6

D.Z.公司
工作表
2019 年 12 月 31 日

账户	调整前试算平衡表		调整账项		调整后试算平衡表		利润表		资产负债表	
	借方	贷方	借方	贷方	借方	贷方	借方	贷方	借方	贷方
现金	$53,000	$22,800			$30,200				$30,200	
应收账款	$5,200		$2,640		$7,840				$7,840	
预付保险	$3,600			$100	$3,500				$3,500	
耗材	$2,500				$2,500				$2,500	
设备	$10,000				$10,000				$10,000	
累计折旧				$150		$150				$150
短期贷款		$8,000				$8,000				$8,000
应付职工薪酬				$360		$360				$360
应付利息				$40		$40				$40
未实现收入		$3,000	$300			$2,700				$2,700
资本		$36,000				$36,000				$36,000
提款	$300				$300				$300	
服务收入		$11,200		$2,940		$14,140		$14,140		

(续表)

租赁费用	$4,000					$4,000	$4,000			
保险费用			$100			$100	$100			
水电费	$600					$600	$600			
薪酬费用	$1,800		$360			$2,160	$2,160			
利息费用			$40			$40	$40			
折旧费用			$150			$150	$150			
总额	$81,000	$81,000	$3,590	$3,590	$3,590	$61,390	$7,050	$14,140	$54,340	$47,250
净利润							$7,090			$7,090
							$14,140	$14,140	$54,340	$54,340

4.7 结账分录

在财务报表完成后的会计期间结束时，结账流程是重要的一步。有了正式的财务报表，就可以开始结账并为下一个会计期间做准备。收入是随着时间的推移而获得的。在此期间结束时，它需要重新开始并计算下一个期间的收入。结算过程的目标是在期末将所有临时账户重置为零余额。将要结转的所有账户都称为临时账户。临时账户包括收入、支出、提款和损益汇总。在期末，这些账户的余额都应为零。永久账户包括资产、负债和所有者的资本。这些账户本质上是永久性的，因为它们从一个会计期间结转到下一会计期间。企业将使用名为"损益汇总"的临时账户来简化结算过程。结账流程仅适用于临时账户，收入、支出、提款和损益汇总。

1. 结转收入类账户到损益汇总账户

日期	摘要	过账参考	借方	贷方
12月31日	服务收入		$14,140	
	损益汇总			$14,140
	结转收入类账户			

2. 结转费用类账户到损益汇总账户

日期	摘要	过账参考	借方	贷方
12月31日	损益汇总		$7,050	
	租赁费用			$4,000
	保险费用			$100
	水电费			$600
	薪酬费用			$2,160
	利息费用			$40
	折旧费用			$150
	结转费用类账户			

3. 结转损益汇总账户到留存收益账户

日期	摘要	过账参考	借方	贷方
12月31日	损益汇总		$7,090	
	留存收益			$7,090
	结转损益汇总账户			

4. 结转提款账户到股利/留存收益账户

日期	摘要	过账参考	借方	贷方
12月31日	留存收益		$300	
	提款			$300
	结转提款账户			

4.8 结账后的试算平衡表

会计循环的最后一步是在结账后准备试算表，这需要确保完成结账日记账和过账。临时账户的余额重置为零。永久账户仍然存在。表4-7显示了结账后的试算平衡表。

表4-7

D.Z.公司
试算平衡表
2019年12月31日

	借方	贷方
现金	$30,200	
应收账款	$7,840	
预付保险	$3,500	
耗材	$2,500	
设备	$10,000	
累计折旧		$150
短期贷款		$8,000
应付职工薪酬		$360
应付利息		$40
未实现收入		$2,700
资本		$36,000
留存收益		$6,790
总额	$54,040	$54,040

Chapter 5

Cash

An asset is defined in *IAS Conceptual Framework* as:

The resources generated through transactions in the past, owned or controlled by the entity at the moment, and predicted to bring economic benefits in the future.

In the field of accounting, the asset refers to economic resources, which are measured by currency values and owned or controlled by an enterprise. Firms may have current assets, fixed assets and other forms of assets. Current assets are expected to be converted to cash, sold or used up in one year or one operating cycle, with the normal operation of the enterprise. The main current assets include cash, receivables and inventories. This chapter will discuss cash firstly.

5.1 Cash and Cash Equivalents

5.1.1 Definition

Cash refers to more than bills and coins. In accounting, it refers to currencies on hand (coins, bills), and deposits in banks or other depositories.

Cash equivalents refer to short-term and highly liquid investments that are easily converted to the known amount of cash and have an insignificant risk of changes in value. Cash equivalents, along with stocks and bonds, are three main asset classes. Cash and cash equivalents, including government treasury bills, bank certificates of deposit, bankers' acceptances, corporate commercial paper and other money market instruments, have the features of low risks and low returns.

Cash equivalents differ from other investments in terms of their short-term existence. They normally mature in three months. However, the existence of short-term investments does not exceed 12 months and that of long-term investments is more than 12 months. Another important requirement for cash equivalents is the low investment risk. Therefore, preferred shares that can be purchased shortly before the redemption date, instead of common shares, can be included in cash equivalents.

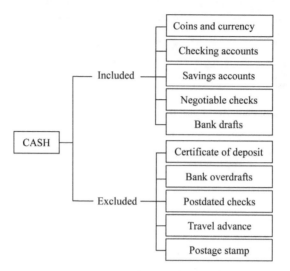

Figure 5-1   The Classification of Cash

Most companies use the term "Cash and Cash Equivalents" when reporting cash. As the most current and liquid asset of all current assets, "Cash and Cash Equivalents" is listed the top of the balance sheet. Bankers, credit managers, or investors who study balance sheets tend to show more interests in the total amount of cash and cash equivalents, compared with those in other balance sheet items, such as accounts payable.

5.1.2　Cash on Hand

Cash on hand refers to the currency deposited in the accounting department of the enterprise and administered by the cashier. Cash on hand is the most liquid asset of an enterprise. An enterprise should strictly abide by the relevant cash management system of the state, correctly carry out the accounting of cash income and expenditure, and supervise the legitimacy and rationality of its use.

According to the *Provisional Regulations on Cash Management*, the enterprise cash management system mainly includes the following aspects:

1. Scope of use of cash on hand

Payable which can use cash on hand includes:
- Wages and allowances for employees.
- Remuneration for personal services.
- Bonuses awarded to individuals in accordance with the provisions of the State for science, technology, culture, art, sports competitions, etc..
- Expenditures on labor insurance, welfares and other aspects stipulated by the State for individuals.
- Individuals' expenditure in purchasing agricultural and sideline products and other related products.
- Travel expenses that must be carried by travelers.
- Sporadic expenditures below the settlement threshold.

2. Maximum amount of cash holdings on hand

The maximum amount of cash holdings on hand refers to the maximum amount of cash that a company is allowed to retain in order to ensure its daily allowance for petty expenses. This limit is approved by the deposit-opening bank according to the actual needs of the enterprise, normally as the daily sporadic expenses for 3-5 days of a company. In remote areas with poor traffic condition, this limit can be determined according to the sporadic expenses for 5-15 days. Companies must strictly execute the cash float, and the cash above the mentioned amount must be deposited in bank on that day. An application shall be required to be submitted to the deposit-opening bank for the approval of any increase or decrease of the cash limit.

3. Regulations on Cash Receipts and Disbursement

The cash receipts and expenditures of the enterprise shall in accordance with the following provisions:

- The cash receipt of the company shall be deposited in the bank on the same day. If it is really difficult, the depositing time shall be determined by the bank.
- When an account-opening entity pays cash, it can pay from cash-on-hand limit or withdraw from the deposit bank. But cannot pay directly from the cash receipts of the entity. When cash is required to be deposited due to special circumstances, it shall be submitted to the depositing bank in advance for examination and approval, and the depositing scope and limit shall also be approved by the depositing bank. Enterprises with cash deposits shall regularly report the amount and use of cash deposits to their account-opening bank.
- While withdrawing cash from the depositing bank, the company shall specify the purpose of the withdrawal, which shall be signed and sealed by the person in charge of the accounting department. The cash shall be paid after the examination and verification conducted by the depositing bank.
- When cash must be used in other special situations, such as uncertain purchasing place, inconvenient transportation, urgent need for production or market and emergency relief, the enterprise shall submit an application to the deposit-opening bank, and the cash shall be paid after the application is signed and sealed by the person in charge of the accounting department and then examined by the deposit-opening bank.

Enterprises should set up the subject "Cash on Hand", in order to reflect and supervise the income, expenditure and deposit of cash on hand. The debit of the subject registers the increase of cash on hand, and the credit of the subject registers the decrease of cash on hand. The debit balance at the end of the period reflects the actual amount of cash on hand at the end of the period. In order to comprehensively and continuously reflect and monitor the receipts, disbursements and deposits of cash on hand, enterprises should also set up general accounts of cash on hand and diaries of cash on hand, and conduct general and explicit classified accounts of cash on hand respectively.

Cash on Hand	
Dr.	Cr.
Increase	Decrease

5.2 Internal Control over Cash

Considering the high risk of cash misappropriation, it is of great necessity to control and supervise the cash.

Due to the large volume and high frequency of cash transactions, errors may occur in executing and recording them. In order to ensure the accuracy and the reliability of accounting records cash, effective internal control over cash is necessary.

An effective internal control system to protect cash assets should follow three principles:

(1) Cash receipt and disbursement should be separated from cash recording.

(2) Cash receipt should be promptly deposited in bank.

(3) Cash disbursement should be made by check.

5.2.1 Separate from Record-keeping

This principle requires a separate management system of cash and account. More specifically, cash receipt, disbursement and custody shall be in the charge of the cashier, while the cashier shall not be in charge of the registration and custody of general ledger.

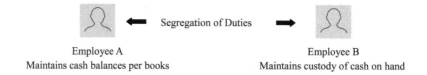

Employee A
Maintains cash balances per books

Employee B
Maintains custody of cash on hand

5.2.2 Internal Control over Cash Receipts

Cash inflows in most businesses come from various sources. The procedures used to attain adequate control may vary. However, the following procedures are of great importance in all situations:

(1) Immediate counting of all cash received.

(2) Immediate recording of all cash received.

(3) Timely depositing of all cash received.

5.2.3 Internal Control over Cash Disbursements

Many cases of the cash defalcation occur during the process of disbursement. The defalcation would be covered up very easily unless the enterprise can establish an effective controlling system with the following principles:

(1) All cash disbursements are made by check with an exception of applying the petty cash system for small amount expenditures. Checks should be signed, stored, and recorded separately. Control will be the most effective if one person is responsible for the only given task.

(2) A petty cash system should be established with tight control and close supervision.

(3) The enterprise should closely supervise all cash-disbursement, related bookkeeping and periodic internal reports, and verify them periodically or on a supervised basis by a third independent party.

Finally, in order to reduce the cash defalcation in the management process, it is necessary to institute a shift work in the financial department.

In order to ensure the safety and integrity of cash, the company should carry out checks of cash on hand regularly or irregularly according to the regulations. The cash checking report should be prepared on the basis of the check results. Any practice of cash misappropriation should be corrected in time. If the accounts are not in conformity and the causes of cash shortage or surplus are unknown, they should firstly be accounted for through the subject of "Wait Deal Assets Loss or Income". After approved by the authority of management, they should be dealt with separately in two cases. In the case of cash shortage, the part that should be compensated by the person responsible or the insurance company shall be included in the subject "Other Receivables", while the part with no clear reasons shall be included in the subject "Administrative Expenses". In the case of cash surplus, the part that should be paid to relevant personnel or units shall be included in the subject "Other Accounts Payable", while the part with no clear reasons shall be included in the subject "Non-operating income".

	Cash Shortage	Cash Overflow
Before Approval	Dr. Wait Deal Assets Loss or Income	Dr. Cash on hand
	Cr. Cash on Hand	Cr. Wait Deal Assets Loss or Income
After Approval	Dr. Other Receivables	Dr. Wait Deal Assets Loss or Income
	Administrative Expenses	Cr. Other Accounts Payable
	Cr. Wait Deal Assets Loss or Income	Non-operating Income

5.3 The Petty Cash Funds

The petty cash fund, also petty cash, refers to a small amount of cash on hand used for payment. A petty cash fund provides convenience for small transactions when issuing a check is unreasonable or unacceptable. Examples of petty cash fund uses include but not are limited to meal payment for a small group of employees, purchasing a small number of inexpensive supplies, or reimbursement claim for small work-related expenses.

For example, company A decided to establish a $500 small reserve (petty cash fund) on June 1. A check is required and exchanged in currency at the bank. The accounting entries for issuing checks are as follows:

  Dr. Petty Cash $500
    Cr. Bank Deposits $500

When the money in the petty cash fund reaches a minimum level or it is at the end of an accounting period, the fund should be reimbursed. The financial management department should examine the receipts and supporting documents to verify whether the payment is proper, and then the amount can be restored to its original level with approval. Meanwhile, all the supporting documents (receipts) are stamped paid so that they cannot be submitted again.

Continuing with the above example, company A used $150 paying for office expenses. The accounting entries are as follows:

  Dr. Administrative Expenses $150
    Cr. Petty Cash $150

And at the end of June, company A will issued a $150 check to replenish the petty cash fund keeping it at $500. The accounting entries are as follows:

Dr. Petty Cash $150
　　Cr. Bank Deposits　　　　　　　　　　　　　　　　　　　　　　　　$150

5.4　Bank Reconciliation

Bank deposits refer to the money deposited in banks or other financial institutions by enterprises. Enterprises shall open accounts in their local banks according to their business needs and regulations, and settle deposits, withdrawals and various revenue and expenditure transfer businesses with this account. The receipt and expenditure of bank deposits shall strictly comply with the provisions of the bank settlement system.

In order to reflect and supervise the receipts, expenditures and deposits of the bank deposits, enterprises should set up the subject "Bank Deposits". The debit of the subject registers the increase of corporate bank deposits, and the credit of the subject registers the decrease of bank deposits. The debit balance at the end of the period reflects the amount of bank deposits actually held by enterprises at the end of the period.

Bank Deposits	
Dr.	Cr.
Increase	Decrease

A company shall set up a general bank deposit account and a bank deposit journal, and carry out the general classification, the sequential classification and the detailed classification of bank deposits, respectively. Enterprises can set up "bank deposit journals" according to the deposit banks and other financial institutions, the types of deposit, etc., and register receipt and payment vouchers one by one according to the order of business occurrence. At the end of the day, the balance should be settled.

The bank presents monthly bank statements to the company, showing the beginning cash balance, each performance of saving and withdrawal within the month, and the ending cash balance of the company account. The bank deposit journal should be checked regularly with the bank statement, with the frequency of at least once per month. The company compares the bank statements with its bank deposit journal, and then examines the errors or difference exists between the two records as well as its reasons. All the errors and difference are recorded in a bank reconciliation statement, beforebeing adjusted. If there are no accounting errors, the balance of both sides after adjustment should be equal.

Difference between the bank deposit journal and the bank statement arise for three reasons:

(1) Error – usually refers to the errors in the recording of cash book

(2) Omission – such as bank charges not posted in the cash book

(3) Timing difference – such as unpresented checks

Bank reconciliation can be made in many forms. Its format can be normally divided into two sections: adjusting the balance based on the cash balance of the bank statement, and adjusting the balance based on the depositor's cash balance. In the end, the two accounts's balance must be equal. The content of the bank reconciliation is outlined as follows:

The balance on the bank statement		The balance on bank deposit journal	
Add:		Add:	
Additions by depositor not on the bank statement		Additions by bank not recorded by depositor	
Bank errors		Depositor account errors	
Minus:		Minus:	
Deduction by depositor not on the bank statement		Deduction by bank not recorded by depositor	
Bank errors		Depositor account errors	
Balance after adjustment		Balance after adjustment	

Let's use ABC Co., Ltd. as an example to explain how to prepare a bank reconciliation. According to the bank statement, on April 30, 2019, ABC has a bank deposit $500 million. However, the bank deposit balance recorded on the company's account was $250 million. The reason for the difference is mainly due to the existence of the following items.

(1) On April 30 (Nonworking days), ABC Co. deposited $25,920,000 into the bank. The bank has not received.

(2) Three checks issued by the company, as follows, the bank has not received.

NO.512, $200 million.

NO.558, $70 million.

NO.653, $6.6 million.

(3) The bank's receivables of $1.4 million have been received, but have not been recorded by ABC.

(4) Due to insufficient customer deposits, the $2 million checks paid to ABC were returned by the bank.

(5) The bank charges a handling fee of $80,000, which is not listed on the bank deposit journal.

In order to reflect the amount of bank deposits in the company, ABC has made the following bank deposit adjustment table.

CO. ABC's Bank Reconciliation

unit: million

The balance on the bank statement	500	The balance on bank deposit journal	250
Add:		Add:	
Unrecorded deposited on 30 Apr.	25.92	Unrecorded bank's receivables	1.4
Minus:		Minus:	
No.512	200	Checks returned by the bank	2
No.558	70	Handling fee	0.08
No.653	6.6	-	-
Balance after adjustment	249.32	Balance after adjustment	249.32

It should be noted that the "bank deposit balance adjustment form" is only used for checking accounts, which cannot serve as a basis for adjusting the accounting records of enterprise bank deposits.

Key Words and Expressions

assets	资产
current assets	流动资产
fixed assets	固定资产
cash and cash equivalents	现金及现金等价物
coins	硬币
currency	货币，通货
checking accounts	支票账户
savings accounts	储蓄账户
negotiable checks	可转让支票
bank drafts	银行汇票
certificate of deposit	存款证明
bank overdrafts	银行透支
postdated checks	远期支票
government treasury bills	国库券
bank certificates of deposit	定期存单
bankers' acceptances	银行承兑汇票
commercial paper	商业票据
cash on hand	库存现金
wages	工资
sporadic expenditures	零星支出
internal control	内部控制
shift work	轮岗
cash receipts	现金收入
cash disbursements	现金支出
wait deal assets loss or income	待处理财产损益
other receivables	其他应收款
administrative expenses	管理费用
other accounts payable	其他应付款
cash shortage	现金短缺
cash overflow	现金溢余
non-operating income	营业外收入
petty cash fund	备用金
check	支票
bank reconciliation	银行存款余额调节表
general bank deposit account	银行存款总分类账
bank deposit journal	银行存款日记账

bank statement　　　　　　　　银行对账单
voucher　　　　　　　　　　　　凭证
transfer check　　　　　　　　　转账支票

Exercises

Ⅰ. **Please select the best answer for the following questions or uncompleted sentences.**

1. The following are all cash expect (　　).
   A. coins
   B. checks
   C. money orders
   D. stamps

2. Petty cash fund is (　　).
   A. a cash fund used to pay for relatively small amounts
   B. set aside by estimating the amount of cash needed for disbursements of relatively small amounts during a specified period
   C. reimbursed when the amount of money in the fund is under the predetermined minimum amount
   D. All of above.

3. Each of the following measures strengthens internal control over cash receipts except (　　).
   A. the use of a petty cash fund
   B. preparation of a daily listing of all checks received through the mail
   C. the deposit of cash receipts in the bank on a daily basis
   D. the use of cash registers

4. All of the following are controls over petty cash except (　　).
   A. keeping an unlimited amount of cash on hand
   B. supporting all fund disbursements with a petty cash ticket
   C. replenishing the fund through normal cash disbursement procedures
   D. designating one employee to administer the fund

5. A fund containing a small amount of cash used to pay for minor expenditures is known as a (　　).
   A. expenditure fund
   B. expense fund
   C. petty cash fund
   D. payments fund

Ⅱ. **Finish the following tasks based on the information given.**

The balance of bank deposit journal of XYZ company on December 31, 2019 is $400,000, and the balance of the bank statement is $300,000. The reason for the difference is mainly due to the existence of the following items.

(1) The enterprise has sent and deposited a transfer check of $1,000,000, and the registered bank deposits have increased, but the bank has not kept accounts.

(2) The enterprise has issued a check of $500,000, and the registered bank deposit has decreased, but the holder has not yet handled the transfer to the bank, and the bank has not kept accounts.

(3) The enterprise entrusts the bank to collect the payment of $800,000 for the purchase of a company. The bank has received the payment and recorded it in the account, but the enterprise has not received the payment notice and has not kept the account.

(4) The bank paid the phone bill of $400,000 on behalf of the enterprise. The bank has registered to reduce the enterprise's bank deposit, but the enterprise has not received the notice of payment from the bank and has not kept accounts.

Please make the bank reconciliation for XYZ Co..

第5章 现金

在《国际会计准则——概念框架》中,资产被定义为:由企业过去的交易或事项形成的、由企业拥有或者控制的、预期会给企业带来经济利益的资源。

会计学中资产是指经济资源,即可以通过货币价值衡量并由企业拥有或控制。公司可能拥有流动资产、固定资产和其他形式的资产。通过经营活动,预计流动资产将在一年或一个营运周期内转换为现金或出售、用尽。主要的流动资产有现金、应收账款和存货。在本章中,我们将首先讨论现金。

5.1 现金及现金等价物

5.1.1 定义

现金不仅仅是指纸币和硬币。在会计中,现金是指手头的货币(硬币、纸币)、银行或其他存放处的存款,如图5-1所示。

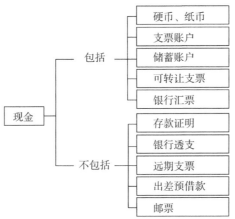

图5-1 现金分类

现金等价物是指短期的、流动性强的、易于转换为确定金额的现金且价值变动风险很小的投资。现金等价物是三种主要资产类别之一,其余两种分别是股票和债券。现金及现金等价物具有低风险、低回报的特征,包括政府国库券、银行存单、银行承兑汇票、公司商业票据和其他货币市场工具。

现金等价物因存续期间较短而不同于其他投资。它们一般在三个月内到期,而短期投资的存续期一般不超过12个月,长期投资则在12个月以上。满足现金等价物的另一个重要要求是投资风险很小。因此,普通股不能被视为现金等价物。但是离赎回日较近的可赎回优先股属于现金等价物。

大多数公司在报告现金时使用"现金和现金等价物"一词。在资产负债表中,"现金和现金等价物"在流动资产中位列第一,因为它是所有资产中流动性最强的资产。与其他资产负债表项目(如应付账款)相比,研究资产负债表的银行家、信贷经理或投资者总是对现金总额更加感兴趣。

5.1.2 库存现金

库存现金是指存放在企业财务部门并由出纳员管理的货币。库存现金是企业中流动性最高的资产。企业应严格遵守国家有关现金管理制度，正确进行现金收支核算，监督现金使用的合法性和合理性。

根据《现金管理暂行条例》，企业现金管理制度主要包括以下内容：

1. 库存现金的使用范围

企业可用库存现金支付的款项有：
- 职工工资及津贴；
- 个人劳务报酬；
- 国家根据科学、技术、文化、艺术、体育比赛的规定给予个人的各种奖金；
- 国家规定的个人劳动保险，福利支出和其他支出；
- 个人购买农副产品及其产品；
- 出差人员必须随身携带的差旅费；
- 低于结算门槛的零星支出。

2. 库存现金限额

库存现金的限额是指需要确保公司的日常零用支出的需要，允许单位留存现金的最高额度。该限额由开户行根据企业的实际需要批准。通常是根据公司 3～5 天的日常零花费用确定。在交通不便的偏远地区，库存现金限额可以根据五天以上但不超过十五天的零星日常开支的需要来确定。公司必须严格遵守现金支付限额。超过库存最高限额的现金应在当日结束前存入银行。需要增加或减少库存的现金限额时，应当向开户行提出申请。

3. 现金收支规定

企业的现金收支按照下列规定处理：
- 公司的现金收据应于当日存入银行。如果确实难以在同一天存款，则存款时间应由存款银行确定。
- 开户单位支付现金时，可以从库存现金限额中支付或从存款银行取款。但不能直接从单位的现金收入中付款。因特殊情况需要坐支的，应当提前交存银行审批，由存款银行核定坐支范围和限额。坐支单位应定期向自己的开户银行报告现金存款的金额和用途。
- 公司在向存款银行提取现金时，应当说明提取的目的，并由会计部门负责人签字盖章。经存款银行审核后予以支付。
- 由于购买地点不确定，交通不便，生产或市场急需或用于紧急救灾等其他特殊情况必须使用现金的，企业应当向开户行提出申请，并由会计部门负责人签字盖章，经开户行审查后予以支付现金。

为了反映和监督现金的收支和结余情况，企业应设立"库存现金"科目。该科目的借方记录库存现金的增加，贷方记录库存现金的减少。期末的借方余额反映期末的实际现金余额。为了全面、连续地反映和监控库存现金的收支、支出和结余情况，企业还应设置库存现金总账和库存现金日记账，分别进行库存现金的总分类核算和明细分类核算。

库存现金	
借方	贷方
增加	减少

5.2 现金的内部控制

现金很容易被盗用,因此对现金的监控是非常必要的。

由于现金交易量大且频繁,在使用和记录它们时可能会出现许多错误。为了确保现金会计记录的准确性和可靠性,有效的内部现金控制是必要的。

有效的内部控制系统可以保护现金资产,它应该符合以下三个原则:

(1) 现金的收付应与现金记录分开。
(2) 现金收入及时存入银行。
(3) 以支票的方式支付现金。

5.2.1 现金的保管应与记录分开

这一原则要求企业建立钱账分管制度。现金的收付及保管由出纳人员负责,其他人员不得接触。出纳人员不得负责总分类账的登记和保管。

雇员A 雇员B
记录现金账簿 保管现金

5.2.2 现金收入的内部控制

大多数企业的现金流入有众多来源。用于实现适当控制的程序可能有所不同。但是,以下程序在所有情况下都很重要:

(1) 立即计算所有收到的现金;
(2) 立即记录收到的所有现金;
(3) 及时把收到的现金存入银行。

5.2.3 现金支出的内部控制

许多现金欺诈的案例都发生在支付过程中,它们十分容易被掩盖,除非企业有如下有效的控制系统:

(1) 所有现金支付均以支票支付,但小额支出适用小额现金系统除外。支票应单独签名、存储和记录。当一个人只负责某一给定任务时,控制是最有效的。
(2) 建立密切监督的备用金制度。
(3) 密切监督所有现金支付、相关账务记录并定期形成内部报告,并定期核对或由第三方独立监督。

最后，为了减少现金管理中欺诈的可能性，财务部门进行轮岗是有必要的。

为保证现金的安全和完整，公司应按规定对库存现金进行定期和不定期检查，并且应根据检查结果编制现金检查报告。如发现有挪用现金、白条顶库的现象，应及时纠正。如果账目不一致，发现现金短缺或盈余，且原因不明，应首先通过"待处理财产损益"科目进行会计处理。按管理权限在批准后，分两种情况处理：现金短缺时，属于责任人或保险公司应当赔偿的部分，计入"其他应收账"；无法查明原因的，计入"管理费用"。如为现金盈余，属于应当支付给有关人员或者单位的，应当计入"其他应付款"；原因不明的，应当计入"营业外收入"。

	现金短缺	现金溢余
审批前	借：待处理财产损溢 　贷：库存现金	借：库存现金 　贷：待处理财产损溢
审批后	借：其他应收款 　　管理费用 　贷：待处理财产损溢	借：待处理财产损溢 　贷：其他应付款 　　营业外收入

5.3　备用金

备用金，也称为小额现金基金，是便于支付费用的少量现金。备用金可以为不适于签发支票的小额交易提供便利。备用金可以用于支付包括但不限于为一小部分雇员的餐费，购买少量廉价用品，或报销员工以支付与工作相关的小额费用。

例如，A 公司决定在 6 月 1 日建立 500 美元的备用金。需要用支票在银行兑换成现金。签发支票的会计分录如下：

　　借：小额备用金　　　　　　　　　　　　　　$500
　　　贷：银行存款　　　　　　　　　　　　　　　　　　　$500

当备用金中的资金达到最低水平或在会计期末时，该备用金将获得补偿。相关凭证和证明文件由财务主管部门进行检查，以确认它们的用途是否合理。经财务主管批准后可将备用金恢复到其确定的金额。同时，所有支持文件(收据)都已加盖印花，因此无法再次提交付款。

继续上面的例子，A 公司使用 150 美元支付办公费用。会计分录如下：

　　借：管理费用　　　　　　　　　　　　　　　$150
　　　贷：银行存款　　　　　　　　　　　　　　　　　　　$150

在 6 月底，A 公司签发一张 150 美元的支票以补充备用金，使其保持 500 美元。会计分录如下：

　　借：备用金　　　　　　　　　　　　　　　　$150
　　　贷：银行存款　　　　　　　　　　　　　　　　　　　$150

5.4　银行存款余额调节表

银行存款是企业存入银行或者其他金融机构的款项。企业应当根据业务需要和规定在其机构所在地银行开立账户，用于办理存款、取款和各项收支转移业务。银行存款的收付应当严格遵守银行结算制度的规定。

为了反映和监督企业银行存款的收支和结存情况，企业应设立"银行存款"科目，借方登记企业银行存款增加额，贷方登记企业银行存款减少额，期末借方余额反映企业期末实际持有的银行存款金额。

银行存款	
借方	贷方
增加	减少

公司应当设立银行存款总账户和银行存款日记账，分别进行银行存款总分类、银行存款顺序分类和银行存款明细分类。企业可以根据存款银行和其他金融机构、存款类型等设立"银行存款日记账"，并根据收付款凭证按业务发生顺序逐一登记。每日终了，应结出余额。

银行向开户单位提供月度银行对账单，显示期初现金余额、当月每笔存款和取款的执行情况以及期末账户余额。银行存款日记账应定期与银行对账单核对，至少每月核对一次。公司将银行对账单与其日记账进行比较，然后确定两个记录之间是否存在错误或差异，以及为什么存在差异。所有错误和差额均记录在银行存款余额调节表中。如果没有会计错误，则调整后双方的余额应相等。

现金簿与银行对账单之间的差异有三个原因：

(1) 错误——通常是指现金账簿的记载有误；
(2) 遗漏——如未在现金账簿上粘贴的银行手续费；
(3) 时间差异——例如未提交的支票。

银行存款余额调节表有多种形式。通常，银行存款余额调节表分为两个主要部分。第一部分是银行的对账单。对账单的现金余额是基点，根据未达账项调整其余额，得到调整后的余额。第二部分是基于公司账上的现金簿余额，根据未达账项调整其余额，得到调整后的余额。最后，两个账户余额必须相等。银行存款余额调节表的内容如下：

银行对账单余额		公司账上的银行存款余额	
加：		加：	
企业已收，银行未收		银行已收，企业未收	
银行错误		记账错误	
减：		减：	
企业已付，银行未付		银行已付，企业未付	
银行错误		记账错误	
调整后的余额		调整后的余额	

接下来以 ABC 股份有限公司为例，说明如何编制银行对账单。根据银行对账单，2019 年 4 月 30 日，ABC 公司有 5 亿美元的银行存款，而该公司账户上记录的银行存款余额为 2.5 亿美元。造成此差异的原因主要是由于以下项目：

(1) 4 月 30 日(非工作日)，ABC 公司向银行存入 25,920,000 美元。银行没有付款。
(2) 公司签发的下列三张支票，银行未支付：512 号，2 亿美元；558 号，7,000 万美元；653 号，660 万美元。
(3) 银行的应收账款 140 万美元已经收到，但 ABC 公司没有记录。
(4) 由于客户存款不足，其给 ABC 公司的 200 万美元支票被银行退回。

(5) 银行收取手续费 8 万元，未列入银行对账单。

为了反映公司真实的银行存款金额，ABC 编制了以下银行存款调节表。

ABC 股份有限公司银行存款余额调节表

单位：百万美元

银行对账单余额	500	公司账上的银行存款余额	250
加：		加：	
企业已付，银行未付(4月30日)	25.92	银行已收，企业未收	1.4
减：		减：	
No.512	200	被退还的支票	2
No.558	70	银行已付，企业未付	0.08
No.653	6.6	-	-
调整后的余额	249.32	调整后的余额	249.32

需要说明的是，"银行存款余额调节表"仅用于核对账目，不能作为调整企业银行存款会计记录的依据。

Chapter 6

Receivables

In order to achieve more sales of services or products, many companies choose the pattern of credit sale. The receivables are generated when sales and transactions are conducted without the immediate receipt of cash, which is a significant portion of the total current assets. Enterprises should pay close attention to the receivables and manage them carefully.

6.1 Classification of Receivables

The term "receivables" refers to amounts due from individuals and companies. Receivables include notes receivable, accounts receivables, other receivables, accounts prepaid expenses, etc. Among them, accounts receivables and notes receivables are two major types of receivables. Accounts receivables, sometimes named as trade receivables, refer to the amounts that customers owe the enterprise. Notes receivables are more formal than accounts receivables. Receivables are prepayments which shall be accounted for according to actual amount.

6.1.1 Accounts Receivable

Accounts receivables serve as the account to record the claims on customers due from the sale of commodities and services. Companies generally expect to collect accounts receivable within 30 to 60 days. Accounts receivables, usually the most significant claim held by a company, are classified as a current asset on the balance sheet.

6.1.2 Notes Receivable

Notes receivable refer to claims for the evidence of the debt when formal instruments of credit are issued. The credit instrument normally extends the payment period to 60-90 days or longer and requires the debtor to pay interest. They are classified as current asset on the balance sheet. Notes and accounts receivable from sales transactions are often named as trade receivables.

6.1.3 Other Receivables

Accounts receivable and notes receivable, together named as operating accounts receivable, are generated by the sale of goods and the provision of services. These two types of receivables are generally considered as the most important one owned by an enterprise. Non-operating accounts receivable, also named as other receivables, refer to receivables resulting from the sale of non-commodity assets or other forms of short-term receivable unrelated to any sale. Examples of nonoperating accounts receivables include loans to officers and company employees, interest and dividends receivables, and claims against insurance companies.

6.2 Accounting for Accounts Receivables

In general, the book value of accounts receivable is equal to the actual transaction price. However, when there are sales discounts or sales subsidies, the confirmation of the receivables will become complicated.

In order to reduce the risk that income cannot be recovered and accelerate cash recovery, enterprises always hope to recover cash more quickly. Therefore, sales discounts are necessary, mainly including trade discounts and cash discounts.

Trade discount refers to a certain amount deducted from the list price offered by suppliers, which encourages customers to purchase more products. Trade discounts reduces the original price of products. Sales subject to trade discount should only be recorded at a net amount, and trade discount should not be recorded separately. For example, the price of a certain product is $100. If a purchaser purchases 1,000 pieces and the supplier offers a trade discount of 20%, the book value of this receivable will be $80,000.

Cash discount refers to the incentive provided for the buyer to encourage payment within a specified period of time. If the amount is paid within short time limit (called discount period), the buyer will receive a discount of X%. For example, A Co. sold products to its customer B Co. for $50,000 on Sep. 10. The credit terms were 2/10, n/30. And B Co. paid the money on Sep.20. A Co.'s journal entries to record the transaction was:

Sep.10	Dr. Accounts Receivable——B Co.	$50,000	
	Cr. Operating Revenue		$50,000
Sep.20	Dr. Cash Deposits	$49,000	
	Finance Expense	$1000	
	Cr. Accounts Receivable——B Co.		$50,000

6.3 Uncollectible Accounts

Regardless of the cautiousness in credit sale and the selected collection procedures, a part of the credit sales will still be not collectible. The operating expense incurred with the failure in collecting receivables is called uncollectible accounts expense, doubtful accounts expense, or bad debts expense.

In accounting, two methods are applied to deal with uncollected receivables. The first method is the direct write-off method, which recognizes the expense only when accounts are judged to be worthless. The second method is the allowance method, which provides an expense for uncollectible receivables in advance of their write-off.

6.3.1 Direct Write-off Method

Under direct write-off method, when an account is determined to be uncollectible, bad debt expense is recorded, and no adjusting entry is recorded to estimate uncollectible at the end of the period. This method fails to match revenues and expenses, unless the write-off occurs in the same period as the related sale does. Although this method is not conceptually sound, it is justified under the materiality principle.

For example, Company an estimated that $1,000 of the accounts receivable will be uncollectible on December 31. Company A's journal entry is:

  Dr. Bad Debts Expense $1,000
    Cr. Accounts Receivable $1,000

If the bad debts recognized in the accounting books are collected back later, subsequent recovery journal entries should be prepared as follows:

  Dr. Accounts Receivable $1,000
    Cr. Bad Debts Expense $1,000
  Dr. Bank Deposits $1,000
    Cr. Accounts Receivable $1,000

Within this method, bad debts expense is recorded in a different period of recording the revenue. Consequently, the direct write-off method cannot be applied in financial report, on the condition that a company expects significant bad debts losses.

6.3.2 Allowance Method

The allowance method of accounting for bad debts estimates the amount of uncollectible receivables at the end of each period. This method can better match expenses with revenues on the income statement. Most enterprises apply this method to account for the receivables. Also, the accounts receivable appears on the balance sheet at the amount of cash proceeds that are expected from their collection (realizable value).

The adjusting journal entry to record the estimated uncollectible is:

  Dr. Bad Debts Expense
    Cr. Allowance for Doubtful Accounts

Allowance for Doubtful Accounts shows the estimated amount of accounts receivables of an enterprise which are predicted to be uncollectible in the future. The credit balance in the allowance account will absorb the specific write-offs when they occur.

When an enterprise exhausts all means but still fails to collect a past-due account, the company should write off the account. The journal entry to record the write-off is:

  Dr. Allowance for Doubtful Accounts
    Cr. Accounts Receivable——×××（Name of customer)

A company may also collect this receivable after the account has been written off as uncollectible. The adjusting journal entries to record the recovery of bad debt are:

  Dr. Accounts Receivable——×××（Name of customer)

　　　　　Cr. Allowance for Doubtful Accounts
　　　　Dr. Bank Deposits
　　　　　Cr. Accounts Receivable——×× × （Name of customer)

It should be noted that the recovery of a bad debt, same as the write-off of a bad debt, only affects balance sheet accounts. The net effect of the two entries is an increase in cash and allowance for doubtful accounts.

6.4　Notes Receivables

6.4.1　Accounting for Notes Receivables

Compared with accounts receivables, notes receivables are favored more by the seller for the following merits:
- Notes mean a strong, legal claim to the maker or its endorsee.
- Notes can be converted into cash by discounting them to banks.
- Interests can be earned with an interest-bearing note.

Notes have several characteristics that affect how they are recorded and reported.

1. Due Date and Interest

Due date, also maturity date, refers to the date when a note is to be paid. Normally, a note specifies the interest generated in the period between the issuance date and the due date. The formula for computing interest is as follows:

Interest = Face Amount × Rate × Time

2. Maturity Value

Maturity value refers to the amount that is due at the due date. The formula for computing maturity value of a note is as follows:

Maturity Value = Face Amount + Interest

For example, assume that a 30-day, 3% note dated January 1, 2019, is accepted in settlement of the account of Company XYZ, which is past due and has a balance of $1,000. The journal entry to the transaction is:

| Jan.1 | Dr. Notes Receivable | $1,000 | |
| | Cr. Sales Revenue | | $1,000 |

When the note matures, the entry to record the receipt of $1002.5 ($1000 principle plus $1000×3%÷12=$2.5 interest) is as follows:

Jan.30	Dr. Bank Deposit	$1,002.5	
	Cr. Notes Receivable		$1,000
	Interest Revenue		$2.5

If the notes receivable fail to be paid on the due date, the entry to transfer the note and the interest back to the customer's account is as follows:

Jan.30	Dr. Account Receivable	$1,002.5	
	Cr. Notes Receivable		$1,000
	Interest Revenue		$2.5

6.4.2 Discounting Notes Receivables

Note receivable refers to negotiable instruments that can be passed to a bank or other companies. This practice is also called discounting. When the former owner sells the receivable, the buyer (a bank in most cases) is buying the right to collect the maturity value of the note at the due date. The basic formula to calculating bank discount is as follows:

Bank Discount Amount = Maturity Value × Bank Discount Rate × Discount Period

Discount period is the numbers of days between the date of sale to the bank and maturity date

Proceeds of Discounted Note = Maturity Value - Bank Discounted Amount

For example, Company A had a 90-day, 5% note dated June 1, 2019. The face amount is $2,000. On July 1, the note is sold to a bank with 6% rate.

$$\text{Interest} = 2{,}000 \times 5\% \times \frac{90}{360} = \$25$$

Maturity Value = 2,000 + 25 = $2,025

$$\text{Bank Discount Amount} = 2{,}025 \times 6\% \times \frac{90-30}{360} = \$20.25$$

Proceeds of Discounted Note = 2,025 − 20.25 = $2,004.75

The entry to record this transaction is as follow:

Jan.30	Dr. Cash	$2,004.75	
	Cr. Interest Income		$4.75
	Notes Receivable Discounted		$2,000

Key Words and Expressions

accounts receivables	应收账款
notes receivable	应收票据
other receivables	其他应收款
accounts prepaid expenses	预付账款
commodities	商品
balance sheet	资产负债表
claims	索赔
book value	账面价值
sales discounts	销售折扣
sales subsidies	销售补贴
trade discounts	商业折扣
cash discount	现金折扣

discount period	折扣期
credit terms	信用条件
finance expense	财务费用
uncollectible accounts	坏账
direct write-off method	直接转销法
materiality principle	重要性原则
allowance method	备抵法
income statement	利润表
realizable value	可变现价值
allowance	备抵、折扣、折让
credit balance	贷方余额
endorsee	持票人
discount	贴现
due date	到期日
maturity date	到期日
maturity value	到期值
face amount	面值
sales revenue	销售收入

Exercises

Please select the best answer for the following questions or uncompleted sentences.

1. Under the direct write-off method of accounting for uncollectible accounts (   ).
    A. The current year uncollectible accounts expense is less than the expense that would be under the allowance approach
    B. The relationship between the current period net sales and current period uncollectible accounts expense illustrates the matching principle
    C. The allowance for doubtful accounts is debited when specific accounts receivable are determined to be worthless
    D. Account receivable is not stated in the balance sheet at net realizable value, but at the balance of the accounts receivable control account

2. October 1, 2018, Citi Bank loaned Company B $300,000, receiving in exchange a nine-month, twelve percent note receivable. Citi Bank ends its fiscal year on December 31 and makes adjusting entries to accrue interest earned on all note receivables. The interest earned on the note receivable from Company B during 2018 will amount to (   ).
    A. $9,000
    B. $18,000
    C. $27,000
    D. $36,000

3. Which of the following statements related to receivables is true? (　　)
   A. On the balance sheet, accounts receivable is usually reported as total accounts receivable plus the allowance for uncollectible accounts.
   B. A dishonored notes receivable should be shown as a current liability.
   C. When a customer overpays his accounts receivable, the resulting balance should be properly shown among the non-current assets on the balance sheet.
   D. When a notes receivable is not paid at maturity, the principal plus any interest due should be charged back to the customer's accounts receivable.
4. A company has received payment for a debt that had been written off as irrecoverable. What double entry should be made to record this transaction? (　　).
   A. Dr. Cash
       Cr. Receivable
   B. Dr. Receivable
       Cr. Bad debt expense
   C. Dr. Receivable
       Cr. Cash
   D. Dr. Cash
       Cr. Bad debt expense
5. A 90-day note issued on April 10 matures on (　　).
   A. July 9
   B. July 10
   C. July 11
   D. July 12
6. The interest accrued on $6,500 at 6% for 50 days is (　　).
   A. $36
   B. $42
   C. $65
   D. $190

第6章　应收款项

为了销售更多的产品或提供更多的服务，许多公司会采取信用销售的模式，即在没有立即收到现金的情况下完成销售和交易，这便产生了应收款项。应收款是流动资产的重要组成部分。公司应密切关注应收款并对其进行认真的管理。

6.1 应收款的分类

应收款一词是指应收个人和公司的款项。应收款项包括应收票据、应收账款、其他应收款、预付账款等。两种主要的应收款项是应收账款和应收票据。应收账款是客户欠企业的钱，这些应收账款有时被称为贸易应收账款。应收票据比应收账款更正式。应收款项是企业预付的项目，按实际金额核算。

6.1.1 应收账款

应收账款是用于记录因销售商品和提供服务而客户应该付给公司的款项的账户类型。公司通常希望在 30 到 60 天内收回应收账款。应收账款通常是公司持有的最重要的债权类型，在资产负债表中归类为流动资产。

6.1.2 应收票据

应收票据是指发行正式信贷工具作为书面凭证的债权。应付票据通常要求债务人支付利息并将付款期延长至 60~90 天或更长的时间。它们在资产负债表中被归为流动资产。销售交易产生的票据和应收账款通常称为贸易应收款。

6.1.3 其他应收款

应收账款和应收票据是由销售商品和提供服务产生的，它们通常被认为是企业拥有的最为重要的应收款。应收非营业账款又被称为其他应收款，顾名思义，它是指销售非商品资产造成的应收款或与任何销售无关的其他形式的短期应收款。例如，向高级职员和公司员工提供的贷款，利息和应收股息以及向保险公司的索赔。

6.2 应收账款的计量

一般而言，应收账款的账面价值等于实际交易价格。但是，当有销售折扣和销售补贴时，应收账款的确认就变得复杂了。

为了降低款项无法收回的风险，加快现金回收速度，企业总是希望更快地收回应收款项。因此，销售折扣就很必要了。销售折扣包括商业折扣和现金折扣两种方式。

商业折扣是从供应商提供的定价中扣除的一定金额，以鼓励客户购买更多产品。商业折扣是对原本销售价格的降低。按商业折扣计算的销售额应仅以净额记录，而不单独记录商业折扣。例如，一种产品的价格是 100 美元。对于一个购买了 1,000 件的采购商，供应商提供了 20%的商业折扣。那么最后，这笔应收账款的入账价值应为 8 万美元。

现金折扣是为鼓励买方在规定时间内付款而提供的奖励。如果账款在短时间内支付，则买方将获得X%的折扣。例如，A 公司在 9 月 10 日以 50,000 美元的价格将产品卖给了客户公司 B。信用条件是 2/10，N/30。B 公司于 9 月 20 日付款。A 公司对该项交易的分录如下：

9月10日	借：应收账款——B 公司	$50,000	
	贷：营业收入		$50,000
9月20日	借：银行存款	$49,000	
	财务费用	$100	
	贷：应收账款——B 公司		$50,000

6.3 坏账

不管在信用销售时如何谨慎，也不管是采用哪种托收程序，总有部分信用销售的款项无法收回。因未收回应收款项而发生的营业费用，称为坏账损失、呆账费用或坏账费用。

未收应收款的会计处理有两种方法。一种是直接冲销法，即只在应收款项确定无法收回时确认费用。另一种方法称为备抵法，是在应收账款核销前，估计无法收回的应收账款并计提相关费用。

6.3.1 直接转销法

直接转销法下，当一个账户被确定为不可收回时，则记录坏账损失。期末不做预计无法收回的调整分录。这种方法没有将对应的收入和费用相匹配，除非该笔坏账和相关销售发生在同一期间。虽然这种方法在概念上不健全，但在实质性原则下是合理的。

例如，12 月 31 日，A 公司有一笔 1,000 美元的应收账款将无法收回。A 公司的账务处理应为：

借：坏账损失	$1,000	
贷：应收账款		$1,000

若已确认的坏账以后又被收回了，应当如下所示编制后续收回分录：

借：应收账款	$1,000	
贷：坏账损失		$1,000
借：银行存款	$1,000	
贷：应收账款		$1,000

在这种方法下，坏账费用记录在与收入不同的期间。因此，在公司预计坏账损失金额较大的情况下，直接转销法不适用于财务报告。

6.3.2 备抵法

债务核算的备抵方法在每个期末会估计当期无法收回的应收款项金额，这样可以更好地将费用与利润表上的收入相匹配。大多数企业采用这种方法来核算应收账款，因为它将应收款项的损失与销售期间的收入相匹配。在备抵法下，应收账款在资产负债表上显示其可变现价值。

预计坏账时的分录为：

借：坏账费用

贷：坏账准备

坏账准备显示了公司预计未来无法收回的应收账款的金额。备抵账户中的贷方余额将在发生坏账时转销。

当公司已用尽各种方法都无法收回逾期账款时，该公司应注销该账款。注销时的分录为：

借：坏账准备

贷：应收账款——××公司

注销应收账款后，公司也有可能收回该笔款项。记录坏账收回的调整分录如下：

借：应收账款——×××公司

贷：坏账准备

借：银行存款

贷：应收账款——×××公司

值得注意的是，坏账的收回和账款的注销一样，只影响资产负债表账户。

6.4 应收票据

6.4.1 应收票据的会计处理

与应收账款相比，应收票据更受卖方的青睐，它具有以下优点：

- 票据是对出票人或者被背书人的强有力的、合法的请求权。
- 票据到期前，都可以向银行申请贴现。
- 带息票据有利息可以收取。

下面我们将学习影响票据的一些因素：

1. 到期日和利息

到期日即支付票据的日期。票据通常会标注在发行日期和到期日之间的利息。计算公式如下：

利息＝票据票面金额×利率×时间

2. 到期价值

到期日到期的金额称为到期价值。计算票据到期价值的基本公式如下：

到期价值＝票面价值＋利息

例如，假设在 XYZ 公司账户的结算中接受了日期为 2019 年 1 月 1 日的 30 天，利率为 3%的票据，该票据已到期并且余额为 1,000 美元。会计分录如下：

| 1月1日 | 借：应收票据 | $1,000 | |
| | 贷：销售收入 | | $1,000 |

当票据到期时，记录收款 1,002.5 美元(本金 1,000 美元加上利息 1,000×3%÷12＝2.5 美元)的分录如下：

1月30日	借：银行存款	$1,002.5	
	贷：应收票据		$1,000
	利息收入		$2.5

如果应收票据未能在到期日支付，则将票据和利息转回客户账户的分录如下：

1月30日	借：应收账款	$1,002.5	
	贷：应收票据		$1,000
	利息收入		$2.5

6.4.2 应收票据贴现

应收票据是可转让票据，可以转让给银行或其他公司，这种转让的做法也被称为贴现。当前所有者出售应收票据时，买方(多数情况下是银行)拥有购买在到期日收取票据到期价值的权利。计算银行贴现的基本公式如下：

银行贴现金额＝票据到期金额×银行贴现率×折扣期

(折扣期是指向银行出售之日和到期日之间的天数。)

票据贴现收益＝到期价值－银行贴现金额

例如，A公司在2019年6月1日有一张90天，5%的票据。面额为2,000美元。7月1日，A公司将该票据以6%的利率出售给银行，则

$$利息 = 2,000 \times 5\% \times \frac{90}{360} = 25 \text{ 美元}$$

到期价值＝2,000＋25＝2,025 美元

$$银行折扣金额 = 2,025 \times 6\% \times \frac{90-30}{360} = 20.25 \text{ 美元}$$

贴现票据收益＝2,025－20.25＝2,004.75 美元

会计分录如下：

借：现金	$2,004.75	
贷：利息收入		$4.75
应收票据		$2,000

Chapter 7

Inventory

Inventories serve as an important barometer of the operating condition of an enterprise. The amount of inventories and the time required for sale should be paid close attention to. Inventories will normally be consumed or converted into cash in less than one year or one operating cycle of the firm, thereby being seen as a current asset.

According to *IAS 2 Inventory*, inventories include:

(1) Assets held for sale in the ordinary course of business (finished goods).

(2) Assets in the process of production used for sale in the ordinary course of business (work in process – WIP).

(3) Materials and supplies consumed in the process of production process (raw materials).

However, *IAS 2 Inventory* excludes certain inventories as follows:

(1) Projects in process under construction contracts.

(2) Financial instruments.

(3) Agricultural products and forest products, agricultural productions, as well as minerals and mineral products.

7.1 Measurement of Inventory upon Initial Recognition

According to *IAS 2 Inventory*, "Inventories shall be measured at the lower of cost and net realizable value." Since acquiring or manufacturing inventory items aims to sell them for profits, inventory will initially be recognized according to its cost. Two specific industries can be exempted from applying the lower of cost and net realizable value rule, namely:

(1) Producers of agricultural products and forest products, agricultural productions, as well as minerals and mineral products. They are measured at net realizable value in accordance with well-established practices in these industries.

(2) Commodity broker-traders who measure their inventories by subtracting sale costs from fair value.

In these cases, the part which subtracts the changing sale costs during this period from net realizable value or fair value is recognized in profits or losses. If inventories in these industries are measured according to the historical cost, the lower of cost and net realizable value rule mandated by paragraph 9 of *IAS 2* could still be applied.

The first step in accounting for inventory is the initial recognition at cost. *IAS 2 Inventory* specifies three components of inventory cost: costs of purchase, costs of conversion, and other costs to make the inventories in the present state. Among them, costs of conversion are more applicable for manufacturing entities where raw materials and other supplies are purchased and then converted to other products.

7.1.1 Costs of purchase

According to *IAS 2*, "the costs of purchase of inventories include the purchase price, import duties and other taxes (other than those subsequently refunded by the taxing authorities), as well as the costs on transport, handling, or the purchase of finished goods, materials and services. Trade discounts, rebates and other similar items should be deducted when enterprises determine the costs of purchase."

(1) Transaction taxes

Many countries impose taxes on transactions involving the exchange of goods and services, and require entities engaged in such activities to pay taxes and remittances. However, some taxes which can be recovered by taxation authorities, such as value added tax, cannot be included in the costs of purchase.

(2) Trade discounts and cash discounts

A trade discount refers to a reduction in the price offered to customers. This discount can serve as an incentive to the purchase, a means of withdrawing from inventory overhang, or a reward for ordering large quantities of goods. The trade discount reduces the purchase cost, so the enterprise will deduct it when determining the cost of inventory.

A cash discount or settlement discount refers to incentives for early payment of amounts owing on credit sales. Credit terms normally appear on invoices or contracts as the form of "2/10, N/30", which means that the buyer will receive a discount of 2% if the invoice is paid within 10 days after the invoice date but will receive no discount if the invoice is paid within 10-30 days after the invoice date. Some entities may also impose an interest penalty for the overdue payment. In November 2004, the International Financial Reporting Interpretations Committee (IFRIC) issued an agenda decision that "settlement discounts should be deducted from the cost of inventories". The International Accounting Standards Board (IASB) also clarified that "rebates of sales return cannot be deducted from the cost of inventories". However, in China, according to *the Accounting Standards for Business Enterprises*, "if cash discount is involved in selling goods, the amount of sales should be determined according to the amount before cash discount is deducted. Cash discount is recorded into current profits and losses when it actually occurs".

(3) Deferred payment terms

If an item of inventory is acquired by cash or short-term credit, the determination of the purchase price will be relatively straightforward. According to *IAS 2*, in this situation, the purchase cost includes a financing element – the difference between the amount paid on normal credit terms and the amount paid actually, which must be recognized as interest expense over the period of deferral.

7.1.2 Costs of Conversion

IAS 2 defines conversion costs as the costs directly related to the production unit such as direct labor, plus a systematic allocation of fixed and variable overheads incurred in converting materials into finished goods. Variable overhead refers to the production overhead that varies indirectly with production volume. It is allocated to each production unit based on the actual use of the production facility. Fixed overhead refers to the production overhead that remains relatively constant regardless of production and is allocated to inventory costs based on normal production capacity, such as depreciation of production machinery. When a production process produces one or more products at the same time, the conversion costs must be distributed between the products on a systematic and reasonable basis. The cost calculation and allocation method is an issue of management accounting, which is not included in the scope of this book.

7.1.3 Other Costs

Other cost can be included only if they are "incurred in bringing the inventories to their present location and condition". Such costs could include specific design expenses incurred in producing goods for individual customers. *IAS 23 Borrowing Cost* allows borrowing costs such as interest to be included in the cost of inventories, but only where such inventories are a qualifying asset; that is, one which "takes a substantial period of time to get ready for its intended use or sale".

The following costs are specifically listed in *IAS 2* as the cost that cannot be included in the cost of inventories and must be recognized as expenses when incurred:

— Abnormal losses are generated from wasted materials, labor or other production costs.
— Storage costs, unless necessary in the production process before a further production stage.
— Administrative overheads without direct relations to inventories.

7.1.4 Lower of Cost and Net Realizable Value

As the measurement rule of inventories is mandated by *IAS 2* as "the lower of cost and net realizable value", an estimate of net realizable value must be conducted to determine if inventory must be written down. This estimate is normally done at the end of the reporting period. If the management realizes during the reporting period that goods or services can no longer be sold at a price above cost, inventory values should be written down to net realizable value. The rationale for this measurement rule, according to *IAS 2*, is that assets should not be carried in excess of amounts which are expected to be realized from their sale or use".

Net realizable value refers to the net amount that an entity expects to realize from the sale of inventory in the ordinary course of business. According to *IAS 2*, it is defined as "the net value which subtracts the completion costs, the estimated sale costs and relevant taxes from the estimated selling price in the ordinary course of business". Net realizable value is specific to an individual entity, which is not necessarily equal to fair value less selling costs. According to *IFRS 13 Fair Value Measurement*, fair value is defined as "the price of selling an asset or transferring a liability which is received in an orderly transaction between market participants at the measurement date".

Net realizable value may be less than the cost on inventories in many situations, including but not limited to:
— A decrease in selling price of inventories (e.g., fashion garments).
— Physical deterioration of inventories (e.g., fruit and vegetables).
— Product obsolescence (e.g., computers and electrical equipment).
— A decision, aimed at a company's marketing strategy, to manufacture and sell products when deficit occurs (e.g., new products).
— Miscalculations or other errors in purchasing or production (e.g., over-stocking).
— An estimated increasing cost when the sale is done (e.g., air-conditioning plants).

(1) Net realizable value

Estimates of net realizable value must be based on the most reliable evidence (normally specific situations in the end of the reporting period), with the net value which subtracts taxes from the expected selling price. Thus, estimates must consist of the following statistics:
— Expected selling price.
— Estimated completion costs (if any).
— Estimated selling costs.

These estimates should consider fluctuations of price or cost after the end of the reporting period. The purpose of holding inventories also be taken into account when net realizable values are reviewed. For example, the net realizable value of inventories held to satisfy firm sales or service contracts is based on the contract price. If the amount in sales contracts is lower than the amount of the held inventories, the net realizable value of the excess is calculated based on general selling prices. All the likely occurring costs to satisfy consumers' demands should be included in estimating selling costs, such as advertising costs, sales personnel salaries, operating costs, and the costs on storing and shipping finished goods.

Formulas based on predetermined criteria can be used to initially estimate net realizable value. These formulas normally consider the movement and estimated scrap value of the inventories. However, the results must be reviewed in the light of any unexpected special circumstances in the formulas, such as changes in the current demand for inventories or the obsolescence.

(2) Materials and other supplies

IAS 2 states that "if materials and other supplies used for the production of inventories are sold at or above their costs, the costs should not be written down". *IAS 2* also states that "the replacement cost of the materials or other supplies can be regarded as an important measure to estimate their net realizable value".

(3) Write-down to net realizable value

Inventories are usually written down to net realizable value on an item-by-item basis, when the book value is higher than net realizable value. According to *IAS 2*, inventory is usually written down to net realizable value on an item-by-item basis. However, in some cases, it is also possible to group similar or related inventories and make provision for impairment, the write-down may be applied on a group basis provided that the products have similar purposes or end uses and are produced and marketed in the same geographical area.

And it is not appropriate to write down the inventory on the basis of its classification, but should be measured separately according to different sub items. The journal entry to process the write down is shown as follows:

Dr. Inventory writes down an expense
　　Cr. Inventory

7.2 Inventory Systems

In fact, there are two alternative systems used to account for inventories: a perpetual inventory system and a periodic inventory system.

7.2.1 Perpetual Inventory System

In the perpetual inventory system, each receipt and each issue of an inventory item is recorded in the inventory records to maintain an up-to-date inventory balance at all times. Thus, this system provides the units and costs of ending inventories as well as the costs on goods sale at any time. In the actual work, a perpetual inventory system is normally applied, especially for items with high unit values of inventories.

The perpetual inventory system requires detailed accounting records, and therefore it tends to be more costly in implementing and maintaining compared with the periodic inventory system. However, the perpetual inventory system should be tested through a physical inventory at least once per year – comparing the records and the actual quantities on hand and then correcting its differences.

7.2.2 Periodic Inventory System

Periodic inventory system refers to a system of accounting for inventories. Under this system, the inventory on the balance sheet date is determined by counting and pricing the goods on hand with a particular cost flow assumption. Costs on of the goods sale are computed by subtracting the ending inventory from the cost of goods available for sale. The periodic inventory system is normally applied by the enterprises selling merchandise with low unit prices, such as a drugstore or hardware store. In these enterprises, to maintain perpetual inventory records would consume a lot of time and money.

Under the periodic inventory system, the amount of inventory is determined periodically (normally once per year), to calculate the value of the inventory on hand through multiplying the unit number by the cost per unit. Then, this amount is recognized as a current asset. This balance remains unchanged until the next count is taken. Purchases and returns of inventories during the reporting period are directly posted to expense accounts. Cost of sales during the year is determined as follows:

$$\text{Cost of sales} = \text{Opening inventory} + \text{Purchases} + \text{Freight inwards} - \text{Purchase returns} - \text{Cash discounts received} - \text{Closing inventory}$$

Accounting for inventories under the periodic inventory system is cost-effective and easily-applicable. However, the exact quantity and cost of inventories cannot be determined on a day-to-day basis, and this major weakness might result in the sales loss or decreasing customer satisfaction. In addition, it is difficult to identify inventory losses, resulting in inaccurate or misleading accounting figures.

7.3 Inventory Measures

Inventories are recorded in accordance with the historical cost principle at the date of acquisition.

Subsequently, when an item is sold, net assets will decline, and expenses will increase with the cost on this item transferring from the inventory to the sold goods. The cost value assigned to the end-of-period inventory is determined by an allocation of the total cost of goods for sale between the sold portion and the portion held as an asset for subsequent sale. This is not a problem when costs remain stable over the period. But when costs change, a problem will arise: which item has been sold? The core of its solution is the order in which the actual unit costs incurred are assigned to the ending inventory and the cost of sold goods. Each of the following assumptions leads to a different method of pricing inventories and a different amount in the financial statement. Three most common ones will be considered, based on which there are three inventory valuation methods: specific identification, average cost, first-in, first-out.

7.3.1 Specific Identification

This method is applicable to inventories of high value but low volume, such as cars and construction equipment. The specific identification method requires that each stocked item should be specifically marked so that its unit cost can be identified at any time. However, since this method requires careful identification of each item because of its need of detailed records, this method is not applicable to inventories of small unit price and large volume.

7.3.2 Average-cost Method

The average cost method (is also called the weighed average) is based on the assumption that cost should be charged against revenue according to the weighted average unit cost of the sold goods. The average figure comes from the following formula:

$$\text{Average Unit Cost} = \text{Total Cost of Goods} \div \text{Total Units}$$

The average cost method is applicable to a large volume of undifferentiated goods stored in the same area. Since the new cost level will be averaged by the old one, the replacement cost of inventories cannot be reflected, which is seen as the weakness of this method. Because of the averaged costs, the gross profit in the statement may not accurately reflect the current profitability of the company.

7.3.3 First-in, First-out Method (FIFO)

The first-in, first-out method is based on the assumption that the first merchandise acquired is the first merchandise sold and the items remaining in inventory at the end of the period are recently purchased or produced. According to this method, more recent purchase costs are assigned to the inventory asset account, while older costs are assigned to the cost of sales expense account.

On 1 December 2019, Co. ABC had 400 units of inventory with a total cost of $2,000. The following transactions occurred during the month:

10 Dec.	Sale 250 unit	$8 per unit
15 Dec.	Purchase 200 unit	$7 per unit
20 Dec.	Sale 300 unit	$8.5 per unit

Under the FIFO method, the COGS would be $3,050 ($250 \times 8 + 150 \times 7 = 3,050$), the closing inventory would be $350 ($50 \times 7 = 350$).

During a period of rising prices, the first-in first-out method will result in a smaller amount assigned as the cost of the ending inventory than that assigned under other methods. Unlike specific identification, FIFO specifies the order of acquisition costs as the order of costs of goods sold, so management cannot affect income by choosing to sell one identical item instead of another.

The selection of inventory measures is determined by management judgment which further depends upon the nature of the inventory, the needs of management and financial statement users, and the cost on different measures. For example, the weighted average method is highly applicable, especially for inventories of homogeneous products being mixed together, such as iron ore or spring water. On the other hand, First-in, First-out (FIFO) can better reflect the actual physical movement of goods. For example, the first produced must be sold (used) first to avoid loss due to obsolescence, spoilage or legislative restrictions. Entities with diversified operations can apply different methods for different types of inventories they have carried. According to *IAS 2*, using diverse methods is acceptable. Meanwhile, it also cautions that "the difference in geographical location of inventories (or in the respective tax rules), itself cannot justify the use of different cost methods". Instead, it is the nature of the inventory itself that serves as the core element in determining the suitable method.

7.4 Inventory Estimation Method

It is impractical to take physical inventory counts when preparing interim financial statements. Thus, it is useful to introduce some methods to estimate inventories. The inventory estimation method consists of two types: the gross profit method, and the retail inventory method. Manufacturing entities determine a standard cost on materials, direct or indirect labor, and overheads of each product based on the normal level of efficiency and capacity utilization. Adjustments are made at the end of the reporting period to account for variances between standard and actual costs.

7.4.1 Gross Profit Method

The gross profit method is a quick, simple method to estimate inventories, which can be applied by almost all types and sizes of enterprises. The calculation formulas are as follows:

$$\text{Gross profit margin} = \text{Sales Gross Profit} \div \text{Net Sales} \times 100\%$$

$$\text{Sales gross profit} = \text{Net Sales} \times \text{Gross Profit Margin}$$

If the rate of gross profit is known, the amount of net sales for period can be divided into two components that are the gross profit and the cost of goods sold. Then the cost of goods sold may be deducted from the cost of goods available for sale to yield the estimated ending inventory.

To illustrate this method, assume that the beginning inventory on January 1 is $10,000. During the month, net purchases amount to $28,000 and net sales total $30,000. The gross profit rate is 20%. The inventory on January 31 may be estimated as follows:

$$\begin{aligned}
\text{Cost of Goods Available for Sale} &= \text{Beginning Inventory} + \text{Net purchases} \\
&= 10{,}000 + 28{,}000 \\
&= \$38{,}000
\end{aligned}$$

Cost of Goods sold = Net Sales × Gross Profit Margin
= 30,000×20%
= $6,000

The inventory on January 31 = Cost of Goods Available for Sale - Cost of Goods sold
= 38,000 - 6,000
= $32,000

Normally, the estimation of the gross profit rate is based on the actual rate for the preceding year, and adjusted according to any changes in the cost and sales prices during the current period. This method helps a lot in preparing interim statements and estimating the loss of merchandise caused by fire or other disasters.

7.4.2 Retail Inventory Method

The retail inventory method is extensively applied by department stores and other types of retail enterprises. These enterprises normally mark each item of merchandise with the retail price and record purchases with both cost price and retail price. A firm can estimate its ending inventory at retail price merely by subtracting the net sales for the month from the retail price of goods available for sale. Then, the ending inventory at retail is converted to cost, according to the ratio of cost to retail price for the current period. Determination of ending inventory by the retail method is illustrated as follows:

	Cost	Retail Selling Price
Beginning inventory, January 1	$20,000	$30,000
Net purchases	$60,000	$70,000
Goods available for sale	$80,000	$100,000
Ratio of cost to selling retail price ($80,000÷$100,000=80%)		
Deduct: Net sales		$80,000
Ending inventory at retail selling price, January 31		$20,000
Ending inventory at cost, January 31	$16,000	

A comparison of the total computed inventory and the total physical inventory (both at retail prices) will show the extent of inventory shortages and the consequent need for corrective measures.

Both the gross profit method and the retail inventory method apply a calculation of cost of goods sold percentage. The gross profit method is based on the past experience, while the retail inventory method relies on the current experience. The gross profit method may be less reliable because of the difference between the past experience and the current situation. These two methods can both enable the accountant to prepare frequent financial statements without a physical count or perpetual inventory records. However, they require a physical count at least once a year, which will disclose losses due to thefts or shrinkage.

Key Words and Expressions

inventory	存货
finished goods	产成品
work in process (WIP)	在制品

raw materials	原材料
financial instruments	金融工具
biological assets	生物性资产
agricultural product	农产品
initial recognition	初始确认
net realizable value	可变现净值
commodity	商品
fair value	公允价值
historical cost	历史成本
purchase price	购买价格
import duties	进口关税
taxing authorities	征税机关
value added tax	增值税
trade discounts	商业折扣
cash discounts	现金折扣
settlement discounts	现金折扣
deferred payment term	延期付款条件
variable production overhead	变动生产性制造费用
administrative overheads	行政管理费用
selling costs	销售费用
estimated scrap value	预计残值
perpetual inventory system	永续盘存制
cost of goods sold	销货成本
periodic inventory system	定期盘存制
opening inventory	期初存货
closing inventory	期末存货
specific identification method	个别计价法
high-value	高价值
low-volume	小批量
average-cost method	平均成本法
gross profit	毛利润
first-in, first-out method	先进先出法
gross profit method	毛利率法
retail inventory method	零售价格法
department stores	百货商店
retail	零售
International Financial Reporting Interpretations Committee	国际财务报告解释委员会
Accounting Standards for Business Enterprises	《企业会计准则》

Exercises

Please select the best answer for the following questions or uncompleted sentences.

1. Which of the following is not the character of a manufacture's inventory ? (   )
   A. It is owned by the company.
   B. It is kept for future sale.
   C. It belongs to current asset.
   D. It will be converted into cash or consumed in the production.

2. The primary purpose for using an inventory flow assumption is to (   ).
   A. parallel the physical flow of units of merchandise
   B. offset against revenue an appropriate cost of goods sold
   C. minimize income taxes
   D. maximize the reported amount of net income

3. Company purchased 100 units of inventory with the following cost details:
   (1) Purchase price $5 per unit.
   (2) Non-recoverable import tax $500.
   (3) Carriage inwards $1,000.
   (4) Trade discount 5% of purchase price.
   (5) Selling costing was $1 per unit.
   How much is the cost of the inventory? (   )
   A. $4,750
   B. $5,250
   C. $6,250
   D. $7,250

4. On September 20, a company's warehouse was destroyed by a typhoon. The following information is the only one that has been retrieved:
   (1) Inventory, beginning: $28,000.
   (2) Purchase in the current period: $17,000.
   (3) Sales in the current period: $55,000.
   (4) Return on current sales: $7,00.
   The company's average gross profit rate is 35%. The estimated cost of lost inventory is (   ).
   A. $9, 705   B. $29, 260   C. $4, 525   D. $45, 370

5. In period of rising prices, FIFO will produce (   ).
   A. higher cost than average costing
   B. lower net income than average costing
   C. the same cost as average costing
   D. higher net income average costing

第7章 存货

存货是企业经营情况的晴雨表。存货的数量和销售库存所需的时间应被密切关注。存货通常能在一年内或公司一个经营周期内被消耗或转换为现金,因此被视为流动资产。

根据《国际会计准则第2号——存货》,存货包括:
(1) 在正常经营过程中持有待售的资产(产成品);
(2) 生产过程中的资产,用于在正常业务过程中出售(在制品——WIP);
(3) 生产中消耗的材料和物资(原材料)。

但是,《国际会计准则第2号》将以下几项排除在存货范围之外:
(1) 施工合同项下的在建工程;
(2) 金融工具;
(3) 农产品和林产品、农产品加工以及矿物和矿物产品。

7.1 存货的初始计量

根据《国际会计准则第2号——存货》的规定,"存货应当以成本与可变现净值孰低计量"。由于取得或制造存货项目的目的是出售存货以赚取利润,因此存货将按成本进行初始确认。以下两个特定的行业不适用成本与可变现净值孰低原则,即:

(1) 农产品和林产品以及矿物和矿物产品的生产者。它们按照在这些行业中已确立的做法,即以可变现净值来计量。
(2) 以公允价值减去销售成本计量存货的商品经纪交易商。

在这些情况下,可变现净值或公允价值减去在此期间发生的销售成本的变动计入损益。如果这些行业的存货是参照历史成本计量的,则《国际会计准则第2号》规定的成本与可变现净值孰低原则仍然适用。

存货核算的第一步是按其成本进行初始计量。《国际会计准则第2号——存货》规定了存货成本的三个组成部分:采购成本、加工成本、使存货达到其当前状态所发生的其他成本。其中,加工成本多适用于购买原材料和其他供应品再加工转化为其他产品的制造企业中。

7.1.1 采购成本

《国际会计准则第2号》规定,"存货的购买成本包括购买价格、进口关税和其他税金(随后可由税务机关退回的税款除外)、运输、装卸和其他由于收购产成品、材料和服务而直接产生的费用。商业折扣、回扣和其他类似项目在确定购买成本时需要扣除。

(1) 交易中的税收

许多国家对涉及货物和服务交换的交易征税,要求从事此类活动的企业向政府缴纳税款。但是如果存在如增值税这类可以由税务机关抵扣的税款,那么这类税款就不再包括在购买成本中。

(2) 商业折扣与现金折扣

商业折扣是指降低给予顾客的销售价格。这种折扣可以作为购买的激励,作为从积压库存中撤出的手段,或者作为订购大量商品的奖励。商业折扣降低了采购成本,在确定库存成本时会扣除商业折扣。

现金折扣是一种鼓励购买者快速支付他们账款的价格卖方激励方式。信用条款通常以"2/10, N/30"的形式出现在发票或合同上。这意味着,如果买方在发票日期后 10 天内付款,将获得原价款 2%的折扣;如果在 10 天后 30 天内付款则不享受折扣。有些公司还可能对逾期付款处以利息罚款。2004 年 11 月,国际财务报告解释委员会(IFRIC)发布了一项议程决定,即"结算折扣应从存货成本中扣除"。国际会计准则理事会还补充了"发生销售退回的费用不可从库存成本中扣除"。但在我国,根据《企业会计准则》,"销售商品涉及现金折扣的,应当按照扣除现金折扣前的金额确定销售商品收入金额。现金折扣在实际发生时计入当期损益"。

(3) 延期付款条件

如果一项存货是通过短期的信用销售或直接支付而获得的,那么确定购买价格就相对简单。在《国际会计准则第 2 号》中规定,在这种情况下,购买成本包含一个融资要素——在正常信贷条件下支付的金额和实际支付价款的差额,这将被确认为延期付款期间的利息费用。

7.1.2 加工成本

《国际会计准则第 2 号》将加工成本确定为与生产产品直接相关的成本,如直接劳动力,加上将材料转换为产成品过程中产生的固定和变动间接费用。变动间接费用是指直接随生产量变化的间接生产费用。它们将根据生产设施的实际使用情况分配给每一生产单位。固定间接费用是指无论产量多少,都保持相对恒定,并在正常生产能力的基础上分配到存货成本的生产费用,如生产机械的折旧。当一个生产过程同时生产一个或多个产品时,加工成本必须在系统和合理的基础上在产品之间进行分配。成本计算、分配方法属于管理会计的范畴,不在本书的讨论范围内。

7.1.3 其他成本

其他成本只有在"为将存货运至预定位置并达到预定状态时发生"的才能计入存货成本。这些费用可以包括为特定对象生产产品所发生的设计费用。《国际会计准则第 23 号——借款成本》规定,在这些存货验收合格的情况下,允许将借款利息列入存货成本。

下列成本在《国际会计准则第 2 号》中被明确指出不应列为存货成本,在发生时必须确认为当期费用:

—— 材料、人工或其他生产成本的非正常损失。
—— 除产成品的储存成本外的储存成本。
—— 与存货无直接联系的管理费用。

7.1.4 成本与可变现净值孰低

由于《国际会计准则第 2 号——存货》规定存货的计量规则是"成本和可变现净值孰低",因此必须对存货进行可变现净值的估计,以确定存货是否需要计提减值。通常,这一估计是在会计报告期末进行的,但是,如果管理层在期中意识到货物或服务将不能以高于成本的价格出售时,存货价值应减记为其可变现净值。根据《国际会计准则第 2 号——存货》的规定,这种计量规则的理由是:资产的金额不应超过预期从其销售或使用中实现的经济利益流入金额。

可变现净值是指企业在正常经营过程中从存货的销售中实现的净额。在《国际会计准则第 2 号——存货》中可变现净值的定义为"在正常经营过程中,以预计售价减去进一步加工成本和预计销售费用以及相关税费后的净值"。可变现净值是针对每一个特定个体的,不一定等于公允价值减销售成本。根据《国际财务报告准则第 13 号——公允价值计量》,公允价值被定义为"在出售日或市场参与者之间有序交易中获取的出售资产或支付债务的价格"。

可变现净值在很多情况下可能低于存货的成本,包括但不限于:

— 存货销售价格的下降(例如时装)。
— 库存的情况恶化(例如水果、蔬菜)。
— 产品过时(例如计算机等电子设备)。
— 出于公司营销战略的需要,在亏损时生产和销售产品的决定(例如生产新产品)。
— 计算错误或采购、生产中的其他错误(例如库存积压)。
— 估计完成销售时需要增加的成本(例如空调设备的调试)。

(1) 可变现净值

可变现净值的估计数必须基于最可靠依据(通常是基于报告期结束时的具体情况),预计库存将可变现的净值。因此,必须估计如下数据:

— 预计售价。
— 预计完工成本。
— 预计销售成本。

在做预计时需要考虑报告期结束后发生的价格或成本的波动等情况。在估算可变现净值时,还应考虑持有存货的目的。例如,为满足公司销售或服务合同而持有的存货的可变现净值是基于合同价格的。如果销售合同低于所持有的存货的数量,超额部分利润的可变现净值是根据一般销售价格计算的。估计销售成本时需包括为满足顾客需求而发生的所有成本,如广告费用、销售人员薪金和经营成本,以及存储和运输成品的成本。

可以使用基于预定标准的公式来初步估计可变现净值。这些公式通常考虑了存货的变动和估计报废价值。但仍需要根据公式中未预料到的其他特殊情况(如当前库存市场需求的变化或已过时),对结果进行审查。

(2) 材料和其他物资

《国际会计准则第 2 号》规定,"如果用于库存生产的材料和其他物资预计以成本或高于成本的价格出售,则不得减记其成本"。同时准则还规定:在估算材料或其他物资的可变现净值时重置成本可作为重要参考依据。

(3) 减记至可变现净值

当账面价值高于可变现净值时,存货通常会逐项减记至其可变现净值。《国际会计准则第 2 号》规定,存货通常以单个项目减记到可变现净值。但在某些情况下,也可以将类似或者相关的存货分组后计提减值。当与同一生产线有关的存货项目具有类似的目的或最终用途、在相同的地理区域生产或销售,并且实际上也不可能将它们与这一生产线上的其他项目分开估价时,就可以采用分组。存货不宜以分组为基础进行减记,而应按照不同的子项目单独计量。会计分录如下所示:

借:存货跌价准备
　　贷:存货

7.2 存货盘存制度

在实际中,存货盘存有两种不同的制度:永续盘存制和定期盘存制。

7.2.1 永续盘存制

在永续盘存制中,存货项目的每一次收货和每一次发出都记录在存货中,以随时保持最新的存货余额。因此,永续盘存制提供了期末存货的数量、成本及产品销售成本。在实际工作中,除少数特殊情况外,一般都应采用永续盘存制,尤其是存货单位价值较高的项目。

永续盘存制需要有详细的会计记录,因此实施和维护永续盘存制的成本往往高于定期盘存制。尽管如此,永续盘存法也需要通过至少每年一次的实物盘点来加以检查,方法是将账务记录和实际库存量进行比较,并对照差异进行修改。

7.2.2 定期盘存制

定期盘存制是一种对存货进行会计核算的制度,在这种制度下,资产负债表日的存货是通过使用特定的成本流假设对现有货物进行计数和定价来确定的。在定期盘存制下,销货成本是用期末存货减去可供出售货物的成本来计算的。定期盘存制一般用于单位商品价值较低的企业,例如药店或五金店。在这样的企业使用永续盘存耗费太大。

在定期盘存制下,存货的数量是定期(通常是每年一次)进行实物清点,通常用数量乘以单位成本来计算现有存货的价值,然后将该金额确认为流动资产的价值。这种平衡将保持到下一次清点。报告期内库存的采购和退货直接计入费用账户。本年度销售成本的公式如下:

销售成本=期初库存+采购成本+运费-采购退货-现金折扣-期末存货

定期盘存制下的存货核算具有成本效益高、适用性强的特点。其主要缺点是存货的准确数量和成本无法按天确定,这可能导致销售损失或降低客户满意度。此外,定期盘存制很难发现库存损失,从而导致会计数据的不准确。

7.3 存货计价方法

存货在取得时按照历史成本原则入账。随后,当一个项目被出售时,由于该项目的成本从库存转移到所售商品的成本,从而使得公司净资产减少,费用增加。分配给期末存货的成本价值是可供出售商品的总成本在已出售部分和作为资产持有以备日后出售部分之间的分配。当成本在这段时间内保持稳定时,这不是问题。但当成本发生变化时,会出现一个问题:哪一件商品被卖掉了?解决这个问题的核心在于将实际发生的单位成本分配到期末存货和销售商品成本的顺序。以下将介绍三种最常见的存货估价方法,每种方法均基于不同的假设,而每种假设都会导致存货得出不同的金额,并计入在财务报表中。这三种方法分别是个别计价法、平均成本法、先进先出法。

7.3.1 个别计价法

这种方法最适用于高价值、小批量的存货,如汽车和工程机械。个别计价法要求对每一个库存项目都有明确的标识，以便随时识别其单位成本。这种方法需要仔细识别每一项，原因是需要详细的记录。当存货的单价较小、数量较大时，不宜采用这种方法。

7.3.2 平均成本法

平均成本法(也称为"加权平均法")是基于这样一种假设，即应根据销售商品的总成本加权均摊至单位商品上，从而得出其平均单位成本。加权平均法的计算公式如下：

$$平均单位成本＝总销货成本\div总销量$$

平均成本法适合于储存于同一处的区别甚小的大量商品。它的缺点是掩盖了存货的重置成本，因为新的成本会被旧的成本平均化。由于成本被平均，报表中的毛利可能无法准确反映公司当前真实的盈利水平。

7.3.3 先进先出法

先进先出法(通常缩写为 FIFO)是基于所购进的第一批商品是第一批售出的商品这一假设。期末存货中剩余的商品则是最近购进或生产的。先进先出法将最近的采购成本分配给库存商品账户，将较旧的成本分配给销售货物的成本账户。

截至 2019 年 12 月 1 日，ABC 公司有 400 件库存，总成本为 2,000 美元。本月发生如下交易：12 月 10 日出售 250 件，每件 8 美元；12 月 15 日，购进 200 件，每件 7 美元；12 月 20 日，出售 300 件，每件 8.5 美元。

在先进先出法下，本月销货成本为 3,050 美元(250×8+150×7=3,050)，期末存货为 350 美元(50×7=350)。

在价格上涨期间，先进先出法将比其他方法下分配的期末存货成本小。与个别计价法不同，先进先出法规定了购进成本的顺序即为销售商品成本的顺序，因此管理层难以操纵销货成本。

存货计价方法的选择取决于管理层的判断。而管理层的判断是基于存货的性质、管理层和财务报表使用者的需求以及不同计价方法的使用成本。例如，加权平均法易于应用，特别适用于同类产品混合在一起的存货，如铁矿石或泉水。而先进先出法可以更好地反映货物的实际移动情况，例如为避免由于过时、变质或立法限制而造成的损失，必须先销售(使用)第一批到达的库存。经营多元化的公司可以对其持有的不同类型的存货采用不同的方法。根据《国际会计准则第 2 号》，采用不同的方法是被允许的，但它同时也指出："库存的地理位置(或各自的税收规则)差异本身不足以证明采用不同的成本方法是合理的"。存货本身的性质才是决定方法的选择的核心要素。

7.4 存货估价方法

在编制中期财务报表时，进行实际盘存盘点是不切实际的。因此，引入一些存货的估算方法是有意义的。主要有两种存货估价方法：一种是毛利法，另一种是零售价格法。制造企业根据正常的效率和产能利用水平，将所消耗的材料、劳动力等直接或间接费用分推至每种产品，作为其计划成本。在报告期末再对计划成本与实际成本之间的差异做出调整。

7.4.1 毛利法

毛利法是一种快速、简单的估算存货的方法，可用于几乎所有类型和规模的企业。计算公式如下：

$$毛利率＝销售毛利÷净销售额×100\%$$

$$销售毛利＝净销售额×毛利率$$

如果毛利率是已知的，则当期净销售额可以分为毛利率和销售成本两部分。进而可以从可供出售商品的成本中扣除已出售商品的成本，从而估算出期末存货的价值。

假设1月1日的期初库存为10,000美元。本月净采购额为2.8万美元，净销售总额为3万美元。毛利率为20%，1月31日的存货估价过程如下：

$$
\begin{aligned}
可供出售商品成本 &＝期初库存＋净采购额 \\
&＝10,000＋28,000 \\
&＝\$38,000 \\
销货成本 &＝净销售额×毛利率 \\
&＝30,000×20\% \\
&＝\$6,000 \\
1月31日存货价值 &＝可供出售商品成本－销货成本 \\
&＝38,000－6,000 \\
&＝\$32,000
\end{aligned}
$$

毛利率的估值通常以上一年的实际利率为基础，并根据当期成本和销售价格的变动进行调整。这种方法在编制中期报表、确定火灾或其他灾害所造成的商品损失方面非常有用。

7.4.2 零售价格法

零售价格法广泛应用于百货公司等零售企业，这些企业一般会用零售价格标记每种商品，并以成本价和零售价记录购买情况。企业只需从可供销售商品的零售价格中减去当月的净销售额，就可以按零售价格估算其期末存货。然后，根据当期成本与销售零售价的比率，将零售期末存货转换为成本。采用零售法确定期末存货如下：

	成本	售价
期初存货，1月1日	$20,000	$30,000
购(进)货净额	$60,000	$70,000
可供出售的货物	$80,000	$100,000
成本与销售零售价之比($80,000÷$100,000＝80%)		
减：净销售额		$80,000
按零售价计算的期末存货，1月31日		$20,000
期末存货成本，1月31日	$16,000	

将计算出的库存总量与实际库存总量(均以零售价计算)进行比较,将显示库存短缺的程度以及随后需要采取的应对措施。

毛利率法和零售价格法都是使用销货成本百分比的计算方法。毛利法以过去的经验为基础，零售库存法采用当前经验。毛利润法有时不太可靠，因为过去的经验可能不同于当前的情况。使用这两种方法都能方便地编制中期的财务报表。然而，在这两种方法下每年依然有必要至少进行一次实地盘存。实物盘存将显示因偷窃或存货缩水而造成的损失。

Chapter 8

Plant Assets

Plant assets, as an important part of a company's assets, include assets that are needed for the daily operations of the company, such as land, office machinery, equipment, warehouses, buildings, factories, retail stores, and delivery trucks. There are many alternative terms of plant assets, such as factory assets, fixed assets, operational assets, as well as Property, Plant and Equipment (PPE).

According to *IAS 16 Property, Plant and Equipment*, plant assets are defined as tangible items that:

(1) are used for the production, the supply of services, rental, or administrative purposes; and

(2) are expected to be used in a period of more the one year.

To be included in plant assets, an asset must have three characteristics:

(1) Assets should be used in production/supply, rental or administration, rather than investment, only in normal business processes. However, assets that are held for sale, including land, or held for investment should not be included. Instead, assets held for sale are accounted for in accordance with *IFRS 5 Non-current Assets Held for Sale and Discontinued Operations*.

(2) The life expectancy of an asset must exceed one year. This asset represents a range of future services that companies will receive during the life of the asset. To be included in plant assets, the benefits must be extended to more than one year or more than one operating cycle.

(3) Assets must be tangible and must have visible and tangible material. In contrast, intangible assets such as goodwill or patents are not entities.

8.1 Acquisition of Plant Assets

IAS 16 Property, Plant and Equipment clarifies the principles for the recognition of fixed assets:

The cost of an item of plant assets shall be recognized as an asset if, and only if:

(1) It is probable that future economic benefits associated with the item will flow to the entity; and

(2) The cost of the item can be measured reliably.

This is a general principle for the recognition of property, plant and equipment. It applies to the initial recognition of an asset. When parts of the asset are replaced or other costs are incurred during the use of the asset, the outlay must give rise to the expectation of future economic benefits, so that the part of costs can be recognized as an asset cost.

After the asset is recognized, the entity must assign a monetary amount to the asset. *IAS 16* also clarifies the principles for initial measurement of fixed assets, "the item of property, plant and equipment that is qualified for the recognition principle of a fixed asset shall be measured at its cost". Meanwhile, *IAS 16* specifies three elements of cost: purchase price, directly attributable costs, and estimated costs of dismantling and removing the item or restoring the site on which it is located. It should be noted that only reasonable and necessary expenditures should be included.

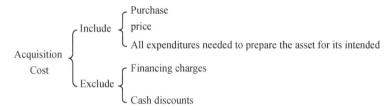

These elements are considered separately in the following sections.

8.1.1 Acquisition by Cash

It is easier to determine the cost of the assets which are purchased by cash. The cost of an asset is equal to the expenditure required to obtain the asset plus any insurance for transportation, installation, commissioning, and other costs required to prepare the asset. If the plant assets are purchased by installment or by issuing notes payable, the interest should be recorded as interest expense rather than a part of the cost of the fixed asset.

8.1.2 Acquisition through Non-cash Exchange

More difficulties arise in the measuring process when the exchange involves assets other than cash. In a non-cash exchange, the acquiring entity receives the non-cash assets and provides the seller with non-cash assets in return. In this situation, a question will arise in the measuring process of the purchased assets: whether the measurement should be based on the value of the asset given up by the acquirer, or by reference to the value of the asset acquired from the seller. In terms of the application of the cost measurement principle, the following aspects should be noted:

(1) Cost is determined according to the fair value of assets given up (exchanged) by the acquirer. This principle is inherent in the definition of cost in *IAS 16*. Further, if the fair values of the assets exchanged and the asset received are both reliably measurable, the fair value of the asset given up will be used to measure the cost of the asset received.

(2) Cost is measured according to the fair value. In *IAS 16*, the term fair value is defined as "the price that would be received in selling an asset or transferring a liability in an orderly transaction between market participants at the measurement date".

(3) *IAS 16* requires the use of fair value to measure the cost of an asset received, unless the exchange transaction lacks commercial substance. Commercial substance means a discernible effect of a business on the economy of an entity. According to *IAS 16*, an exchange transaction has commercial substance in the following

situations:

① the configuration (risk, timing and amount) of the cash flows of the asset received differs from the configuration of the cash flows of the asset transferred, in terms of risk, timing and amount. This would not occur if similar assets (e.g., an exchange of commodities such as oil or milk) were exchanged as would occur where, for example, suppliers exchanged inventories in various locations to fulfill demand on a timely basis in a particular location; or

② the entity-specific value of the portion of the entity's operations affected by the transaction changes as a result of the exchange. *IAS 16* defines entity-specific value as "the present value of the cash flows an entity expects to arise from the continuing use of an asset and from its disposal at the end of its useful life or expects to incur when settling a liability". If there is no change in the expected cash flows to the entity as a result of the exchange, as in the case of the exchange of similar items, the transaction will lack commercial substance; and

③ the difference between ① and ② is significantly relative to the fair value of the assets exchanged. In both ① and ②, the change in cash flows or configuration must be material, with materiality being measured in relation to the fair value of the assets exchanged.

(4) *IAS 16* also includes the situation that neither the fair value of the assets given up nor the fair value of the assets acquired can be measured reliably in an exchange of assets. This situation may occur when the assets exchanged are all traded in weak markets with infrequent market transactions. In this situation, the acquirer measures the cost of the asset acquired at the carrying amount of the asset exchanged.

8.1.3 Acquisition through Self-construction

Sometimes buildings and equipment are constructed by a company itself. The cost of construction includes contract price, architect fees, building permits and excavation fees. In addition, with a long construction period of the fixed asset, the cost also includes interest charges for financing the project. In this case, the cost of interest is considered to be as necessary as materials and labors. However, only the cost of interest in the construction period is included in the cost of fixed assets of self-construction. After the construction, the subsequent payment of the funds borrowed for construction financing is debited for interest expenses.

8.2 Accounting for Depreciation

Depreciable assets are tangible assets used by a business in the production of goods and services. Apart from land, the typical fixed assets have a limited life span. In order to understand the accounting principles for depreciation, it is necessary to introduce the definitions of depreciation, depreciable amount, lifespan and residual value described in *IAS 16*:

— Depreciation refers to the systematic allocation of the depreciable amount of an asset over its useful life.

— Depreciable amount refers to the amount which deducts the residual value from the cost of an asset or the amount of other substituting cost.

— The residual value of an asset refers to the estimated amount that an entity would currently obtain from disposal of the asset after deducting the estimated costs of disposal, if the asset were already of the age and in the condition expected at the end of its lifespan.

— Lifespan refers to the period over which an asset is expected to be available for use by an entity, or the number of production or similar units expected to be obtained from the asset by an entity.

Fixed assets added in the current month will not be depreciated in the current month, but from next month. Fixed assets disposed in the current month will be depreciated in the current month, instead of from next month. Depreciation is calculated by subtracting estimated salvage value from cost and then allocating the remainder over the expected lifespan. A formula is shown as follows:

Depreciable Amount = Initial Cost - Residual Value

There are four common methods of computing depreciation: (1) Straight-line, (2) unit-of-production, (3) double-declining-balance, and (4) sum-of-the-years'-digits. Once a method is chosen, it should be used consistently all over the lifespan of the asset. However, a company does not need to apply the same method of depreciation for all of its assets.

8.2.1 Straight-line Method

The straight-line method is based on the assumption that depreciation depends only on the time. Within this method, the amount of depreciation expense remains fixed for each year. The formula is shown as follows:

Annual Depreciation = (Initial Cost - Residual Value) ÷ Expected Useful Life

For example, if a delivery truck costs $8,500 and has an estimated residual value of $500 at the end of its estimated useful life of five years, the annual depreciation would be $1,600 ($\frac{8,500-500}{5}=1,600$) under the straight-line method.

The journal entry is:

  Dr. Depreciation Expense —— Delivery Truck $1,600
    Cr. Accumulated Depreciation —— Delivery Truck $1,600

The straight-line method is a simple and widely used method. It is reasonable to convert costs into periods, when the use of assets and related income are generated during the same period.

8.2.2 Unit-of-production Method

The unit-of-production method is based on the assumption that depreciation is solely the result of use and that time plays does not affect the depreciation process. When the amount of use of a plant asset varies from year to year, it is more suitable to use the unit-of-production method than the straight-line method.

The formula of the unit-of-production method is as follows:

  Depreciation Expense = Depreciation per unit × Number of Units Produced
  Depreciation per Unit = (Initial Cost - Residual Value) ÷ Total Units of Production

If the delivery truck from the example above has an estimated useful life of 80,000 miles, the mileage use of the truck was 15,000 miles for the first year. Then we can calculate that the depreciation cost per mile is $0.1 ($\frac{8,500-500}{80,000}=0.1$). The annual depreciation of the first year under the unit-of-production method should be

$1,500 (15,000 miles × $0.1 per mile = 1,500).

8.2.3 Double-declining-balance Method

The double-declining-balance method and sum-of-the-years'-digits method are time-based methods of accelerated depreciation, with the assumption that many types of plant assets are the most efficient when they are new and thus more and better service can be provided in their early lifespan. It is consistent with the matching rule to allocate more depreciation to early stages than to later stages with greater received benefits or services in the early stage.

The formula of the double declining balance method is as follows:

Annual depreciation = Carrying amount × Double declining balance rate

Within the double-declining-balance method, the depreciation rate for the first several years is doubled, compared to that within the straight-line method. For example, the double-declining-balance rate for the above-mentioned delivery truck is 40% (20% × 2=40%) for the first three years. When the double-declining-balance method is used, the estimated residual value is not considered in determining the depreciation rate. Moreover, the asset should not be depreciated below its estimated residual value. In the last two years of depreciation, the annual average method should be used and the residual value should be considered. To illustrate, the annual double-declining-balance depreciation for the truck from the example above is shown below.

Year	Carrying Amount at Beginning of year ($)	Depr. Rate	Depr. for Year ($)	Carrying Amount at End of year ($)
1	8,500	40%	3,400	5,100
2	5,100	40%	2,040	3,060
3	3,060	40%	1,224	1,836
4	1,836	50%	(1,836-500)÷2=668	1,168
5	1,168	50%	668	500

8.2.4 Sum-of-the-years'-digits Method

Under the sum-of-the-years'-digits method, the depreciation rate to be used is a fraction, of which the numerator is the remaining years of lifespan. The formula of calculating depreciation under the sum-of-the-years'-digits method is shown as follows:

$$\text{Annual Depreciation} = (\text{Original Cost} - \text{Residual Value}) \times \frac{\text{Remaining Useful Life}}{\text{Sum-of-the-years-digits}}$$

In the above-mentioned example of the delivery truck, the denominator of the fraction will be 15 (1+2+3+4+5=15). The numerator of the first year will be 5, and those of the second, the third, the fourth and the fifth year will be 4, 3, 2 and 1, respectively. The annual depreciation for the truck under the sum-of-the-years'-digits method is shown as follows:

Year	Depr. Rate	Depr. for Year ($)	Carrying Amount at end of year ($)
1	5/15	2,666.67	5,833.33
2	4/15	2,133.33	3,700

(Continued)

Year	Depr. Rate	Depr. for Year ($)	Carrying Amount at end of year ($)
3	3/15	1,600	2,100
4	2/15	1,066.67	1,033.33
5	1/15	5,33.33	500

Once an asset has been fully depreciated, no more depreciation should be recorded on it, even though the property is in good condition and is still in use.

8.3 Plant Assets Disposals

Plant assets may be disposed by the ways of being retired, sold, or exchanged. Upon the disposal of a depreciable asset, the cost of the property should be deducted from the asset account, and the accumulated depreciation should be deducted from the related contra-asset account. Assume, the delivery truck mentioned above which has been fully depreciated is sold for $500. The journal entry to record this transaction is as follow:

  Dr. Cash $500
    Accumulated Depreciation——truck $8,000
    Cr. Interest Income $8,500

In practice, it is rare to see that the disposal price and the book value are equal. In most circumstances, the book value of the asset and the proceeds received from the disposal is not exactly different. If proceeds exceed the book value, a gain on disposal will occur. If proceeds are less than the book value, a loss on disposal.

Plant Assets Disposals
$$\begin{cases} \text{Proceeds} > \text{Book Value, record a gain (credit)} \\ \text{Proceeds} > \text{Book Value, no gain or loss} \\ \text{Proceeds} < \text{Book Value, record a loss (debit)} \end{cases}$$

Assume, the delivery truck mentioned above which has been fully depreciated is sold for $550. The journal entry to record this transaction is as follow:

  Dr. Cash $550
    Accumulated Depreciation——truck $8,000
    Cr. Vehicles——truck $8,500
      Gain on Disposal of Plant Assets $50

If the truck is sold for $400, the journal entry to record this transaction is as follow:

  Dr. Cash $400
    Accumulated Depreciation——truck $8,000
    Loss on Disposal of plant assets $100
    Cr. Vehicles——truck $8,500

Key Words and Expressions

plants assets	固定资产
warehouses	仓库
tangible	有形的
IFRS (International Financial Reporting Stand)	国际财务报告准则
intangible assets	无形资产
goodwill	商誉
financing charges	融资费用
interest expense	利息费用
cost principle	历史成本原则
fair value	公允价值
commercial substance	商业实质
depreciation	折旧
residual value	净残值
straight-line method	直线法
initial cost	原值
expected useful life	预计可使用年限
estimated residual value	预计净残值
unit-of-production method	产量法
double-declining-balance method	双倍余额递减法
matching rule	配比原则
carrying amount	账面价值
sum-of-the-years'-digits method	年数总和法
remaining useful life	尚可使用年限
disposal	处置
accumulated depreciation	累计折旧

Exercises

Ⅰ. **Please select the best answer for the following questions or uncompleted sentences.**

1. Which of the following is not a characteristic of fixed assets? (　　)

    A. Tangible.

    B. Long-lived.

    C. Unchanged outlook.

    D. For resale.

2. Which of the following statement is correct? (   )

   A. Accumulated depreciation represents a cash fund being accumulated for the replacement of plant assets.

   B. An entity may use different depreciation method in its financial statements and its income tax return.

   C. The use of an accelerated depreciation method causes an asset to wear out more quickly than that the use of the straight-line method.

   D. None of above statement is correct.

3. In accounting, which of the following factors is not an estimate to determine the depreciation rate of a fixed asset? (   ).

   A. Cost

   B. Useful life

   C. Salvage value

   D. Total units of output

4. Company A acquired a new car. The purchase price of the car was $100,000. The transportation cost was bringing the car from manufacturer to carport that cost $50000. And company A paid $2,000 consulting fees. Therefore, what cost should be recorded into the asset register? (   ).

   A. $152,000

   B. $150,000

   C. $102,000

   D. $95,000

5. Management should select the depreciation method that (   ).

   A. is easiest to apply

   B. best measures the plant asset's market value over its useful life

   C. best measures the plant asset's contribution to revenue over its useful life

   D. has been used most often in the past by the company

6. Company B sold a fixed asset which originally cost $1,000 for $100 cash. If the company correctly reports a $40 gain on this sale, the accumulated depreciation on the asset at the date of sale must have been (   ).

   A. $ 900

   B. $ 940

   C. $ 860

   D. $ 60

II. Finish the following tasks based on the information given.

HYX Co. purchased a new machine for its assembly process on December 1, 2015. The cost of this machine was $120,000. The company estimated that the machine would have a salvage value of $20,000 at the end of its service life. Its life is estimated at 5 years and its working hours are estimated as following.

Year Hours	2015	2016	2017	2018	2019
Working Hours	150	200	250	210	190

Please compute the depreciation expense for each year under the
(a) Straight-Line method.
(b) Unit-of-production method.
(c) Double-declining-balance methods.
(d) Sum-of-the-years'-digits method.

第8章 固定资产

固定资产是企业资产的重要组成部分,它包括公司日常运营所需的资产,如土地、办公机械、设备、仓库、建筑物、工厂和送货车。固定资产的英文表述有很多,如:factory assets、fixed assets、operational assets、Property,Plant and Equipment(简称 PPE)。

《国际会计准则 16 号——固定资产》对固定资产的定义是:

(1) 用于生产产品、提供服务、出租或者行政管理的;

(2) 预计使用时间至少在一年以上。

若要被归为固定资产,则该资产必须具有三个特征:

(1) 必须为使用而非投资持有。应包括在正常业务流程中使用的资产,但闲置土地或建筑物不包括在内,它们应单独列为投资。持有待售资产按照《国际财务报告准则第 5 号——持有待售非流动资产和终止经营》进行会计处理。

(2) 预期寿命必须超过一年。该资产代表了公司在资产寿命期间将获得的一系列未来服务。能被定义为固定资产的,收益必须延长至一年以上或一个以上的运营周期。

(3) 资产必须是有形的。相反,公司的商誉或专利等无形资产并非实体物质,故不属于固定资产。

8.1 固定资产的取得

《国际会计准则 16 号——固定资产》中明确了固定资产的确认原则:

当且仅当满足下列条件时,才能将一项固定资产的成本确认:

(1) 与该资产有关的未来经济利益很可能流入该企业;

(2) 该资产的成本能够被可靠地计量。

这是确认固定资产的一般原则。它适用于对资产的初始确认。当该资产的部分被替换,或该资产在其使用寿命内发生其他成本时,若要将此类成本确认为资产的成本,那么这部分成本必须引起预期未来经济效益的增加。

在固定资产得以确定后,企业必须给其确定一个货币金额。《国际会计准则第 16 号》还明确了固定资产的初始计量原则:"符合固定资产确认条件的不动产、厂房和设备项目应按其成本计量"。同时准则规定了构成成本的三个要素,即:购买价格、直接归属与固定资产的成本、使固定资产达到预定可使用状态所花费的成本。

以下将详细叙述这 3 个要素。

8.1.1 购入固定资产

用现金(银行存款)购入的固定资产的成本较容易确定。资产的成本等于获得资产所需的支出加上运输、安装、调试的保险费,以及准备资产所需的其他成本。以分期付款或发行应付票据的方式购买的固定资产,其利息应当记入利息费用,而不是固定资产成本的一部分。

设备成本包括购买和使设备达到预计可使用状态的一切合理费用。这些费用包括发票上注明的价款(减去现金折扣)、运输费、保险费、消费税和关税、安装费用以及调试费用。

8.1.2 资产置换

如果取得资产的交易涉及现金以外的其他资产,则在计量的时候会比通过支付现金的方式更复杂。在非现金交换中,收购企业接收非现金资产,并向卖方提供非现金资产作为回报。在计量所购资产的成本时便会出现一个问题:计量应当以购买方放弃的资产价值为基础,还是以购买方取得的资产价值为基础。关于成本计量原则的应用,应注意以下几点:

(1) 成本应当参照购买方放弃的资产(即置换出去的资产)的公允价值确定。成本代表收购方做出的牺牲。这一原则是《国际会计准则第 16 号》中成本定义所规定的。此外,如果收购方放弃的资产和收到的资产的公允价值都是可靠计量的,则放弃的资产的公允价值用于计量收到的资产的成本。

(2) 成本参照公允价值计量。《国际会计准则第 16 号》将"公允价值"定义为"在计量日市场参与者之间有序交易中,出售资产或转移负债所收到的价格"。

(3) 《国际会计准则第 16 号》要求使用公允价值来衡量所收资产的成本,除非该交易行为缺乏商业实质。商业实质是指交易是否对一个实体的经济有明显的影响。准则规定,在下列情况下,交易行为具有商业实质:

① 换入资产的未来现金流量在风险、时间和金额方面与换出资产显著不同。交换类似的资产(如石油或牛奶等商品的交换)不属于这种情况。但供应商在不同地点交换库存以及时满足特定地点的需求则属于这种情况。

② 实体的特定价值会由于交换而发生变化。《国际会计准则第16号》将实体的特定价值定义为"一个实体预期从资产的持续使用和在其使用寿命结束时的处置产生的现金流的现值,或在清偿债务时预期产生的现金流的现值"。如果该实体的预期现金流没有因交换而发生变化,则该交易将缺乏商业实质。

③ 第 1 和第 2 项之间的差异与交换资产的公允价值显著相关。在第 1 和第 2 项中,现金流量或配置的变化必须是重大的,其重要性根据所交换资产的公允价值计量。

(4) 《国际会计准则第 16 号》还包括了资产交换中,放弃资产的公允价值和取得资产的公允价值均不能可靠计量的情形。这可能发生在交换的资产都在市场交易不频繁的弱市中交易。这种情况下,收购方以置换的资产的账面价值计量所收购资产的成本。

8.1.3 自建

有时建筑物和设备是由公司自己建造的。施工成本包括合同价格、建筑师费、建筑许可证和开挖费。此外,当固定资产的建设期较长时,其成本还包括项目融资的利息费用。在这种情况下,利息成本被认为与材料和劳动力一样必要。但是,只有建设期内的利息费用包含在自建的固定资产成本中。建设完成后,建设融资借款的后续款项借记利息费用。

8.2 折旧

企业用于生产产品或提供劳务的有形资产应计提折旧。除土地外，典型的固定资产具有有限的使用寿命。为了理解折旧的会计原则，有必要介绍《国际会计准则第 16 号》所表述的折旧、折旧(总)额、使用寿命和残值的定义：
— 折旧是一项资产在其使用寿命内的应计折旧额的系统分配。
— 折旧(总)额是指资产的成本，或其他替代成本的金额减去其残值。
— 资产的剩余价值(也称"残值")是一家企业估计从资产处置中获得的金额，即固定资产报废清理时收回的一些残余材料的价值。
— 使用寿命是一个企业预期资产可供使用的期限。

当月增加的固定资产，当月不提折旧，从下月起计提折旧；当月减少的固定资产，当月照提折旧，从下月起不提折旧。折旧额的计算是从成本中减去估计残值，然后在预计使用期限内分配应计折旧额。它的计算公式是：

$$折旧总额＝固定资产原值－固定资产净残值$$

最常用的四种折旧方法是：直线法、产量法、双倍余额递减法、年数总和法。折旧方法一经选择，在该资产的整个使用寿命内不得随意变更。但是，一家公司不必对其所有的资产使用相同的折旧方法。

8.2.1 直线法

直线法的基础假设是折旧只取决于时间的推移。该方法下每年的折旧费用都一样。利用直线法计算折旧额的公式如下：

$$年折旧额＝(资产原值－资产净残值)÷资产预计使用年限$$

例如，一辆卡车的成本为 8,500 美元，估计在其五年的估计使用寿命结束时，残值为 500 美元，按直线法计算，年折旧应为 1,600 美元（$\frac{8,500-500}{5}=1,600$）。

会计分录应为：

借：折旧费——货车　　　　　　　　　　　　$1,600
　　贷：累计折旧——货车　　　　　　　　　　　　　　$1,600

直线法是一种简单且应用广泛的方法。当资产的使用和相关收入在同一期间发生时，将成本转换为各期费用是合理的。

8.2.2 产量法

产量法建立在这样的一个假设基础上：即折旧仅仅是使用的结果，时间的推移不影响折旧过程。当固定资产的使用量逐年变化时，用产量法进行折旧比直线法更合适。

产量法下的计算公式为：

$$折旧额＝单位产量折旧额×产量$$
$$单位产量折旧额＝(资产原值－资产净残值)÷预计总产量$$

如果上述示例中的货车的估计使用寿命为 80,000 英里，第一年货车的使用里程为 15,000 英里，则可以计算出的折旧成本是 0.1 美元/英里（$\frac{8,500-500}{80,000}=0.1$）。第一年的年折旧应为 1,500 美元(15,000 英里×0.1 美元/英里＝1,500)。

8.2.3 双倍余额递减法

双倍余额递减法和年数总和法是基于时间推移的加速折旧法，假定许多类型的固定资产在初始的时候效用是最高的，使用寿命的初期可以提供更多更好的服务。如果早期获得的收益或服务很多，则应将更多折旧分配给早期，而不是后期，这与配比原则的要求是一致的。

双倍余额递减法公式如下：

年折旧额＝账面价值×双倍余额法下的折旧率

采用双倍余额递减法，前几年的折旧率在直线法下的折旧率基础上翻一番。例如，上例中的货车前三年在双倍余额递减法下的折旧率为 40%(20%×2＝40%)。采用双倍余额递减法时，在确定折旧率时不考虑预计残值。此外，资产的折旧不应低于其估计残值。在最后两年的折旧中，应采用年平均法，并考虑残值。上例中的货车在双倍余额递减法下的折旧情况如下所示：

年	年初账面价值($)	折旧率	年折旧额($)	年末账面价值($)
1	8,500	40%	3,400	5,100
2	5,100	40%	2,040	3,060
3	3,060	40%	1,224	1,836
4	1,836	50%	(1,836-500)÷2=668	1,168
5	1,168	50%	668	500

8.2.4 年数总和法

按年限总和法计算，年折旧率的分子为尚可使用的年限。年数总和法折旧计算公式如下：

年折旧额＝(固定资产原值－固定资产净残值)×(尚可使用年限÷剩余使用年数总和)

前例中的货车，在年数总和法下其年折旧率的分母是 15(1＋2＋3＋4＋5＝15)。第一年的分子是 5，第二年的分子是 4，第三年的分子是 3，第四年的分子是 2，第五年的分子是 1，如下所示。

年	年折旧率	年折旧额($)	年末账面价值($)
1	5/15	2,666.67	5,833.33
2	4/15	2,133.33	3,700
3	3/15	1,600	2,100
4	2/15	1,066.67	1,033.33
5	1/15	533.33	500

已提足折旧的固定资产，即使该资产状况良好且仍在使用，也不再提折旧。

8.3 固定资产的处置

固定资产可以通过报废、出售或交换的方式进行处置。处置应计折旧资产时，应当将该资产的成本从资产账户中移除,并将累计折旧从相关的资产抵销账户中移除。假设上述已完全折旧的货车售价为 500 美元,记录该交易的会计分录如下:

  借:库存现金   500
    累计折旧——货车   8,000
    贷:固定资产——货车   8,500

  实际上,资产处置价格与账面价值相等的情况比较少见。在多数情况下,资产的账面价值和处置所得不尽相同。如果处置所得超过账面价值,则产生处置收益。如果处置所得低于账面价值,则发生处置损失。

$$\text{固定资产处置} \begin{cases} \text{处置所得} > \text{账面价值,处置收益} \\ \text{处置所得} = \text{账面价值,平衡} \\ \text{处置所得} < \text{账面价值,处置损失} \end{cases}$$

假设上面提到的已计提完折旧的货车售价为 550 美元。记录此交易的会计分录如下:

  借:库存现金   550
    累计折旧——货车   8,000
    贷:固定资产——货车   8,500
      资产处置损益   50

如果货车售价为 400 美元,则记录此交易的会计分录如下:

  借:库存现金   400
    累计折旧——货车   8,000
    资产处置损益   100
    贷:固定资产——货车   8,500

Chapter 9

Intangible Assets and Natural Resource

9.1 Intangible Assets

Assets are resources of the entity generated from past transactions and events from which future economic benefits are expected to flow to the entity. Intangible assets, as a part of assets, refer to identifiable non-monetary assets without physical substance. Company frequently incurs expenditure on all types of intangible resources. The definition of an intangible asset should be identifiable and controllable, with the possibility of the future economic benefits. If the expenditure does not meet the definition, it will be expensed when incurred, unless it is generated in the context of an acquisition which will be involved in the calculation of goodwill. Several important characteristics are included in the definition of intangible assets.

- No physical existence

This is the key characteristic and evidence to identify an intangible asset. With this characteristic, intangible assets differ from plants asset.

- For long-term service

This characteristic makes intangible assets different from current assets. An intangible asset is expected to bring benefits to an entity in more than one operating periods.

- Monopolistic

Intangible assets are exclusive rights often monopolized by a single entity. The monopoly over intangible assets is protected by laws or other governmental regulations.

- Identifiable

If an asset meets any one of the following requirements, it meets the criteria of identifiability in the definition of intangible assets:

(1) Can be separated from the enterprise, and can be used for sale, transfer, licensing, leasing or exchange separately or with relevant contracts, assets or liabilities.

(2) Originating from contractual rights or other legal rights, whether or not these rights can be transferred or separated from enterprises or other rights and obligations.

9.1.1 Types of Intangible Assets

Intangible assets mainly include patents, trademark, copyright and franchise right.

1. Patents

Patents are granted by relevant governmental institution (National Intellectual Property Office), enabling the owner to have exclusive rights to the patent. The initial cost of purchasing a patent should include any related legal fees. The most commonly-used amortization method for patents is the straight-line method.

2. Copyrights

Copyright is granted by governmental institution, giving its owner exclusive right to publish, reproduce and sell writings and other forms of artistic works. For individuals, the term of copyright is 50 years after death, and the duration of spiritual rights such as the right of signature is unlimited. For enterprises and artificial persons, the term of copyright is 50 years after the first publication of the work.

3. Trademarks

Trademark refers to a word, phrase, or symbol that identifies a particular enterprise or product. Several examples are "HUAWEI", "Lenovo", the letter "KFC" for "Kentucky Fried Chicken". Trademark right refers to the exclusive right of the owner to the trademark.

4. Franchises

Franchise refers to the right of an enterprise to conduct operations or sell a particular commodity in a certain area, or the right of an enterprise to allow others' use of its trademark, trade name, technical secrets, etc. The former is normally authorized by governmental agencies, allowing enterprises to use the privileges of operating certain business in certain areas, such as water, telecommunications, posts and telecommunications, tobacco monopoly. The latter refers to certain rights of enterprises to use another enterprise for a limited or indefinite period in accordance with the signed contract, such as the use of the name of the head store in a chain store branch, etc. The most common franchise case between companies is in the catering industry. For example, units of milk tea chains such as Coco, KOI are owned by headquarters and operated locally according to the terms of the franchise agreement. The initial cost paid for obtaining the franchise will be capitalized. During the operation period, the continuing franchise fee the franchise paid for the franchiser's services for the subsequent years will be expensed in accordance with the normal matching criteria. If the franchise is granted permanently, it will be deemed to have an indefinite life and the test will be impaired at least annually. However, most franchises are legally effective as defined in their operating agreements. For these franchises, the franchisee amortizes the relevant initial franchise costs over its lifespan.

$$\text{Types of Intangible} \begin{cases} \text{Patents} \\ \text{Trademark} \\ \text{Copyright} \\ \text{Franchise} \end{cases}$$

9.1.2 Initial Measurement of Intangible Assets

Intangible assets shall be initially measured according to their acquisition cost. The main ways for enterprises to acquire intangible assets include purchasing, self-research and development, etc. The accounting treatment differs with different ways of acquisition.

1. Purchased by cash

The cost of an intangible asset equals to the cash expenditure required to purchase the asset, plus the related taxes and fees as well as any other costs to make the asset available for use. It is worth note that the following costs are not included in the initial costs of intangible assets:

① advertising costs, management costs, and other indirect costs on new product promotion;
② costs generated after the use of intangible assets;
③ value-added tax (VAT) input tax that can be deducted from the amount of write-off tax.

ABC Company, as a general VAT taxpayer, purchases a patented technology with bank deposit. The price indicated on the special VAT invoice obtained is $60,000, and the VAT amount is $3,600. ABC Company shall prepare the following accounting entry:

```
Dr. Intangible asset ——Patent                   $60,000
    Taxable Fees ——VAT (Input Tax)              $3,600
Cr. Bank Deposits                                          $63,600
```

It should be noted that the cost of goodwill incurred in business combination also needs to be capitalized as an intangible asset. According to *IAS38 Intangible Asset*, internally-generated goodwill should not be recognized in the financial statements.

2. Self-research and development

Expenditures incurred in internal R&D projects should be distinguished between research expenditures and development expenditures. Research is original and planned investigation undertaken with the prospect of gaining new scientific or technical knowledge and understanding. Development is the application of research findings or other knowledge to a plan or design for the production of new or substantially-improved materials, devices, products, processes, systems or services before the start of commercial production or use. Research costs are not included in calculating the cost of an intangible asset. However, recognition of an intangible asset in the development phase is allowed by accounting standards because the development phase of a project is more advanced than the research phase, which proves that the asset will generate probable future economic benefits.

(1) Research

Basically, the research stage is exploratory, aimed at doing preparations for information and related aspects for further development activities. It is uncertain whether the conducted research activities will be transferred to development in the future and whether intangible assets will be formed after development.

According to *IAS 38 Intangible Assets*, research expenditure cannot directly generate future economic benefits, so research expenditures on internal research and development projects of an enterprise shall be recorded into the profit or loss for the current period. This is in compliance with the principle of prudence.

Examples of activities of development include:
— Tests or experiments aimed at obtaining new knowledge.
— The application of research findings or another knowledge.
— Experiments aimed at searching for product or process alternatives.
— The formulation and design aimed at improving product or process alternatives.

(2) Development

According to *IAS 38 intangible assets*, development expenditure must be capitalized into intangible assets, when all the following conditions are met:
— Possible economic benefits which will flow into the entity in the future,
— Intention to complete and use/sell assets,
— Adequate and available resources,
— Ability to use/sell assets,
— Technical capability of assets for use/sale,
— Reliable measurement of expenditures.

The cost included in R&D are listed as follows:
— Salaries, wages and other employment-related expenses for persons engaged in R&D activities.
— Depreciation of assets, plant and equipment within the scope of these assets used for R&D activities.
— Indirect costs other than general management costs associated with R&D activities. These costs are allocated to the cost of intangible assets based on the allocation of indirect costs.
— Other costs, such as the amortization of patents and licenses.

3. Acquired by exchange

The amount of the transaction assets is its fair value. The cost of the transaction assets is equal to the fair value of the transaction assets plus the relevant taxes and fees.

4. Invested by investors

If the production, operation and management activities of an enterprise require certain intangible assets, investors can invest certain intangible assets into the enterprise and meanwhile obtain the rights and interests of the enterprise in exchange. Under the premise of fair value stipulated in the contract or agreement, the cost of the intangible assets invested by investors is the value stipulated in the contract or agreement. If the value stipulated in the contract or agreement is unfair, the cost of the intangible assets formed by investment will be its fair value.

9.1.3 Amortization of Intangible Assets

A key determinant in the amortization of intangible assets is the lifespan of intangible assets. With finite span, the asset must be amortized over this period. With indefinite span, there would be no annual amortization charge. According to *IAS 38*:

"An entity shall assess whether the lifespan of an intangible asset is finite or indefinite. If the span is finite, it should be assessed. Based on an analysis of all the relevant factors, an intangible asset shall be regarded by the entity as having an indefinite lifespan, when there is no foreseeable limit to the period over which the asset is expected to generate net cash inflows for the entity."

The term "indefinite" does not mean that the asset has an infinite life, that is, the asset will exist forever. As noted in *IAS*, an indefinite life means that there is no foreseeable end to the life of the asset with the proper maintenance. *IAS* also provides a list of factors that should be considered in determining the lifespan of the asset:

— The expected use of the asset by the entity, and whether the asset could be efficiently managed by another management team.
— Typical product life cycles for the asset, and public information on estimates of the lifespan of similar assets.
— Technological advance, the stability of the industry, changes in market demand, and the competition in the market.
— The level of required maintenance expenditure and the entity's ability and intention to reach such a level.
— The period of control over the asset and legal limits or similar limits on the use of the asset.
— Whether the lifespan of the asset depends on that of other assets of the entity.

In general, assets whose lifespan depends on contracts or legal documents will be amortized over the span (the comparatively shorter period in varied cases). If renewal can be allowed with small costs, the applied lifespan can include the renewal period.

An example can be illustrated from cases of lifespan assessment listed in *IAS 38*.

According to the rules, if the entity provides at least an average level of service for its customers and complies with the relevant legislative requirements, the broadcasting license will be renewable every 10 years. The license may be renewed indefinitely at a low cost. An entity is acquired by another entity recently, and the license had been renewed twice before acquisition. In this situation, the acquiring entity intends to renew the license indefinitely. Historically, it is not difficult to renew the license. The technology used in broadcasting is not expected to be replaced by another technology at any time in the foreseeable future. Therefore, the license is expected to contribute to the entity's net cash inflows indefinitely. The broadcasting license would be regarded as having an indefinite lifespan, because it is expected to contribute to the entity's net cash inflows indefinitely. Therefore, the license would not be amortized until its finite lifespan is confirmed. According to *IAS 36 Impairment of Assets*, the license would be tested for impairment annually, and it would be impaired whenever there is an indication.

As noted above, the amortization does not apply to the use of intangible assets with indefinite lifespan. However, these assets should still be reviewed regularly, as those tangible assets. Intangible assets with indefinite lifespan are subject to annual impairment tests.

The amortization period of intangible assets with finite lifespan shall start from the date of its usability (achieving the intended purpose) and end with the date of termination of confirmation. That is to say, the starting and ending dates of amortization of intangible assets are as follows: the increased intangible assets in the current month shall be amortized in the same month; the reduced intangible assets in the current month shall not be amortized in the same month.

The amortization method of intangible assets chosen by an enterprise should reflect the expected the economic benefits related to the intangible assets and be consistently applied through the lifespan of the asset. For example, intangible assets such as patents and proprietary technologies, which are greatly affected by technology obsolescence, can be amortized by accelerated amorization. On the other hand, franchises or patents with specific output restrictions should be amortized by unit-of-production method. If it is impossible to reliably determine the expected realization mode, the straight-line method shall be adopted for amortization.

Normally, the amortization amount of intangible assets shall be recorded into the current profits and losses (e.g., administrative expenses, other business costs, etc.). If the economic benefits contained in an intangible asset are realized through the products or other assets produced, the amortized amount shall be recorded into the cost of the relevant asset.

The enterprise shall review the service life and amortization method of intangible assets with limited service life at least in the end of each year. If the service life and amortization method of intangible assets are different from previous estimates, the amortization period and method shall be changed.

9.1.4 Disposal of Intangible Assets

Accounting for the retirements and disposals of intangible assets is identical to that for property, plant and equipment under *IAS 16 Property, Plant and Equipment*. According to *IAS 38 Intangible assets*:

Intangible assets are to be derecognized on disposal or without expected future benefits from the asset. Gains or losses on disposal are calculated as the difference between the proceeds on disposal and the carrying amount at point of sale, with amortization calculated up to the point of sale. Amortization of an intangible with a finite useful life does not cease when the asset becomes temporarily idle or is retired from active use. There are three categories of disposal of intangible assets are selling, renting and scrapping.

1. Sale

When an enterprise sells intangible assets, the accumulated amortization and provision for intangible assets should be transferred. The profits and losses shall be recorded in the accounts of non-operating income or non-operating expenditure.

2. Rent

When an enterprise rents an intangible asset to others, the journal entries normally consist of a debit to "Cash" or "Bank deposit", a credit to "Other Operating Income", and a debit to "Other Operating Cost", and a credit to "Accumulated Amortization" account.

3. Scrapping

If intangible assets no longer bring economic benefits to the enterprise, they should be transferred. The net book value of intangible assets should be transferred to "Non-operating Expense" account.

9.2 Natural Resource

Natural resources refer to assets physically consumed by entities. For example, forests, mineral deposits, natural gas, and oil fields are included in natural resources. Since these resources are consumed at the time of use, they are also referred to as wasting assets. Such assets will soon become an inventory of raw materials that can be converted into one type or various types of products through logging, mining and extraction. Before conversion, they were non-current assets listed on the balance sheet by names such as forestland, mineral deposits or oil reserves. Natural resources are either listed under intangible assets or shown as a separate category. For example, some companies normally list their natural resources under the term of property, plant and equipment items on the balance sheet.

Natural resources are recorded according to costs, including all expenditures to acquire the resource and prepare it for its intended use. For discovered resources, such as an existing coalmine, the cost is the price paid for the property.

The term "depletion" is used to describe both the exhaustion of a natural resource and the proportional allocation of the cost of a natural resource to the units extracted. The costs are allocated in a similar way to the production method used for depreciation. On the balance sheet, natural resources are reported as the amount which deducts depletion from costs. The depletion expense per period is usually calculated based on units extracted from cutting, mining, or pumping.

To illustrate, assume there is a mining property with an estimated 1,500,000 tons of available ore. It is purchased for $3 million, with the expected salvage value of zero. The company mines 200,000 tons during the first year. The computation of the depletion rate and journal entries that would be made to record this series of events are shown as follows.

$$\text{Depletion Rate} = \$3,000,000 \div 1{,}500{,}000 = \$2 \text{ per ton}$$

$$\text{Depletion for the first year} = \$2 \times 200{,}000 = \$400{,}000$$

The journal entry to record the depletion is:

Dr. Depletion Expense——Mineral Deposit　　　　　　400,000
　　Cr. Accumulate Depletion——Mineral Deposit　　　　　　　　400,000

Key Words and Expressions

intangible assets	无形资产
identifiable	可辨认
non-monetary assets	非货币性资产
physical substance	实物形态
goodwill	商誉
monopolistic	垄断的
patents	专利
national intellectual property office	国家知识产权局
invention patent	发明专利
utility model patent	实用新型专利
design patent	外观专利
copyright	版权

exclusive	独有的，排他的
date of application	申请日
artificial persons	法人
trademark	商标
trademark right	商标权
franchise	特许经营权
tobacco monopoly	烟草专营
chain store	连锁店
branch	分支机构
headquarter	总部
capitalized	资本化
expensed	费用化
indirect costs	间接费用
value added tax (VAT)	增值税
VAT input tax	增值税进项税额
general VAT taxpayer	一般增值税纳税人
special VAT invoice	专用增值税发票
the development phase	开发阶段
the research phase	研究阶段
principle of prudence	谨慎性原则
amortization	摊销
fair value	公允价值
impairment of assets	资产减值
other operating income	其他营业收入
other operating cost	其他营业成本
accumulated amortization	累计摊销
scrapped	报废
non-operating expense	营业外支出
net book value	账面净值
natural resources	自然资源
wasting assets	递耗资产
depletion	折耗

Exercises

Please select the best answer for the following questions or uncompleted sentences.

1. Cost allocation of an intangible asset is referred to as (   ).
    A. amortization
    B. depletion

C. accretion

D. capitalization

2. Goodwill (   ).

A. can be subdivided and sold in parts

B. can only be identified with the business as a whole

C. is only recorded when generated internally

D. can be defined as normal earnings less accumulated amortization

3. Which intangible assets are amortized over their useful life? (   )

A. Trademark.

B. Goodwill.

C. Patents.

D. All above.

4. The exclusive right to use a certain name or symbol is called a (   ).

A. patent

B. copyright

C. franchise

D. trademark

5. A patent has a legal life of 10 years. It should be (   ).

A. expensed in the year of acquisition

B. amortized over 10 years regardless of its useful life

C. amortized over its useful life if less than 10 years

D. amortized over 20 years

第9章　无形资产和自然资源

9.1 无形资产

资产是一个由企业过去的交易或事项形成的，预计未来的经济利益将流入企业的资源。无形资产是资产的一部分，它是指没有实物形态的、可辨认的非货币性资产。公司在各种无形资源上经常会产生支出。无形资产的定义要求具有可辨认性、可控制性和未来经济利益的可能性。如果支出不符合定义，则在发生时将予以费用化，除非该支出是在收购的背景下产生的，而收购可能会涉及商誉的计算。无形资产的定义包括以下几个重要特征：

- 没有实物形态

这是识别无形资产的主要特征和主要证据。这一特点使得无形资产有别于固定资产。

- 长期性

这一特点使无形资产不同于流动资产。一项无形资产预计能在至少一个以上的经营期为一家企业带来收益。

- 垄断性

无形资产是一种排他性权利，通常由一个实体垄断。对无形资产的垄断受法律或其他政府法规的保护。

- 可辨认性

资产满足下列条件，即符合无形资产定义中的可辨认性标准：

(1) 能够从企业中分离或者划分出来，并能够单独或者与相关合同、资产或负债一起，用于出售、转移、授予许可、租赁或者交换。

(2) 源自合同性权利或其他法定权利，无论这些权利是否可以从企业或其他权利和义务中转移或者分离。

9.1.1 无形资产的种类

1. 专利

专利由相关政府机构(国家知识产权局)授予，使其拥有专利专有权。购买专利的初始成本应当包括相关的法律费用。最常用的专利摊销方法是直线法。

2. 版权

版权也称著作权，是政府机构(国家版权局)授予的，赋予其所有者专有的出版、复制和出售其著作和其他形式的艺术作品的权利。版权的期限，对个人而言，是其去世后五十年。署名权等精神权利期限无限制。对企业和法人而言，是作品首次发表后五十年。

3. 商标

商标是用于标识特定的企业或产品的词、短语或符号。比如"华为"、"联想"、代表"肯德基"的"KFC"等。商标权是指所有者对其商标的专有权。

4. 特许经营权

特许经营权，是指企业在一定区域内经营、销售特定商品的权利，或者企业接受他人使用其商标、商号、技术秘密等的权利。前者一般由政府机关授权，允许企业在某些领域使用经营某些业务的特权，如水、电信、邮电、烟草专卖等。后者是指企业根据签订的合同，有限制或无限期地使用另一家企业的某些权利，如在连锁店分店使用总店名称等。企业之间的特许经营权多存在于餐饮业，COCO 或 KOI 等奶茶连锁企业的单位都是其总部拥有的，并根据特许经营协议的条款在当地进行经营。获得特许经营权所支付的初始成本将被资本化。在经营期，特许经营权人按照正常标准支付的后续年份的服务费将按费用处理。如果特许经营权是永久授予的，它将被视为期限不确定的资产，每年都要进行减值测试。然而，大多数特许经营权都已在其经营协议中规定了法定授权时效。对于这些特许经营权，被特许人要在特许权使用寿命内摊销相关的初始特许经营成本。

$$\text{无形资产}\begin{cases}\text{专利}\\\text{商标}\\\text{版权}\\\text{特许经营权}\end{cases}$$

9.1.2 无形资产的初始计量

无形资产应当按照其取得成本进行初始计量。企业获取无形资产的主要方式是外购、自主研发等。获取方式不同，会计处理方式也不同。

1. 外购

无形资产的成本等于购买资产所需的现金支出，加上相关的税费，以及为使资产达到预定可使用状态所发生的一切合理、必要的支出。值得注意的是以下费用不得计入无形资产的初始成本：①广告费、管理费和新产品促销等其他间接费用；②无形资产投入使用后产生的费用；③可以从销项税额中抵扣的增值税进项税额。

ABC 公司是一般增值税纳税人，以银行存款购买一项专利技术。取得的增值税专用发票上标明的价款是 60,000 美元，增值税为 3,600 美元。ABC 公司应编制以下会计分录：

借：无形资产——专利技术　　　　　　　　　　　　60,000
　　应交税费——应交增值税(进项税额)　　　　　　 3,600
　　贷：银行存款　　　　　　　　　　　　　　　　　　　　63,600

值得注意的是，企业合并中产生的商誉成本也需要资本化为无形资产的取得成本。根据《国际会计准则第 38 号——无形资产》，内部产生的商誉不应在财务报表中确认。

2. 自主研究开发

企业内部研究开发项目所产生的支出应当区分研究阶段支出和开发阶段支出。研究是为了获得新的科学或技术知识和认知而进行的有计划的原始调查。开发是指在商业性生产或使用开始之前，将研究成果或其他知识应用于新的或实质上改进的材料、装置、产品、工艺、系统和服务的生产计划或设计。研究成本不包括在计算无形资产的成本中。但是，会计准则允许开发阶段发生的符合条件的支出确认无形资产的成本，因为项目的开发阶段比研究阶段更为先进，更能证明该资产将产生可能的未来经济利益。

(1) 研究

研究阶段基本上是探索性的，是为进一步开发活动进行资料及相关方面的准备，已进行的研究活动将来是否会转入开发、开发后是否会形成无形资产等均具有较大的不确定性。

根据《国际会计准则第 38 号——无形资产》，企业内部研究开发项目的研究支出因为不能直接导致经济利益流入，故应当在发生时计入当期损益，这符合谨慎原则。

— 为获得新知识的试验
— 研究发现或其他知识的应用
— 寻找产品或工艺替代品的实验
— 为改进产品或工艺方案而进行的试验

(2) 开发

根据《国际会计准则第 38 号——无形资产》，当满足以下所有条件时，必须将开发支出资本化为无形资产的成本：

— 未来可能会有经济利益流入企业
— 为了完成和使用/出售资产而产生的
— 企业有足够且可用的资源
— 企业有使用/出售资产的能力
— 用于使用/销售的成套资产的技术可行性
— 支出可以可靠地计量

以下列出了包含在研究开发阶段中的成本：

— 为从事研究开发活动人员支付的薪金、工资和其他相关费用
— 在这些资产用于研究开发活动的范围内对资产、厂房和设备的折旧
— 与研发活动有关的一般管理费用以外的间接费用。这些费用是根据与分配间接费用的依据分配至无形资产成本之中
— 其他费用，例如专利的摊销

3. 以物易物

交易资产的金额就是它的公允价值，交易资产的成本等于交易资产的公允价值加上相关税费。

4. 投资者投入

如果企业的生产、经营、管理活动需要某些无形资产，投资者可以向企业投入这些无形资产并取得企业的权益作为交换。在合同或协议约定的价值公允的前提下，投资者投入无形资产的成本是合同或协议约定的价值。如果合同或协议约定的价值不公允，投资形成的无形资产的成本就是它的公允价值。

9.1.3 无形资产的摊销

无形资产摊销中的一个关键因素是无形资产的使用寿命。如果无形资产的使用寿命是有限的，那

么资产必须在这一期限内摊销。如果资产的使用寿命不确定,则无须每年计提摊销费用。《国际会计准则第38号》规定:

"一家企业应评估无形资产的使用寿命是有限的还是不确定的,如果是有限的,则评估该使用寿命。基于对所有相关因素的分析,当无形资产预计为实体产生净现金流入的期限没有可预见的限制时,实体应将该无形资产视为具有无限期使用寿命。

"无限期"一词并不意味着资产的寿命是无限的。《国际会计准则》指出,无限期的使用寿命是指:在适当的维护下,资产的使用寿命是不可预见的。准则还提供了在确定资产使用寿命时应当考虑的因素:

— 企业对资产的预期使用情况,以及资产是否可以由其他管理团队进行有效管理;
— 与该资产类似的典型产品生命周期的公开信息和以类似方式使用的资产;
— 技术的进步、行业的稳定性、市场需求变化、市场的竞争情况;
— 所需的维修支出水平以及实体达到这一水平的能力和意图;
— 对资产的控制期和对资产使用的法律或类似限制;
— 该资产的使用寿命是否取决于实体其他资产的使用寿命。

一般来说,已被合同或其他法律文件规定了寿命的无形资产应在规定寿命期内摊销(若存在规定不一致的情况,以其中较短的期限为准)。如果该无形资产可以续期,则其使用寿命可包括所续的期限。

《国际会计准则第38号》所列举有关使用寿命评估的示例中有如下这个例子。

根据相关规定,如果公司向客户提供符合相关法律要求的服务,则广播许可证每10年可续期一次。许可证的续期所需费用较少。某公司于近期被另一家企业收购,在收购前广播许可证已经续期过两次。收购方打算无限期地延长许可证。从历史上看,许可证续期并没有什么难度。在可预见的未来任何时候,广播中使用的技术也不会被另一技术取代。因此,该广播许可证有望无限期地为企业的净现金流入做出贡献。这时广播许可证将被视为具有无限期使用寿命,因为预计它将无限期地对公司的净现金流入做出贡献。因此,在确定许可证的使用寿命有限之前,不会对其进行摊销。根据《国际会计准则第36号——资产减值》,许可证将每年进行一次减值测试,只要有迹象表明许可证可能受到减值,就要进行相应的账务调整或披露。

上文已说明,使用寿命不确定的无形资产,不进行摊销,但是它们和确定使用寿命的无形资产一样,需要定期检查。即使用寿命不确定的无形资产每年也需进行减值测试。

使用寿命确定的无形资产的摊销期限自其可使用(达到预定目的)之日起至终止确认之日止,即无形资产摊销的起始和终止日期如下:当月增加的无形资产应于当月开始摊销;当月减少的无形资产不在当月摊销。

企业选择的无形资产摊销方法,应当能够反映与无形资产有关的经济效益的预期实现情况,并在资产的使用年限内始终如一地使用。例如,专利、专有技术等无形资产受技术进步影响较大,可以通过加速折旧法摊销。而具有特定产量限制的专营权或专利权则应按生产方式摊销。如果不能可靠地确定预期利益的实现方式,则应采用直线法摊销。

无形资产的摊销金额一般应当计入当期损益(如管理费用、其他业务费用等)。无形资产所包含的经济利益,通过生产的产品或其他资产实现的,其摊余金额计入相关资产的成本。

企业应当至少在每年年度终了,对使用寿命有限的无形资产的使用寿命和摊销方法进行复核。无形资产的使用寿命和摊销方法与以前估计不同的,应当改变摊销期限和方法。

9.1.4 无形资产的处置

无形资产的报废和处置与《国际会计准则第 16 号——固定资产》中的财产固定资产和设备相同。

根据《国际会计准则第 38 号——无形资产》，无形资产在处置时或在资产预期未来不再能给企业带来经济利益时需要终止确认。处置无形资产的利得或损失按处置收益与出售时账面价值之间的差额计算。使用寿命有限的无形资产在暂时闲置或停止使用时，不得停止摊销。处置无形资产的方式主要有出售、出租、报废。

1. 出售无形资产

企业出售无形资产，应当将无形资产的累计摊销和减值准备结转，其损益应当计入营业外收入或者营业外支出账户。

2. 出租无形资产

企业向他人出租无形资产时，会计分录通常包括借记"现金"或"银行存款"，贷记"其他营业收入"；借记"其他营业成本"，贷记"累计摊销"账户。

3. 无形资产的报废

如果一项无形资产不能再为企业带来经济效益，应当将其予以结转。无形资产的账面净值应当转入营业外支出。

9.2 自然资源

自然资源是指企业在使用时实际消耗的资产。例如，森林、矿藏、天然气和油田。由于这些资源是在使用时被消耗的，因此也称为递耗资产。这些资产很快将成为原材料的来源，可以通过砍伐、开采和提取将其转换为一种或多种产品。在进行转换之前，它们是非流动资产，并在资产负债表上按名称(例如林地、矿藏或石油储备)列出。在资产负债表中，自然资源要么列示在无形资产下，要么作为单独一类列示。例如，一些公司一般会将其列示在资产负债表中的无形资产名下。

自然资源按成本入账，其成本包括获取资源和使其达到预定用途所需的一切支出。对于已被发现的资源，比如一个现有的煤矿，其成本是获取煤矿所支付的价格。

"折耗"一词不仅用来描述自然资源的消耗，而且还用来描述自然资源的成本按比例分配到每单位的产量中。折耗的分配方式与折旧的产量法非常相似。自然资源在资产负债表中按成本减去累计损耗的金额列报。每期消耗费用通常基于从采伐、采矿或抽水中提取的单位来计算。

举个例子，假设一个矿区预计有 150 万吨可供开采的矿石，购买价格是 300 万美元，预计净残值为零。公司第一年开采了 20 万吨。那么

$$损耗率 = 3,000,000 \div 1,500,000 = 2 \text{ 美元/吨}$$
$$第一年损耗 = 2 \times 200,000 = 400,000 \text{ 美元}$$

记录折耗的会计分录是：

借：折耗费用——矿产　　　　　　　　　　400,000
　　贷：累积损耗——矿产　　　　　　　　　　　　　　400,000

Chapter 10

Liability

In *IAS Conceptual Framework*, a liability is defined as:

A present obligation of the entity generated from previous transactions or events, the settlement of which is expected to result in an outflow of embodying economic benefits from the entity.

Several aspects should be noted in terms of this definition:

(1) A liability includes but is not limited to a legal debt. The present obligation is the feature of a liability, as a duty or responsibility of the entity to act or perform in a certain way. A present obligation may be imposed by notions of equity or fairness (referred to as an "equitable" obligation), custom or normal business practices (referred to as a "constructive" obligation), and legally enforceable contracts. For example, if an entity decides to rectify faults in its products even after the warranty period has expired, its liability will be increased at the same time. Therefore, the amounts that are expected to be spent on goods which have been already sold are also liabilities. It is not sufficient for a corporate merely to have an intention to sacrifice economic benefits in the future. A present obligation needs to be distinguished from a future commitment. Management's decision to buy an asset in the future does not generate a present obligation. Obligations are normally generated at the time of asset delivery, or when the entity has made an irrevocable agreement (a substantial penalty will be generated if the agreement is revoked).

(2) Liabilities must lead to the abandonment of resources that reflect economic interests in the future, but businesses have little discretion in avoiding such sacrifices. This settlement may need to be made on a specified date or when a specified event occurs in the future. In this situation, guarantees under loan agreements are regarded as a liability because obligations need to be fulfilled in a particular event (e.g., a loan default).

There are many ways to fulfill current obligations, such as paying in cash, transferring other assets, providing services, converting obligation to equity, replacing obligation with another obligation, etc.

(3) Liabilities must be caused by a past transaction or event. For example, the procurement of goods and the work conducted by staff will increase accounts payable and wages payable respectively. However, the wage to be paid to staff for their future work is not a liability as there is no past transaction or event and no current obligation.

Recognizing a current obligation as a liability should not only meet the definition of liability, but also satisfy two conditions at the same time.

Firstly, the economic benefits related to the obligation are likely to flow out of the enterprise. From the definition of liabilities, it can be seen that the expected outflow of economic benefit from enterprises is a feature of liabilities. In practice, the economic benefits of fulfilling obligations are uncertain, especially those related to presumptive obligations which usually depend on a large number of estimates. Therefore, the confirmation of liabilities should be combined with the judgment of the uncertainty degree of the outflow of economic interests. If evidence proves that the economic interests related to current obligations are likely to flow out of enterprises, it should be recognized as liabilities. On the contrary, if the enterprise undertakes the current obligations with small possibility of causing the outflow of economic interests, it should not be recognized as liabilities.

Secondly, the future outflow of economic benefits can be measured reliably. The confirmation of liabilities should take account of the outflow of economic benefits, and the amount of future outflow of economic benefits should be measured reliably. Normally, the outflow amount of economic interests related to legal obligations can be determined according to the amount stipulated in the contract or the law. Considering that the outflow amount of economic interests is usually reflected in the future and sometimes realized after a long period, the influence of the time value of money and other factors should be considered in the measurement of the relevant amount. For the outflow amount of economic benefits related to the presumptive obligation, the enterprise should take into account the influence of the time value and risk of the relevant currency.

On a balance sheet, liabilities are separated into current liabilities and non-current liabilities to help users assess the company's short-term and long-term financial conditions.

10.1 Current Liability

Current liabilities refer to the obligations that are expected to be paid on demand from existing current assets or through the creation of other current liabilities. The time limit for the payment is one year. If a company's normal operating cycle is longer than one year, the payment of current liabilities will be conducted within one operating cycle.

Current liabilities include accounts payable, notes payable, unearned revenue, cash dividends payable, current maturities of long-term debt, wages payable, income taxes payable, interest payable, etc. Since the payment of current liabilities should be finished within a relatively short time, they generally are shown at their face amount on the balance sheet.

Creditors and analysts often use the current ratio and quick ratio to determine whether a firm has enough resources to pay its debts over the next 12 months.

Current ratio = Current Assets ÷ Current Liabilities

Quick ratio = (Current Assets − Inventories) ÷ Current Liabilities

The current liability accounts are commonly presented as the first classification in the liabilities and stockholders' equity section of the balance sheet. In some cases, current liabilities are presented as a group below current assets, with the total of the current liabilities deducted from the total current assets to obtain "working capital" or "current assets in excess of current liabilities". In the current liability section, the accounts may be listed in order of maturity, according to amount (from largest to smallest), or in order of liquidation preference.

10.1.1 Accounts Payable

Accounts payable are short-term debts to suppliers for the purchase of goods or acquisition of services. Accounts payable normally consist of trade accounts payable and other accounts payable. Trade accounts payable include short-term liabilities for merchandise. Other accounts payable include liabilities for any goods and services other than merchandise. Accounts payable usually do not require the payment of interest. This makes the form of liability very desirable, because it represents an "interest-free" loan from the supplier.

Accounts payable should be recorded when the risks and rewards associated with the ownership of the goods purchased have been transferred or services have been accepted. In practice, we should take different situations into consideration:

(1) Material and invoice bills arrive at the same time.

Generally, accounts payable is registered according to invoice bills only after material acceptance and storage. This helps to confirm whether the quality, quantity and variety of the purchased materials are in accordance with the conditions stipulated in the contract. In this case, some problems, such as mistake, leakage and breakage of the purchased materials can be found in the acceptance and storage before the accounting adjustment.

(2) Material and invoices arrive at different time.

When the goods have been checked and stored but the invoice bill has not arrived, since the buyer's debt to the supplier has been formed, it is necessary to estimate the amount of the relevant accounts payable and record it in the accounting book at the end of the accounting period. In the beginning of the next month, the accounts payable tentatively assessed at the end of the last month will be written off.

The process of reviewing the accounts payable involves an enormous amount of detail, to ensure that only legitimate and accurate amounts are recorded in the accounting system. More specifically, the documents that should be strictly reviewed are listed as follows:

- Purchase orders issued by the company
- Receiving reports issued by the company
- Invoices from the company's vendors
- Contracts and other agreements

The accuracy and completeness of the company's financial statements depend on the management of the accounts payable. A well-functioning accounts payable process should include:

- The timely processing of accurate and legitimate vendor invoices
- Accurate recording in the appropriate general ledger accounts
- The accrual of obligations and expenses that have not yet been completely processed

The efficiency and effectiveness of the accounts payable process will also affect the company's cash position, credit rating, and relationship with suppliers.

The balance in accounts payable serves as an important indicator of a company's financial condition, especially in the retail industry where suppliers are heavily relied upon to provide merchandise.

Some suppliers offer payment discounts to their clients, such as "2/10, N/30". This means that the buyer can deduct 2% of the amount owed if payment is made within 10 days. For example, if the buyer can pay $980 within 10 days, the invoice amount of $1000 can be settled in full. In this example, the buyer can save $20 (2% × $1,000) by paying 20 days ahead of the normal due date. That means the percentage for this saving is about 2%(the saved $20 ÷ the used $980).

On the other hand, if the buyer borrows $980 from the bank for 20 days with the annual borrowing rate of 6%, the interest in this 20-day period would be only $3.22 ($980 × 6% × 20/365). By paying interest of $3.22 to the bank, the buyer will save $20 paid to the seller, thus earning a profit of $16.78 ($20 – $3.22). If it happens 18 times a year, the net annual savings will be about $301 [$16.78 × 18 times, or $360 – the annual interest paid to the bank $59 ($980 × 6%)]. With a 1% discount for the payment 20 days in advance, the annual interest rate is about 18%.

Obviously, buyers with sufficient cash balances or available credit lines should take advantage of the discount on advance payment. However, some buyers have little cash and can hardly borrow extra money. In order to avoid the risk of overdraft checking accounts, these buyers would better give up the discount for the payment in advance. An overdraft may cause greater losses than an early payment discount. If overdraft causes several buyers' checks to be returned to the seller, the total overdraft cost will be greater. If the buyer's check is returned due to insufficient funds, the supplier may be concerned about the buyer's ability to pay. This may result in one or more suppliers demanding payment on delivery. Cancellation of a 30-day credit line by a supplier will bring devastating consequences to the buyer with very little money and for the credit line that has been used up.

10.1.2 Notes Payable

Notes payable refers to obligations in the form of written promissory notes. Transactions which may generate notes payable include the purchase of merchandise, the purchase of real estate or costly equipment, and the substitution of a note for a past-due account payable. The borrower is the maker of the note, and the lender is the payee who is also the note holder.

In accounting, notes payable is a general ledger liability account in which a company records the face amounts of the promissory notes that it has issued. The balance in "Notes Payable" represents the amounts that remain to be paid. Since a note payable requires the issuer/borrower to pay interest, the issuing company will undertake the interest expense. Under the accrual method of accounting, the company should set up another liability account entitled "Interest Payable". In this account, the company records the interest that has incurred but has not paid as by the end of the accounting period.

For most companies, the amounts in Notes Payable and Interest Payable are reported on the balance sheet. The amount due within one year of the balance sheet date is a current liability, and the amount not due within one year of the balance sheet date is a non-current or long-term liability. The company should also disclose pertinent information for the amounts owed on the notes, including the interest rates, maturity dates, collateral pledged, limitations imposed by the creditor, etc.

10.1.3 Unearned Revenue

Unearned revenue refers to the money received by an individual or company for a service or product that has yet to be fulfilled. Unearned revenue can be seen as a "prepayment" for goods or services. With the prepayment, the seller has a liability equal to the revenue earned until the delivery of the good or service. The business would make the following entry to record the receipt of the advance payment:

Dr. Cash
    Cr. Unearned revenue

Unearned revenue is the most common among companies that sell subscription-based products or other services requiring prepayments. Typical examples include prepaid rent, prepaid insurance premiums, statutory reserve, airline tickets, newspaper subscriptions, and annual prepayments through software.

It is beneficial to sellers that receiving money before the service completion. Cash flows received in advance can be used for other activities, such as paying interest on debt and purchasing more inventories.

Unearned revenue is recorded on a company's balance sheet as a liability. It is seen as a liability, because the revenue has still not been earned and represents products or services owed to a customer. As the prepaid service or product is gradually delivered over time, it is recognized as revenue on the income statement.

If a publishing company receives a one-year subscription of $1,200, the amount is recorded as the increase in cash and unearned revenue. Both are balance sheet accounts, so the transaction does not immediately affect the income statement. If it is a monthly publication, as each periodical is delivered, the liability or unearned revenue will be reduced by $100 ($1,200 ÷ 12 months), while revenue will increase by the same amount.

Unearned revenue is usually disclosed as a current liability on a company's balance sheet. However, if services or goods are provided with 12 months or more after the payment date, the unearned revenue will appear as a long-term liability on the balance sheet.

10.1.4 Cash Dividends Payable

A company often declares a dividend before actually paying investors the cash. Cash dividends declared but not yet paid will be reported as a current liability, if they are to be paid within one year or an operating cycle. Declared dividends are reported as a liability between the date of declaration and payment, because declaration gives rise to an enforceable contract.

Normally, the dividend only applies to shares held by a certain date, which prevents new investors purchasing shares just to earn dividends to some extent. Once a company declares a dividend, it must record a liability. This indicates the company has a future cash payout that will occur per management agreement. The Dividend Payable account is a liability that resides on the company's balance sheet. The amount included in the account is the cash the company will pay as designated on the dividend declaration date.

10.1.5 Current Maturities of Long-term Debt

Long-term liabilities to be matured and payable within one year or an operating cycle shall be shown as a separate item under current liabilities.

The current portion of long-term debt (CPLTD) is the portion of a long-term liability that is coming due within the next year. Suppose a company has a 15-year bank loan of $200,000 for a financed construction project. The company needs to pay $1,500 per month. For the sake of simplicity, we assume that each payment of $1500 includes $800 for principal payment and $700 for interest payment. In this case, the current portion of this debt is $9,600 (the monthly payment of $800 × 12 months). This is the principal amount due in this period or the next year. The CPLTD is separated out on the company's balance sheet, because it needs to be paid by highly liquid assets, such as cash. The CPLTD is an important tool for creditors and investors to identify whether a company has the ability to pay off its short-term obligations as they come due.

10.1.6 Wages Payable

Wages payable refers to the wages earned by employees of a company but have not yet been paid. Under the accrual method of accounting, this amount may be recorded with an adjusting entry at the end of the accounting period so that the company's balance sheet will include the amount as a current liability (the adjusting entry typically debits Wages Expense and credits Wages Payable).

For example, suppose the company pays wages to the employees on every Friday. It is Tuesday on December 31, 2019. Since employers pay employees on Friday, employees have to wait until January 3 for the full wage for December. This means that on January 1 of the next year, the employer owes the employee two days' salary, that is, that for the last Monday and Tuesday in December, 2019. In the end of December, this part of owed wage should be recorded as the liability in the accounting system and be displayed in the financial statement.

By December 31, the company's current liabilities on its balance sheet must include the salaries earned by employees for the last Monday and Tuesday of December, as well as other salaries owed by the company on December 31 (the company's income statement by December 31 must also include that amount as part of its wage expenditure).

The amount in the account Wages Payable (or Accrued Wages Payable) will often be reported on the balance sheet as part of a current liability description such as accrued compensation, accrued payroll liabilities, accrued expenses, accrued liabilities, etc.

10.1.7 Income Taxes Payable

Income tax payable is shown as current liabilities, because the liabilities will be settled within one year. However, any income tax payable that is not planned to be paid within the next 12 months is classified as long-term liabilities.

Income tax payable is a necessary part of calculating deferred income tax liabilities of enterprises. In the process of reporting the difference between the company's income tax liabilities and income tax expenses, deferred income tax liabilities will be generated. The difference may be caused by the expiration time of the actual income tax. For example, under the current accounting standards, an enterprise may owe an income tax of $1,000. However, according to the tax law, the company owes the income tax of only $850, and the rest $150 will be seen as a liability in a later period. Conflicts exist between the tax law and Generally Accepted Accounting Practice (GAAP), which leads to the deferral of certain liabilities in the future.

According to the tax law in the home country of the company, the tax is calculated on the basis of its net income. The taxable rate is calculated on the basis of the company's tax rate. For companies that should receive tax credits from their tax authorities, the amount of income tax payable will be reduced.

10.1.8　Interest Payable

Interest payable refers to the interest expense that has been generated but has not been paid by the date of the balance sheet. Interest payable does not include the interest in periods after the date of the balance sheet.

Let's assume that on December 1 a company borrowed $100,000 at an annual interest rate of 12%. The company agrees to repay the principal amount of $100,000 plus 9 months of interest when the note comes due on August 31. The company's accounting entries are as follows:

Dr. Bank Deposits	100,000	
Cr. Short-term Loan		100,000

On December 31, the amount of interest payable is $1,000 ($100,000 × 12% × 1 ÷ 12) and the company's balance sheet should report the following current liabilities:

— Short-term loan of $100,000

— Interest payable of $1,000

The company's accounting entries are as follows:

Dr. Interest Expenses	1,000	
Cr. Interest payable		1,000

Nothing is reported for the $8,000 ($100,000 × 12% × 8 ÷ 12) of future interest.

The company's January 31 balance sheet should report the following current liabilities:

— Short-term loan of $100,000

— Interest payable of $2,000

On August 31, the company was supposed to pay the principal of the loan of $100,000 and the nine-month interest on the loan $ 9,000 ($1,000 + $8,000 = $9,000). The company's accounting entries are as follows:

Dr. Interest Expenses	8,000	
Cr. Interest Payable		8,000
Dr. Short-term Loan	100,000	
Interest Payable		9,000
Cr. Bank Deposit		109,000

10.2　Non-Current Liability

Non-current liability, also long-term liability, refers to company obligations that extend beyond the current year or alternatively beyond the current operating cycle, as opposed to current liabilities which are short-term debts with maturity dates within the next 12-month period.

The comparison between non-current liabilities and cash flows helps to show whether a company can meet its financial obligations in the long term. Lenders focus primarily on short-term liquidity and the amount of current liabilities, while long-term investors use non-current liabilities to gauge whether there is a problem of excessive leverage in the company. With a fixed risk of default, the more stable a company's cash flow is, the more debt it can support.

Analysts also use coverage ratios to assess a company's financial health, including the cash flow-to-debt and the interest coverage ratio. The cash flow-to-debt ratio determines how long it will take a company to repay its debt if it devotes all the cash flow to debt repayment. The higher the index value is, the stronger the cash inflow guarantees the liquidity of the current debt, which indicates that the liquidity of the enterprise is better. The interest coverage ratio, which is calculated by dividing a company's earnings before interest and taxes (EBIT) by its debt interest payments for the same period, gauges whether enough income is being generated to cover interest payments. The larger the value of the index is, the stronger the ability of enterprises is to pay interest costs.

Cash flow-to-debt ratio = Cash Flow ÷ Total Debt

Interest coverage ratio = Earnings before Interest and Taxes ÷ Interest
= (Net Profit + Interest + Income Tax) ÷ Interest

With the long repayment period of non-current liabilities and the large amount, large difference may exist between future cash outflows (interest and principal paid in future) and its present value. From a theory-based perspective, non-current liabilities should be accounted for at their present value. It is not appropriate to account for its future repayment amount.

Non-current liabilities include long-term loans payable, long-term accounts payable, bonds payable, deferred income taxes, etc.

10.2.1 Long-term Loans Payable

Long-term loans payable includes the loans borrowed from financial institutions and other units. It shall be accounted independently according to the different characters of the loan and at the amount actually incurred.

Long-term loans are one of the main sources of funds in project investment. An investment project relies on a lot of funds instead of merely on its own funds. The amount of long-term borrowing should be limited to the part of funds that enterprises lack for long-term investment (except for some international institutions), because of the high cost of long-term borrowing. When borrowing long-term loans, policy makers should fully consider the expected cash flow status of investment projects and future changes in interest rates in order to curtail the financing costs.

The advantages of long-term borrowing are listed as follows:

(1) Shorter period of raising capitals. To issue securities, the process to application, approval, and issuance takes a certain time. Compared with issuing securities, bank loans generally take less time and can quickly raise capitals.

(2) Lower loan cost. The interest paid on bank loans is much lower than the interest paid on bond issuance, and there is no need to pay a large amount of issuance costs.

(3) High flexibility in borrowing. A direct contact can be established between enterprises and banks, through direct negotiations to determine the time, quantity and interest of loans. During the period of borrowing, if the situation of the enterprise changes, the negotiation with the bank will also be allowed to modify the amount and conditions of borrowing. After the maturity of the loan, the repayment may be postponed with acceptable reasons.

The disadvantages of long-term borrowing are listed as follows:

(1) High financial risks. Like bonds, long-term loans must be repaid on a regular basis. When the company is not operating well, there may be risks that the loan cannot be repaid, or even the company may suffer from bankruptcy.

(2) Many restrictions. In the loan contract signed by the enterprise and the bank, there are generally some restrictive clauses, such as submitting relevant statements regularly and forbidding changing the use of the loan. These terms may limit the business activities of the enterprise.

(3) Limited amount of financing, and small possibility of obtaining huge long-term loans.

10.2.2　Long-term Accounts Payable

Long-term accounts payable include accounts payable for imported equipment in compensation trade and accounts payable for leased fixed assets. Long-term accounts payable shall be accounted for at actual amounts.

Generally speaking, leasing can be divided into two forms: one is operating leasing, and the other is financial leasing. An operating lease allows the lessee to redeem the transaction as a lease, with neither an asset nor a liability recorded. But it is a different case for financial leasing. Financial leasing is a lease in the legal sense, but practically it is the lessee' purchasing behaviors on installments. Under capital leases, companies show both the asset and the liability on the balance sheet. Under financial leasing, companies display both assets and liabilities on their balance sheet. The liabilities to be paid in the next year is listed as current liability, while the remainder is classified as long-term liability.

10.2.3　Bonds Payable

Bonds are the most important instrument used by enterprises to finance their long-term investment projects. Bonds are a means of dividing long-term debt into a number of small units. Each bond is, in essence, a long-term interest-bearing note payable.

There are many different types of bonds, each with its own unique characteristics. Some bonds can be converted into common stock at the option of the bondholders, and they are known as convertible bonds. Other bonds that are repurchased by the issuer at a specified amount prior to maturity are called callable bonds. Furthermore, there are secured bonds and unsecured bonds depending on whether bonds have specific assets pledged as collateral; term bonds and serial bonds depending on whether maturing at a specified date or maturing in installments; registered bonds and bearer bonds depending on whether they are issued in the name of owner. In either case, a bond is an interest-bearing note payable.

The market price of a bond is determined by the difference between the effective interest rate and the nominal or coupon rate. If the effective interest rate is identical to the coupon rate, the bonds will be sold at face amount. If the effective interest rate is higher than the coupon rate, the bonds will be sold at a discount. Conversely, if the effective interest rate is less than the coupon rate, the bonds will be sold at a premium.

$$\text{The Market Prices of Bonds} \begin{cases} \text{the effective interest rate} > \text{the coupon rate} \rightarrow \text{Discount issue} \\ \text{the effective interest rate} = \text{the coupon rate} \rightarrow \text{Parity issue} \\ \text{the effective interest rate} < \text{the coupon rate} \rightarrow \text{Premium issue} \end{cases}$$

If A Co. issues bonds at par value, the company's accounting entries are as follows:

Dr. Bank Deposit
  Cr. Bonds Payable —— Principal
When interest accrued:
  Dr. Construction / Manufacturing / Finance / R&D Expenditure
   Cr. Bonds Payable —— Accrued Interest
When the bond is repaid and interest accrual:
  Dr. Bonds Payable —— Face Value
        —— Accrued Interest
  Cr. Bank Deposits

10.2.4 Deferred Income Taxes

A deferred income tax is a liability recorded on a balance sheet due to a difference in income recognition between tax laws and the company's accounting methods. For this reason, the income tax payable by the company may not be equal to the total reported tax expense. As companies defer payments based on accounting rule differences, the total tax expense for a particular fiscal year may differ from the taxes owed.

10.3 Provision

10.3.1 Definition

A provision is a subset of liabilities (i.e., it is a type of liability), whose repayment time or amount generally cannot be determined in according with *IAS 37 Provisions, Contingent Liabilities and Contingent Assets*. It is this uncertainty that distinguishes provisions from other liabilities.

The current *IAS Conceptual Framework* states that an essential characteristic of a liability is that an entity has a present obligation. An obligation is a duty or responsibility to act or perform in a certain way. Obligations may be legally enforceable as a consequence of a binding contract. For example, generally speaking, the amounts payable for goods or services received are described as "payables" or "trade creditors". However, legal enforceability is not a necessary requirement to demonstrate the existence of a liability. An entity may have a constructive obligation, arising from normal business practice or custom, to act in an equitable manner. It is often more difficult to determine a constructive obligation than identifying a legal obligation. A constructive obligation is defined as an obligation that derives from an entity's actions where an established pattern of past practice (including published or sufficiently specific current statements) indicates to other parties that the entity will accept certain responsibilities, consequently creating a reasonable expectation from those parties that the entity will discharge those responsibilities. For example, an enterprise has worked out and implemented a sales policy for many years, providing after-sales warranty services within a certain period of time for the goods sold. It is assumed that the warranty service provided for the sale of goods is a constructive obligation and should be recognized as a liability.

According to *IAS Conceptual Framework*, "A present obligation exists only has no realistic alternative but to settle the obligation". For example, suppose a company makes a public announcement that it will provide financial assistance to the victims of a natural disaster. Out of past practical and ethical considerations, the enterprise will have to provide assistance. In this case, the events have already taken place. The natural disaster and the public announcement are the events of obligations. Importantly, the decisions made by the company's management or governing bodies do not in themselves constitute a constructive obligation because they retain the ability to revoke the decision. When the decision is publicly communicated to those affected, a current obligation will exist. It would result in an effective expectation that the entity would fulfill the obligation, thus leaving it with little or no discretion to avoid an outflow of economic benefits.

10.3.2　Distinguishing from Other Liabilities

A provision may arise from either a legal or constructive obligation. *IAS 37 Provisions, Contingent Liabilities and Contingent Assets* illustrates the differences between provisions and other kind of liabilities. As stated previously, the key distinguishing factor is the uncertainty relating to either the timing of settlement or the amount to be settled. Comparatively speaking:

(1) Accounts payable refer to liabilities paid for goods or services received or provided, invoiced or formally agreed with suppliers.

(2) Accrued items refer to liabilities paid for goods or services received or provided but not yet paid, invoiced or formally agreed with suppliers, including amounts payable to employees (e.g., amounts related to accrued vacation payments). Although it is sometimes necessary to estimate the amount or time of an accrued item, the uncertainty is much less than that faced in preparing the provision. Accruals are generally reported as part of trade and other items payable, whereas provisions are reported separately.

10.4　Contingent Liabilities

10.4.1　Definition

In the standard, a contingent liability is defined as:

(1) A possible obligation that arises from past events and whose existence will be confirmed only by the occurrence or non-occurrence of one or more uncertain future events not entirely within the entity's control; or

(2) A present obligation that arises from past events but is not recognized because:

(i) The possibility of fulfilling the obligation is not large, namely, the outflow of resources embodying economic benefits is not likely to occur; or

(ii) The outflow of economic benefits cannot be measured with sufficient reliability.

The definition of a contingent liability is interesting because it involves two distinct concepts. The first part of the definition (1) is the concept of a possible obligation. It seems to be at odds with one of the essential characteristics of a liability, which is to require a present obligation of an entity. If there is no present obligation but only a possible one, there is no liability. Hence, Part (1) of the definition is not what liability is exactly defined, which is the possible reason for the argument that the term "contingent liability" is misleading because an item in category (1) is not a liability by definition.

Besides, Part (2) is defined as dealing with liabilities that do not meet the recognition criteria. They are present obligations, so they meet the essential requirements of the definition of liabilities, but do not meet the recognition criteria (probability of outflow of economic benefits and reliability of measurement).

However, the definition needs to be considered together with the criteria for recognizing a provision in the standard. A possible obligation that has not yet been confirmed does not conform to the definition of a liability; and a present obligation, in respect of which an outflow of resources is not probable, or which cannot be reliably, measured, does not qualify for recognition. On that basis a contingent liability under *IAS 37* means one of the following:

(1) An obligation whose likelihood for existence is less than 50% (i.e., it does not conform to the definition of a liability). Where it is more likely that there is a present obligation at the end of the reporting period, a provision is recognized. Where it is more likely that there is no present obligation, a contingent liability is disclosed (unless the possibility is remote); or

(2) A present obligation whose likelihood for requiring an outflow of economic benefits is less than 50% (i.e., it conforms to the definition of a liability but does not meet the recognition criteria). Where an outflow of resources is not likely, a contingent liability is disclosed by an entity (unless very unlikely); or

(3) A present obligation for which a sufficiently reliable estimate cannot be made (i.e., it conforms to the definition of a liability but does not meet the recognition criteria). In these rare cases, a liability cannot be recognized, but is disclosed as a contingent liability.

10.4.2 Contingent Liabilities VS Provisions

As mentioned earlier, contingent liabilities are not recognized in the financial statements, but must be disclosed in the financial statements, unless the likelihood of outflow at settlement is very small. All provisions can be seen as being 'contingent', as they are uncertain in timing or amount. However, in this standard, however, the term 'contingent' specifically refers to unrecognized liabilities and assets, since their existence can only be recognized by the occurrence or non-occurrence of one or more uncertain future events that are not entirely within an entity's control. A contingent liability in *IAS 37* is also defined as a liability that does not meet the recognition criteria.

The following example illustrates the difference between a contingent liability and a provision.

Legal proceedings against ABC Co. began after several people became ill, possibly as a result of taking the health supplements manufactured and sold by ABC Co., ABC Co. contests any liability until the authorized release of its financial statements on 31 December 2015, its lawyers advised that Lemmon would most likely not be held legally liable. However, when ABC Co. prepared its financial statements for December 31, 2016, its lawyers advised that Lemon would be likely to be held liable in light of the development of the case and can make a reliable estimate of the amount of damage.

— For 31 December 2015, no provision was recognized, and the matter was disclosed as a contingent liability unless the probability of any outflow was regarded as remote. On the basis of the evidence available when the financial statements were approved, there was no obligation arising from a past event.

— For 31 December 2016, a provision was recognized for the best estimate of the amount required to settle the obligation. The fact that an outflow of economic benefits is now believed to be likely and estimates can be reliably made means that this is no longer a contingent liability, but a provision.

Note that the reporting standard gives no guidance regarding the meaning of the terms of possibility. One possible interpretation is as follows:

Virtually certain > 95%

Likely: 51%~95%

Possible: 5%~50%

Unlikely < 5%

Key Words and Expressions

liabilities	负债
present obligations	现时义务
constructive obligation	推定义务
economic interests	经济利益
loan default	贷款违约
legal obligations	法定义务
balance sheet	资产负债表
current liabilities	流动负债
current ratio	流动比率
quick ratio	速动比率
working capital	营运资本
accounts payable	应付账款
trade accounts payable	购销应付账款
other accounts payable	其他应付账款
invoice	发票
accounting book	会计账簿
financial statement	财务报表
general ledger accounts	总分类账
credit rating	信用评级
notes payable	应付票据
payee	收款人
accrual method	权责发生制
interest rates	利率
maturity dates	到期日
collateral pledged	抵押物
unearned revenue	预收收益
income statement	利润表
long-term liabilities/non-current liability	长期负债

wages payable	应付职工薪酬
Generally Accepted Accounting Practice (GAAP)	一般公认会计准则
coverage ratio	偿还能力系数
cash flow-to-debt ratio	现金比率
interest coverage ratio	利息保障倍数
earnings before interest and taxes (EBIT)	息税前利润
long-term loans payable	长期借款
financial institutions	金融机构
financing costs	筹资成本
securities	证券
bank loan	银行贷款
bankruptcy	破产
principal	本金
long-term accounts payable	长期应付款
operating leases	经营租赁
capital leases	融资租赁
financial leasing	融资租赁
rental	租赁
bonds payable	应付债券
common stock	普通股
convertible bonds	可转换债券
callable bond	可赎回债券
secured bonds	抵押债券
unsecured bonds	信用债券
collateral	抵押品
registered bonds	记名债券
bearer bonds	不记名债券
effective interest rate	实际利率
nominal/coupon rate	名义利率
face amount	面值
par value	票面价值
deferred income tax	递延所得税
provision	准备金
contingent liability	或有负债
recognition criteria	确认条件
disclose	披露

Exercises

I. Please choose the best answer for the following questions or uncompleted sentences.

1. If a corporation plans to issue $2000000 of 12% bonds at a time when the market rate for similar bonds is 10%, the bonds can be expected to sell at ( ).

   A. their face amount

   B. a premium

   C. a discount

   D. a price below their face amount

2. The term used for bonds that are issued in the name of the owner is ( ).

   A. bearer bonds

   B. registered bonds

   C. secured bonds

   D. callable bonds

3. In December 2019, an entity agreed a five-year loan agreement with a bank and undertook to comply with certain covenants. The agreement stipulated that, in the event of a failure by the entity to fulfill any of the contractual obligations, the bank had the right to terminate the agreement and the entity would have to repay the loan unless agreement had been made to reschedule the loan. As at 31 December 2019, the entity was not in compliance with the covenants stipulated in the agreement but had negotiated in writing a rescheduling of the loan over a longer period. How should the loan be treated in the financial statements at 31 December 2019? ( )

   A. The loan should be shown as a current liability.

   B. The loan should be shown as a non-current liability.

   C. The loan should be re-recognized from the financial statements.

   D. The loan should be offset against any other amounts due from the bank irrespective of any agreement to do so.

4. If bonds are issued at a discount, it means that the ( ).

   A. financial strength of the issuer is suspect

   B. market interest rate is higher than the contractual interest rate

   C. market interest rate is lower than the contractual interest rate

   D. bondholder will receive effectively less interest than the contractual rate of interest

II. Finish the following tasks based on the information given.

On January 1, 20×0, a company borrowed $800,000 from the bank for a period of nine months with an annual interest rate of 4.5%. The interest on the loan was paid quarterly and the principal was repaid at maturity. Please prepare accounting entries related to the above economic operations.

第10章 负债

根据《国际会计准则——概念框架》,负债被定义为:"企业因过去的交易或事件而产生的现时义务,且预计该义务的履行将导致经济利益从企业流出。"

关于负债的定义,有几个要点需要注意:

(1) 负债包括但不限于法定债务。负债的基本特征是现时义务,这是公司需要以某种特定的方式行使或履行的义务或责任。现时义务可能是由权益或公平概念(称为"公平"义务),习惯或常规商业惯例(称为"推定"义务)以及由具有法律效力的合同所产生的。例如,公司做出维修已超出保修期的残次品的决定将被视为公司的负债增加。因此,预期在已经售出的商品上花费的金额也是负债。现时义务需要与未来的承诺区分开。管理层在未来购买资产的决定不会产生现时义务(负债)。负债通常产生在资产交付时或企业订立了不可撤销的协议(如果该协议被撤销,则将处以重罚)时。

(2) 负债几乎必将导致经济利益未来流出企业。企业在避免这样的牺牲方面几乎没有什么酌处权。公司需要在指定日期或将来发生指定事件时履行义务。因此,贷款协议下的担保被认为是一种负债,因为在特定事件(例如,贷款违约)的情况下,(偿还贷款的)义务需要被履行。

履行这样的现时义务(清偿负债)有许多方式,如支付现金、资产置换、提供服务、将债务转化为权益、以另一种义务取代该义务等。

(3) 负债的最后一个特征是:它必须是由过去的交易或事件造成的。例如,采购货物和工作人员所做的工作分别会增加企业的应付账款和应付工资。但是支付给工作人员将来工作的工资不是一项负债,因为没有过去的交易或事件,也没有现时义务。

将现时义务确认为负债,不仅要符合负债的定义,而且要同时满足以下两个条件:

首先,与债务相关的经济利益很可能流出企业。从负债的定义可以看出,预期会导致企业经济利益外流是负债的一个本质特征。在实践中,履行义务的经济效益是不确定的,特别是与推定义务有关的经济效益,往往依赖于大量的估计。因此,负债的确认应与经济利益流出不确定性程度的判断相结合。有确凿证据表明与流动负债相关的经济利益很可能流出企业的,应确认为负债。相反,如果企业承担现时义务,但导致企业经济利益流出的可能性很小,则不符合确认负债的条件,不应确认为负债。

再者,经济效益的未来流出能被可靠地计量。负债的确认应当考虑经济利益的流出,并对未来经济利益流出的金额进行可靠计量。与法定义务有关的经济利益流出额,通常可以根据合同或法律规定的数额确定。考虑到经济利益的流出量通常是在未来,有时是较长一段时间后才能实现,在计量相关金额时需要考虑货币时间价值等因素的影响。对于与推定义务相关的经济利益流出额,企业在进行估计时应当考虑相关货币的时间价值和风险的影响。

在资产负债表中,负债被分为流动负债和非流动负债,以帮助会计信息使用者评估公司短期和长期的财务状况。

10.1 流动负债

流动负债是指将在需要时通过现有流动资产或通过产生其他流动负债来偿还的一种债务。流动负债的付款期限为一年或在一个正常经营周期内。

流动负债主要包括应付账款、应付票据、预计收益、应付股利、一年内到期的长期负债、应付职工薪酬、应交税费、应付利息等。由于流动负债需要在相对较短的时间内支付的，因此通常在资产负债表上按其面值列示。

会计信息使用者通常使用流动比率和速动比率来确定公司是否有足够的资源在未来12个月内偿还债务。

流动比率 = 流动资产÷流动负债

速动比率 =(流动资产-存货)/ 流动负债

在资产负债表的负债和股东权益部分，流动负债账户通常位列第一。在某些情况下，流动负债列示在流动资产后，流动资产总额减去流动负债总额被称为"营运资本"或"流动资产超过流动负债"。在流动负债部分，账户可按到期日、金额(从大到小)或清算的优先顺序列出。

10.1.1 应付账款

应付账款是企业因向供应商购买货物或获得服务所产生的短期债务。应付账款通常分为购销应付账款和其他应付账款。购销应付账款是指供应商预先提供货物而产生的短期负债。其他应付账款是指与企业的主营业务没有直接关系的应付款项。应付账款通常不要求支付利息，这使得该种形式的负债有很大的吸引力。因为这意味着购买方可以从供应商那里获得"无息贷款"。

应付账款应在与所购货物所有权有关的风险和报酬转移或服务被接受时入账。在实践中，我们应该分不同的情况处理：

(1) 材料和发票同时到达。

一般情况下，应付账款只有在材料验收入库后才能按发票金额进行登记。这主要是为了确认采购物资的质量、数量、品种等是否符合合同的规定，避免出现差错。也为了避免因先入账而在验收入库时发现购入物资有错、漏、破损等问题再进行调账。

(2) 材料和发票不同时到达。

当货物已清点入库，但发票未同时到账时，由于买方对卖方已经形成债务，在会计期末，需将所购材料、商品和相关的应付账款暂估入账。待下月初还需用红字将上月末暂估入账的应付账款予以冲销。

审查应付账款涉及大量细节，为确保应付账款以合法且准确的金额计入会计系统中，应对以下文件进行严格审查：

- 公司发出的采购订单。
- 本公司的收货单。
- 收到的供应商的发票。
- 合同及其他协议。

公司财务报表的准确性和完整性很大程度上取决于应付账款的管理。良好的应付账款管理应包括：

- 及时处理准确合法的供应商发票
- 在适当的总分类账中准确记录
- 尚未完全处理的债务和费用的计提

应付账款流程的效率和有效性还将影响公司的现金状况、信用评级以及与供应商的关系。

应付账款余额的大小是衡量公司财务状况的一个重要指标，特别是在零售业。

一些供应商会为客户提供现金折扣，如"2/10，N/30"。这意味着如果在10天内付款给卖方，买方可以扣除原所欠金额的2%。例如,如果买方在10天内支付账款,则可以以980美元全额结算原本1,000美元的款项。在本例中,如果买方提前20天付款,则可以节省20美元(2%×1,000)。这意味着每次节约的百分比约为2%(收入20美元÷使用的980美元)。

从另一种角度来看,如果买方以6%的借款利率(年利率)向银行借入980美元,为期20天,那么20天的利息仅为3.22美元(980×6%×20÷365)。通过向银行支付$3.22的利息,买方将节省向卖方支付的20美元,因此可以得到16.78美元(20.00-3.22)的收益。如果一年发生18次,那么每年的净节省额约301美元(每年节省的360美元减去向银行支付的年息59美元)。若提前20天还款可以享受1%的折扣,那么相当于年利率18%左右。

显然,如果拥有足够的现金或可用信贷额度,那么买家应该利用预付款的折扣。然而,一些买家的现金储备较少,而且融资能力较弱。为了避免透支的风险,这些买家最好放弃现金折扣,因为透支的代价可能大于提前付款所享受的折扣。如果透支导致几张支票被退回,那么透支总成本将更高。而且如果买方的支票因资金不足而被退回,供应商可能会担心买方的支付能力。这可能导致其他供应商要求该企业在交货时就付款。供应商取消30天的信用付款期可能会给几乎没有钱的买方或已经用完信用额度的买方带来毁灭性的后果。

10.1.2 应付票据

以书面期票形式表现的票据性债务被称为应付票据。可能产生应付票据的交易行为包括购买商品,购买房地产或昂贵的设备。逾期应付账款可以转为应付票据,欠款方是应付票据的出票人,而收款人是债权方。

在会计中,应付票据负债类账户,该账户中记录公司发行的应付票据的票面金额。应付票据余额是指公司尚未支付的票据的金额。由于应付票据要求发行人/借款人支付利息,因此发行公司将承担利息费用。根据权责发生制,公司还应设立另一个负债账户,名为"应付利息"。在该账户中,本公司记录截至会计期末已发生但尚未支付的利息。

对于大多数公司来说,应付票据和应付利息中的金额在资产负债表中列报。资产负债表日后一年内到期的为流动负债;资产负债表日后一年内未到期的为非流动负债或长期负债。公司还应披露票据所欠金额的相关信息,包括利率、到期日、抵押物、债权人施加的限制等。

10.1.3 预收收入

预收收入是指个人或公司为尚未实现的服务或产品而收到的款项。预收收入可被视为个人或公司预期为买方生产的货物或服务的"预付款"。由于这种预付款,卖方将一直持有该现时义务,直至交付货物或提供劳务。在发生预收收入时,企业将编制如下分录:

 借:现金
   贷:预收收入

预收收入在销售基于订阅的产品或其他需要预付款的服务的公司中最为常见。典型的例子包括预付租金、预付保险费、法定准备金、机票、订阅报纸和使用软件的年度预付款。

在服务完成前就收到价款对卖方是有益的。预先收到的现金流可用于其他活动,如支付债务利息和购进更多库存。

预收收入作为负债记录在公司的资产负债表上。它被视为一项负债,因为尚不能确认为收入,公司负有为客户提供产品或服务的义务。随着预付服务或产品的逐步交付,再在损益表中确认为收入。

如果一家出版公司收取 1,200 美元的一年期订阅费，则该金额将记录为现金和预计收益的增加。两者都是资产负债表账户，因此该交易不会立即影响利润表。如果是月刊，在每一期期刊交付时，负债或未实现收入减少 100 美元(1,200 美元除以 12 个月)，而收入也会增加相同数额。

未实现收入通常在公司资产负债表上作为流动负债披露。但如果商品或服务是在客户付款日期后 12 个月或更长的时间后再提供，未实现收入将在资产负债表上显示为"长期负债"。

10.1.4　应付股利

公司通常在实际向投资者支付现金之前会宣布发放股利。在一年内或一个营业周期内发放的已宣告但尚未发放的现金股利，作为流动负债列示。股利在宣告日和支付日之间作为负债报告。

通常，股利只适用于在某一特定日期之前持有股票的股东。这在一定程度上防止了新投资者仅仅为了赚取股息而购买股票。一旦公司宣告派息，就必须记录负债。应付股利是公司资产负债表上的负债。账户中包含的金额是公司在股利宣告日公告的现金股利金额。

10.1.5　一年内到期的长期负债

一年或一个营业周期内到期应付的长期负债，在流动负债项下单独列示。

一年或一个营业周期内到期应付的长期负债(CPLTD)是下一年或一个营业周期内到期的长期负债部分。假设一家公司有一笔用于融资建设项目的 20 万美元的 15 年期银行贷款。公司每月需支付 1,500 美元，为了简单起见，我们假设每笔 1,500 美元的付款包括 800 美元的本金付款和 700 美元的利息付款。那么，这笔债务的流动部分为 9,600 美元(每月 800 美元 × 12 个月)。这是一年内需要偿还的本金。CPLTD 在公司的资产负债表中被分离出来，因为它需要以现金等高流动性资产支付。CPLTD 是债权人和投资者用来确定公司是否有能力偿还到期的短期债务的重要指标。

10.1.6　应付职工薪酬

应付职工薪酬是指公司员工已赚取但公司尚未支付的工资。按照权责发生制，该金额很可能在会计期末用调整项记录，以便公司的资产负债表将其列为流动负债。(调整分录通常从"工资支出"中扣除，并在计入"应付职工薪酬"贷方。)

假定某公司在每周五时发放上周的工资。2019 年 12 月 31 日是星期二。由于雇主在周五向员工付款，因此这些员工必须等到 1 月 3 日才能获得 12 月份的全部工资。这意味着，从第二年的 1 月 1 日，雇主欠雇员两天的薪水，即 2019 年 12 月最后一个星期一和星期二的工资。在 12 月底，雇主所欠雇员两天的薪水应该在会计系统中记录为负债并将其显示在财务报表中。

截至 12 月 31 日，公司资产负债表上的流动负债必须包括 12 月最后一个周一和周二员工赚取的薪水，以及 12 月 31 日公司所欠的其他薪水。(该金额作为公司工资支出的一部分也必须计入截至 12 月 31 日的公司年度损益表中。)

应付职工薪酬中的金额通常在资产负债表上作为流动负债表的一部分进行报告。

10.1.7　应交所得税费用

应交所得税费用显示为流动负债，因为这些负债将在一年内支付。但是，任何不计划在未来 12 个月内支付的应交所得税都归为长期负债。

应交所得税费用是计算企业递延所得税负债的必要部分。当报告公司的所得税负债和所得税费用之间的差额时，会产生递延所得税负债。差异可能是实际所得税的到期时间导致的。例如，在当前使用的会计准则下，企业欠缴所得税款为 1,000 美元。如果根据税法计算，公司仅欠 850 美元的所得税，剩余 250 美元将在以后期间被视为负债。税法与公认会计准则之间的规则差异而产生冲突，导致将来某些负债的递延。

根据公司所在国的税法，纳税额是根据其净收入计算的。应税率是根据公司的税率计算的。对于应从其税务部门获得税收抵免的公司，应缴纳的所得税额将会减少。

10.1.8 应付利息

应付利息是截至资产负债表日已发生但尚未支付的利息支出。应付利息不包括资产负债表日后边一段时间的利息。

假设一家公司在 12 月 1 日借了 100,000 美元，年利率为 12%。该公司同意在下一年的 8 月 31 日到期时偿还本金 100,000 美元，外加 9 个月的利息。公司取得借款时的会计分录如下所示：

　　借：银行存款　　　　　　　　　　　　　　$100,000
　　　贷：短期借款　　　　　　　　　　　　　　　　　$100,000

则 12 月 31 日，应付利息金额为 1,000 美元(100,000×12%×1÷12)，公司的资产负债表应报告以下流动负债：

— 短期借款 100,000 美元
— 应付利息 1,000 美元

记录该经济业务的会计分录如下：

　　借：财务费用　　　　　　　　　　　　　　　$1,000
　　　贷：应付利息　　　　　　　　　　　　　　　　　$1,000

对于将来需要支付的 8,000 美元利息(100,000×12%×8÷12)不在 12 月 31 日的资产负债表中记录。

公司 1 月 31 日的资产负债表应报告以下流动负债：

— 短期借款 100,000 美元
— 应付利息 2,000 美元

在 8 月 31 日，公司按照约定应支付借款本金 100,000 美元及 9 个月的借款利息(1,000+8,000=9,000 美元)。记录该经济业务的会计分录如下。

　　借：财务费用　　　　　　　　　　　　　　　$8,000
　　　贷：应付利息　　　　　　　　　　　　　　　　　$8,000
　　借：短期借款　　　　　　　　　　　　　　　$100,000
　　　　应付利息　　　　　　　　　　　　　　　$9,000
　　　贷：银行存款　　　　　　　　　　　　　　　　　$109,000

10.2 非流动负债

非流动负债又称长期负债，是指超过一年或者一个经营周期的公司债务。非流动负债是相对于流动负债而言的。

将非流动负债与现金流量进行比较，可以分析出公司是否有长期履行其财务义务的能力。债权人方主要关注公司的短期流动性和流动负债数量,而长期投资者则使用非流动负债来衡量公司是否存在杠杆过高的问题。在违约风险不变的情况下,公司的现金流量越稳定,可以筹措到的债务就越多。

分析师们还通过偿还能力系数来评估公司的财务状况,包括现金流债务比率和利息保障倍数。现金流量与债务比率决定了如果一家公司将其全部现金流用于偿还债务,它将需要多长时间。该指标值越高,表示公司现金流入量越能保证流动负债的偿还,说明企业的流动性越好;反之,说明企业的流动性较差。利息保障倍数是通过将公司的息税前利润(EBIT)除以同期的债务利息支出来计算的,它用于衡量公司是否有足够的收入来支付利息支出。利息保障倍数越大,表示企业长期偿债能力越强。

$$现金流债务比率 = 现金流量 \div 总负债$$
$$利息保障倍数 = 息税前利润 \div 利息$$
$$= (净利润 + 利息 + 所得税) \div 利息$$

由于非流动负债的还款期长且金额大,其未来现金流出量(未来支付的利息和本金)与其现值之间可能存在较大差异。从理论上讲,非流动负债应按其现值入账,而不宜按其未来应偿付金额入账。

非流动负债主要包括长期借款、长期应付账款、应付债券、递延所得税等。

10.2.1 长期借款

长期借款包括向金融机构和其他单位的借款。按照借款的不同性质和实际发生额分别核算。

长期借款是项目投资的主要资金来源之一。一个投资项目一般需要大量的资金,依靠公司自己的资金往往是不够的。长期借款的筹措应以企业进行长期投资所缺少的那部分资金为限,因为长期借款的成本很高(除了一些国际机构)。政策制定者在借入长期贷款时,应充分考虑投资项目的预期现金流状况和未来利率的变化,以获得较低的融资成本。

长期借款的优点有:

(1) 可以迅速筹集资金。发行证券时,申请、批准、发行的程序需要一定的时间。与发行证券相比,银行贷款通常需要的时间更短,可以迅速筹集资金。

(2) 贷款成本低。银行贷款支付的利息远低于债券发行支付的利息,而且无须支付大额的发行成本。

(3) 借款灵活。企业和银行可以直接联系,通过直接谈判确定贷款的时间、数量和利息。在借款期内,如果企业情况发生变化,还可以与银行协商修改借款金额和条件。贷款到期后,如果有合理的理由,可以推迟还款。

长期借款的缺点有:

(1) 财务风险高。像债券一样,长期贷款必须定期偿还。当公司经营不善时,可能存在贷款无法偿还的风险,甚至会导致公司破产。

(2) 有很多限制。在企业与银行签订的贷款合同中,一般都有一些限制性条款,如定期提交财务报表、不允许改变贷款用途等。这些条款可能会限制企业的经营活动。

(3) 融资额度有限,且获得巨额长期贷款的可能性较小。

10.2.2 长期应付款

长期应付账款包括应付补偿贸易引进设备款、租赁固定资产应付账款。长期应付款应当按实际发生额记账。

租赁一般分为两种形式:一种是经营租赁,另一种是融资租赁。经营租赁允许承租人将交易视为租赁,既不记录资产也不记录负债。融资租赁则不同。融资租赁是一种法律意义上的租赁行为,而实际意义是承租方的分期付款购买方式。在融资租赁下,公司在资产负债表上同时显示资产和负债。预计在下一年偿付的负债部分列为流动负债,其余部分列为长期负债。

10.2.3 应付债券

债券是企业为长期投资项目融资的最重要工具。债券是将长期债务划分为若干小单位的一种手段。债券实质上是一种长期有息票据。

债券有许多不同的种类,每一种都有其独特的特点。有些债券可以根据债券持有人的选择转换成普通股,称为可转换债券。其他由发行人选择在到期日前按规定数额回购的债券称为可赎回债券。此外,还有担保债券和无担保债券,这取决于债券是否有特定资产作为抵押;定期债券和系列债券取决于是否在指定日期到期或分期到期;记名债券和无记名债券取决于它们是否以业主的名义签发。不管是哪种,债券都是一种有息的应付票据。

债券的市场价格由实际利率与票面利率之间的差额决定。如果实际利率与票面利率相同,债券将按面值出售。如果实际利率高于票面利率,债券将折价出售。相反,如果实际利率低于票面利率,债券将溢价出售。

$$债券的发行价格 \begin{cases} 实际利率 > 票面利率 \ 折价发行 \\ 实际利率 = 票面利率 \ 平价发行 \\ 实际利率 < 票面利率 \ 溢价发行 \end{cases}$$

企业按票面价值发行债券时的会计分录如下:
  借:银行存款
    贷:应付债券——本金
计提利息时的会计分录如下:
  借:在建工程/制造费用/财务费用/研发支出
    贷:应付债券——应计利息
债券还本计息时的会计分录如下:
  借:应付债券——面值
     ——应计利息
    贷:银行存款

10.2.4 递延所得税

递延所得税是由于税法和公司会计核算之间的收入确认差异而在资产负债表上记录的负债。公司应缴纳的所得税可能不等于报告的总税收费用。由于公司基于会计规则差异推迟付款,因而特定会计年度的总税务费用可能不同于所欠税款。

10.3 预计负债

10.3.1 定义

预计负债也属于一种负债,根据《国际会计准则第 37 号——预计负债、或有负债和或有资产》,

预计负债一般无法确定其偿还时间或金额。正是这种不确定性将预计负债与其他负债区分开来。

根据《国际会计准则——概念框架》的规定，负债的一项基本特征是该企业具有的现时义务。由于具有约束力的合同，义务可能在法律上具有强制性，例如，通常情况下，收到的商品或服务的应付款项被称为"应付款项"。但是，法律意义上的可执行性不是证明负债存在的必要条件。企业可能因正常的商业惯例而具有推定义务。确定是否存在推定义务通常比确定法律义务困难。推定义务的定义是：根据企业多年来的习惯做法、公开的承诺或者公开宣布的政策而导致企业将承担的责任，这些责任也是有关各方形成了企业将履行义务解脱责任的合理预期。例如，企业制定了一项销售政策且已执行多年：在一定时间内为售出的商品提供售后保修服务。预期将为商品销售提供的保修服务是一项推定义务，应确认为一项负债。

《国际会计准则——概念框架》规定"现时义务是指企业在现行条件下已承担的义务"。例如，假设一家公司发布公开声明，它将向自然灾害的受害者提供经济援助。出于过去的实践和道德考虑，该企业将必须提供援助。发布声明后，公司将确认负债增加。在这种情况下，自然灾害和公告是定义中所指的"过去的交易和事项"，是确认该项负债必不可少的事件。公司管理层或理事机构的决定本身并不构成推定义务。这是因为管理层或理事机构保留有撤销该决定的权利。但当该决定被公开传达给受其影响的人时，一项现时义务就出现了。这将导致对公司将履行义务的有效预期，从而使公司几乎没有裁量权来避免经济利益外流。

10.3.2 预计负债与其他负债的区别

预计负债来自法律义务或推定义务。如前所述，关键的区别因素是结算时间或结算金额的不确定性。《国际会计准则第37号——预计负债、或有负债和或有资产》中介绍了预计负债与其他负债的区别：

(1) 应付账款指为已收或已提供的、并已开出发票或已与供应商达成正式协议的货物或劳务进行支付的负债；

(2) 应计项目指为已收或已提供的、但还未支付、开出发票或与供应商达成正式协议的货物或劳务进行支付的负债，包括应付给雇员的金额(例如，与应计的假期支付有关的金额)。虽然有时需要对应计项目的金额或时间进行估计，但其不确定性要比对估计预计负债时面临的不确定性小得多。应计项目经常作为应付账款和其他应付款的部分进行报告，而预计负债则单独进行报告。

10.4 或有负债

10.4.1 定义

或有负债的标准中定义为：

(1) 由过去事件引起的可能的义务,其存在只能通过一个或多个不确定的未来事件的发生或不发生而得到确认，而这些事件并不完全在公司的控制范围内；

(2) 由于过去的事件而产生但因为下列原因而未被确认的当前义务：

(i) 履行义务的可能性不大，即经济利益外流的可能性较小；

(ii) 经济利益外流的金额不能被充分可靠地计量。

或有负债的定义值得深入讨论，它包含两个截然不同的概念。定义的第一部分(1)是可能发生的义务。这似乎与负债的一项基本特征——企业的现时义务相违背。或有负债只是存在的可能的义务，而非现时义务。因此，定义的(1)部分不符合负债的定义，这可能导致学术界有争辩说"或有负债具有误导性"，因为从定义上来说，属于(1)类别的项目并不是负债。

另一方面，定义的(2)满足负债定义的基本要求，但不满足负债的确认标准——流出企业的经济利益可被可靠计量。

但是，定义中的(1)和(2)需要一起考虑。尚待确认的可能义务不符合负债的定义；现时义务很可能导致经济利益外流但无法可靠计量的，不符合负债的确认条件。在此基础上，《国际会计准则第37号》规定满足下列其中一项的即可定义为或有负债：

(1) 估计存在的可能性小于50%的义务(即不符合负债的定义)。如果在报告期末很可能存在现时义务，则确认一项准备金。如果很可能不存在当前义务，则企业应披露或有负债(可能性极小的情况下可以不披露)；

(2) 该项现时义务导致经济利益流出企业的可能性小于 50%(即它符合负债的定义但不符合负债确认标准)。如果不太可能出现经济利益流出，则企业应披露或有负债(可能性极小的情况下可以不披露)；

(3) 无法对其进行足够可靠的估计的现时义务(即它符合负债的定义，但不符合确认标准)。在这种罕见情况下，无法确认负债，因此将其披露为或有负债。

10.4.2 或有负债 VS 预计负债

如前所述，或有负债不在财务报表中确认。除非与或有负债相关的经济利益流出的可能性极小，否则必须在财务报表中披露。所有预计负债都可以视作"或有"，因为它们在时间或金额上具有不确定性。在国际会计准则中，"或有"一词专门指未确认的负债和资产，因为它们只在特定的条件成就时才能确认。《国际会计准则第37号》中的或有负债还指不符合确认条件的负债。

以下的例子将说明预计负债与或有负债的区别。

由于几位客户在食用 ABC 公司生产和销售的保健品后出现了身体不适，于是对 ABC 公司提起了诉讼。截至 2015 年 12 月 31 日 ABC 公司财务报表的授权发布日期，公司律师已告知 ABC 公司可能不会被追究责任。然而，当 ABC 公司编制其 2016 年 12 月 31 日的财务报表时，其律师建议，由于案件的发展，公司很可能会被认定负有责任，并对损害赔偿额作出可靠估计。

2015 年 12 月 31 日，没有确认预计负债，该事项被披露为或有负债，除非任何流出的可能性被视为是遥远的。根据财务报表批准时提供的证据，过去的事件不产生任何债务。

但是在 2016 年 12 月 31 日，该事项会确认一项预计负债，用于对将来要清偿债务所需的金额进行估计。事实上，经济利益的外流现在被认为是可能的，而且是能够被相对可靠地计量的，这意味着这不再是一项或有负债，而是一项预计负债。

值得注意的事，准则并未对可能性的含义做出详细说明。以下对比可作为参考：

几乎肯定>95%

可能：51%～95%

可能：5%～50%

几乎不可能<5%

Chapter 11

Owners' Equity

There are three typical legal organizations that a business may take: sole proprietorship, partnership, and corporation.

- Sole proprietorship

A sole proprietorship enterprise, also known as an individual business or a sole proprietorship enterprise, is an enterprise legal person owned and operated by a natural person. In a sole proprietorship enterprise, there is no legal difference between its owner and the enterprise. In a sole proprietorship, the individual and business are one and the same. The owner of a sole proprietorship has direct control over the entire organization and assume unlimited liability for the debts, loans and losses of the enterprise.

The advantage of a sole proprietorship enterprise is that it is easy to establish and does not need to pay corporate income tax. Meanwhile, sole proprietorship also has its disadvantages. Owners assume unlimited liability for all its losses and debts, which is very risky. The survival of a sole proprietorship enterprise is influenced by the living conditions of its owners. And it is difficult to provide a lot of money for its daily operation.

- Partnership

A partnership is a type of business organization in which two or more individuals pool money, skills, and other resources, and share profit and loss in accordance with terms of the partnership agreement. There are several types of partnership arrangements. It can be divided into general partnership and limited partnership.

The partnership has the following advantages. Firstly, compared with sole proprietorship enterprises, partnership is more capable of raising funds. Secondly, compared with a corporate enterprise, the interests of creditors are more protected because at least one of the partners bears unlimited liability. Theoretically, under the pressure of unlimited liability, a company's reputation can be enhanced even more. Thirdly, partnership only needs to pay individual income tax, not corporate income tax. A major disadvantage of a partnership is unlimited liability. General partners assume unlimited liability for all debts contracted and errors made by the partnership. This makes partnerships too risky in most cases. Partnerships may have a limited life. Upon the withdrawal or death of a partner, the partner may terminate.

- Corporation

Corporate enterprises refer to economic organizations that are established, operated independently, responsible for their own profits and losses, and have legal personality, funded by more than a quorum of investors (or shareholders) in accordance with the laws. At present, there are two forms of corporation in China: limited liability company and joint stock company limited.

The organizational structure of a company is an organizational form commonly used in many countries, especially because it provides limited liability protection for shareholders. These companies are funded by a mix of equity and debt. This chapter focuses on the interests of corporate entities. The components of equity generally recognized by companies include share capital, other reserves and retained earnings. In particular, various financial instruments developed in the financial market affect equity and provide investors with a range of alternatives to risky returns. Each of these equity alternatives has its own accounting implications. The provision is determined by the limitation of traditional accounting and current accounting standards. The increase in wealth partially directly comes from equity rather than current income. Despite the clear distinction between the various components of equity, it is important to recognize that they are equity, with differences in jurisdiction over dividend distribution, tax implications, and restrictions on owner's rights. *IAS 1 Presentation of Financial Statement* requires detailed disclosures in relation to each of the components of equity.

According to *IAS Conceptual Framework*, equity, namely, owners' equity, is defined as the residual interest in the assets of an entity after deducting all its liabilities. Defining equity in this way makes it clear that equity cannot be defined in isolation from other factors in the statement of financial position. The characteristics of equity are as follows: Equity is a residual, that is, something left over. It is a residual amount of the book value that represents the value of the owners' entity in the company. Expressed by the formula:

$$Equity = Assets - Liabilities$$

Owner's equity is normally increased in two ways. One is from contribution by investors in exchange for capital share, which is called paid-in capital. And the other is from the retention of profits earned by the corporation over time, which is called retained earnings. Similarly, equity is diminished by unprofitable operations and by distributions to owners (drawings and dividends).

In preparing general financial statements, owner's equity is influenced by the measurement system of assets and liabilities and by the concepts of capital and capital maintenance. Owner's equity is one of the factors reflecting the financial status of an enterprise.

11.1 Share

Ownership in a corporation is evidenced by a certificate of stock. Share is also named stock or capital stock. The capital or property contributed by a shareholder as the financial basis of a company. Shares are issued with specific rights attached. Shares are then given different names to signify differences in rights. The capital share may be either common or preferred.

11.1.1 Common Share

1. Overview

Common shares are shares with common rights and obligations, and they are the most basic form of company shares. Shareholders of common stocks enjoy equal rights to the management and earnings of the company, and dividend according to the company's operating benefits, which is risky. Common share is the basis of company capital, a basic form of share, and the most important share with the largest circulation. At present, shares traded on the SSE (Shanghai Stock Exchange) and SZSE (Shenzhen Stock Exchange) are common stock.

Stock is often issued by a company at a price other than its par. The price of the issued shares and their par value are not necessarily related. If a company issues par value stock at a price above par value, the stock is said to be issued at a premium. If a company issues par value stock at a price below par value, the stock is said to be issued at a discount.

In China, par value is ¥1 for all the listed corporations and no discount is allowed. The price of a company's shares depends on a variety of factors, such as record of profits, record of dividends and general economic conditions. When stock is issued at premium, the cash or other asset account increases based on the amount received. The excess of the amount paid over par is a part of the total capital contributed by the stockholder of the company. This amount is usually recorded in an account called "Capital Reserve". In most cases, capital stock is sold and issued in cash.

HYX Co. issues 100,000 shares of common share, par ¥1, for cash of ¥1.5 per share. The entry is recorded as follow:

```
Dr. Bank Deposit                              150,000
    Cr. Capital Stock- Common Stock                      100,000
        Capital Reserve                                   50,000
```

When stock is issued in exchange for assets such as equipment, buildings, and land, other than cash, the asset acquired should be recorded at their fair market value. If the fair market value of the assets cannot be objectively determined, the fair market price of the stock issued may be used.

The shareholders of ordinary shares have no right to decide on dividend distribution. Whether to pay dividends depends on the decision of the board of directors. Regulations in some countries may specify which equity accounts from which the dividends can be paid, or whether the company has to meet solvency tests before paying dividends. In some cases, Directors may propose a dividend at the end of the year, but that proposal may need to be approved at an annual meeting.

2. The Right of Common Shareholders

Common shareholders have the rights to ①vote for major issues; ②receive dividends declared by the board of directors; ③share cash or other assets if the corporation is liquidated; and④preemptive right to purchase additional shares of capital share in proportion to present holdings in the event that the corporation increases the amount of share outstanding.

(1) Generally, common shareholders have the right to speak and vote, that is, they have the right to speak

and vote on major issues of the company. Ordinary shareholders have one share of voting rights when they hold one share, and those who hold two shares have two voting rights. Any common shareholder shall be entitled to attend the annual shareholders' meeting, the highest meeting of the company, but may, if he does not wish to attend, exercise his right to vote by entrusting an agent.

(2) Shareholders who hold common stock are entitled to dividends, but only after the company has paid the debt and dividends of the preferred share. The amount of common stock dividends depends largely on a company's net profit, which means it is not fixed. When a company is well managed and its profits are increasing, common shares can get more dividends than preferred shares, and the dividend rate can even exceed 50%. However, in the years when the company is not well managed, it may not even get a penny, or even lose its capital.

(3) When a company is liquidated due to bankruptcy or dissolution, common shareholders have the right to share the remaining assets of the company. But the company must repay its creditors and preferred shareholders before it can distribute its surplus assets to common shareholders. Common shareholders cannot benefit financially from the bankruptcy or dissolution of a company without the residual property distributed to creditors and preferred shareholders. Thus, common shareholders and their company share weal and woe. Common shareholders are the main beneficiaries when the company is profitable, and they are the main losers when it is losing money.

(4) Common shareholders generally have preferred warrants. In other words, when a company issues new common shares, existing shareholders have the priority to buy new shares, in order to maintain the original shareholding ratio of the enterprise unchanged, thus maintaining their rights and interests in the company. For example, if a company has 10,000 common shares, and Jennifer owns 100 shares or1%, suppose the company decides to issue 10% more common shares, then Jennifer has the right to buy 1% or 10 shares so as to keep her shareholding ratio unchanged.

3. Category of Common Share

Incorporated company can issue different types of common stock in accordance with relevant regulations for the purpose of raising funds and the needs of investors.

(1) Registered Shares VS Unregistered Shares

According to whether the shares are registered or not, they can be divided into registered shares and unregistered shares.

A registered share is a stock that bears the name of a shareholder on the face of a stock. No one other than a registered shareholder may exercise his shares, and there are strict legal procedures for the transfer of shares, which all require the transfer of shares.

An unregistered share is a stock that does not bear a shareholder's name. The holder of such shares, that is, the owner of the shares, is qualified as a shareholder, and the transfer of shares is relatively free and convenient without having to go through the transfer formalities.

(2) Par Value Stock VS Non-par Value Stock

According to whether the amount of the stock is marked or not, it can be divided into par value stock and non-par value stock.

A par stock is a stock marked with a certain amount of money. The rights and obligations of shareholders holding such stocks to the company depend on the proportion of the par value of the stocks they hold to the total par value of the stocks issued by the company.

Shares of non-par value are those subscribed for only in proportion to the total share capital or number of shares of the company, rather than in the amount specified at par. The value of a stock without par value varies with the increase or decrease of the company's property, and the rights and obligations of shareholders to the company are directly determined by the proportion of the stock.

(3) State Share VS Legal Person Share VS Individual Share

According to investors, it can be divided into state-owned share, legal person share, and individual share.

State-owned shares are shares formed by departments or institutions that have the right to invest in companies on behalf of the state.

Corporate stock is a share formed by an enterprise legal person investing in a company with its lawfully available property or investing in a legal person institution or social organization operated by a company with assets permitted by the state.

Individual shares are formed by social individuals or employees who invest their legal property in the company.

11.1.2 Preferred Share

Preferred stock, also known as preferred stock, is a type of stock that gives shareholders more rights than common shareholders.

1. Preferred share generally has four major characteristics

(1) Preference as to dividends at a stated rate or amount.

Since the interest rate of preferred shares is fixed, it means that the dividend of preferred shares will not increase or decrease according to the operating conditions of the company, and generally cannot participate in the dividend distribution of the company. But preferred stock can get dividend before common stock. For a company, preferred shares do not affect the distribution of profits because dividends are fixed.

(2) The owner of preferred stock has priority over the assets in the liquidation of the company.

When a meeting of shareholders is required to discuss claims related to preferred stock, the claims of preferred stock precede the common stock and are next to creditors.

(3) Preferred share can be redeemed at the option of the corporation.

Preferred shares are, in effect, a form of debt financing because of the need to pay a fixed dividend to preferred shareholders. But preferred shares are different from corporate bonds and bank loans. This is because the preferred shareholders' right to share profits and the company's assets can only be exercised if the company meets the demands of creditors.

(4) Absence of voting rights.

Preferred shareholders generally have no right to vote and stand for election, and no right to vote on major business activities of the company. There are strict restrictions on the voting rights of preferred shareholders in financial management. The preferred shareholders have limited voting rights in general shareholders' meetings. However, the right to vote may be enjoyed under certain circumstances. When a meeting is held to discuss matters related to the interests of preferred shareholders, preferred shareholders have the right to vote.

2. Category of Preferred Share

(1) Participating VS Non-participating

Participating preferred stock: When corporate profits increase, in addition to enjoying fixed interest rates, enterprises can also participate in profit distribution with common shares.

Non-participatory preferred stock: Preferred stock no longer participates in the distribution of profits, except for the established dividends.

Generally speaking, participating preferred shares is more beneficial to investors than non-participating preferred shares.

(2) Cumulative VS Non-cumulative

Cumulative preferred stock refers to the preferred shareholder's claim to the undistributed dividends of the previous year when the company's earnings for a particular operating year are insufficient to distribute the dividends.

For non-cumulative preferred shares, although the company is entitled to dividends over common stock, shareholders of preferred stock cannot require the company to pay back the dividend if their current year's earnings are insufficient to pay dividends in the following years.

Generally speaking, cumulative preferred shares have more advantages than non-cumulative preferred shares for investors.

(3) Convertible VS Non-convertible

Convertible preferred shares are shares that allow preferred shareholders to convert preferred shares into a certain amount of common shares under specific conditions. Preferred shares are not more valuable than common shares when a company is doing well because dividend is fixed. To make their stocks more attractive to investors, companies sometimes increase their exchange rates. This means that when somebody buys convertible preferred shares, if the value of common stock rises, he or she can choose to convert them into a certain number of common stocks. To make shares more attractive to investors, companies sometimes raise the exchange rate, which means that when someone buys convertible preferred stock, he or she can choose to convert it into a certain amount of common share if the value of common are rises. This feature is attractive if you want to start with low risk. If a company performs better than expected, it will generate higher returns.

Otherwise, it is non-convertible preferred stock.

Convertible preferred stock is more popular than non-convertible preferred stock.

(4) Redeemable VS Non-redeemable

Redeemable preferred stock refers to the fact that a company that is allowed to issue such stock to recover the preferred stock that has been incurred at the original price plus a certain amount of compensation. Companies usually exercise this right when they think they can replace preferred stock with a lower dividend.

Conversely, it is non-redeemable preferred stock.

11.2 Dividends and Retained Earnings

When a company generates a profit, management has two choices: they can either pay it out to shareholders as a cash dividend or retain the earnings and reinvest them in the business. A portion of the profit being distributed to shareholders in the form of a dividend. The rest is called retained earnings or retained capital.

11.2.1 Dividends

Whenever a company generates surplus income, a portion of the long-term shareholders may expect some regular income in the form of dividends as a reward for putting their money into the company. Investors looking for short-term gains may also prefer dividends that provide immediate gains. Dividends are preferred as many jurisdictions allow dividends as tax-free income, while gains on shares are subject to taxes.

A dividend is a distribution of cash or capital share by a company to its shareholders. The term dividend, without any qualifier, usually is understood as cash dividend. Dividends must be approved by the company's board of directors before they can be paid. The following examples illustrate the declaration and payment of cash dividends.

On March 1, 2011, the board of directors of Company A declared an annual cash dividend of $1 per common share of record (100,000 outstanding shares) as of the closure of business on March 5, payable on March 28.

This announcement includes three important dates: the date of declaration (March 1), the date of record (March 5), the date of payment (March 28). During the period of time between the record date and the payment date, the share price is usually quoted as selling ex-dividends. This means that new investors (those who bought after March 5) will not receive dividends because the equity registration date has passed.

At the date of declaration, the following entries should be recorded:

    Dr. Retained Earnings   100,000
        Cr. Dividend Payable   100,000

At the date of payment, the following entries should be recorded:

    Dr. Dividend Payable   100,000
        Cr. Bank Deposits   100,000

A distribution of shares to shareholders is called a share dividend or scrip dividend. Normally, this is allocated to common shareholders. A stock dividend does not change a company's assets, liabilities, or owners' equity, nor does it change the proportion of equity held by shareholders.

Dividends are sometimes divided into interim and final dividends. An interim dividend is paid at the middle of the financial year, whereas a final dividend is paid at a time at the end of the financial year declared by the directors. In most companies, the eventual payment of the final dividends is subject to the approval of the annual general meeting. As for the year-end dividend, there is some debate about when companies should recognize liabilities, especially if the payout is subject to shareholders' approval. Some argue that, pending approval, there are only contingent liabilities and that the company has no current obligation to pay dividends. Others argue that at the end of the year, constructive obligations already exist, and by convention companies are required to recognize liabilities at the end of the reporting period.

In this regard, *IAS 10 Events after the Reporting Period* clearly states:

If an entity declares dividends to holders of equity instruments (as defined in *IAS 32 Financial Instruments: Presentation*) after the reporting period, the entity shall not recognize those dividends as a liability at the end of the reporting period. If dividends are declared after the reporting period but before the financial statements are authorized for issue, the dividends are not recognized as a liability at the end of the reporting period because no obligation exists at that time. Such dividends are disclosed in the notes in accordance with *IAS 1 Presentation of Financial Statements*.

If the dividends are not declared at the end of the reporting period, no liability is recognized at the end of the reporting period. Where shareholder approval is required for a dividend to be declared before the end of the reporting period, liabilities shall be recognized only when the dividend is approved at the annual general meeting, as there is no current debt prior to that date. Until that occurs, declared dividend is only a contingent liability.

11.2.2 Retained Earnings

Retained earnings are the net income remaining after a company pays dividends to its shareholders. A business generates earnings that can be positive (profits) or negative (losses).

Company management may believe that they can put money to better use if it is retained within the company. Similarly, there may be some shareholders who believe in management's potential and are willing to let them retain earnings in the hope of higher returns (even if there are taxes). The decision to retain or distribute earnings among shareholders is usually left to the company's management. A growth-focused company may not pay dividends at all or pay very small amounts, as it may prefer to use the retained earnings for more financing activities.

When evaluating a company's fundamentals, investors need to look at how much money the company is holding back from shareholders. Just as generating profits for shareholders should be the primary goal of a company, investors tend to focus most on reported profits. Profits are surely important, but so is what the company does with the money. Investors should look closely at how a company puts retained earnings and generate returns from them.

11.3 Treasury Stock

A company may reduce the number of shares it issues by buying back its own shares. A key feature of such rules on company shares buy-backs is protection for creditors, as companies are reducing their equity by using cash that could have been used to repay creditors. A company may undertake a share buy-back to:
— Increase earnings-per-share (EPS).
— Manage the capital structure by reducing equity.
— Most efficiently return surplus funds held by the company to shareholders, rather than pay a dividend or reinvest in other ventures.

Repurchased shares are also known as treasury shares. *IAS 32 Financial Instruments: Presentation* requires that the amount spent on buying back treasury shares to be deducted from equity. The standard, however, does not specify which element of equity should be reduced.

Take CFD Inc., which has issued 500,000 shares at $1 par value each over a period of years as an example. Further assume the total equity of CFD Inc. consists of:

Equity	Amount ($)
Share Capital	500,000
Share Premium	270,000
Retained Earnings	230,000
Total Amount of Equity	1,000,000

If CFD Inc. now buys back 50,000 shares for $2.2 per share, the amount of treasury shares is $110,000 (50000 shares $\times$ $2.2 per share), This is recorded as follows:

  Dr. Treasury Shares   110,000
    Cr. Bank Deposits   110,000

The equity section after CFD Inc. bought back its shares should be as follow:

Equity	Amount ($)
Share Capital	500,000
Share Premium	270,000
Retained Earnings	230,000
Treasury Shares	(110,000)
Total Amount of Equity	890,000

Note that the treasury shares account is a contra-equity account, as it appears in equity, but with a negative sign.

There are different laws and regulations in different countries and regions on whether to allow companies to buy back their shares or not. In the United States, in principle, companies are allowed to buy back stocks, and the rules on share repurchase are relatively relaxed. However, there are differences in state corporate law in many states of the United States. In Germany, except in exceptional cases, companies are prohibited by law from buying or selling shares in companies. Under German law, companies are allowed to acquire shares of the company with a capital of less than 10% under certain circumstances. The specific circumstances include: (1) avoiding major losses; (2) providing for employees; (3) canceling stocks based on capital reduction resolutions; (4) inheriting stocks. There are legal barriers to share repurchase and holding of listed companies in China. The *Securities Law of the People's Republic of China* does not provide the disposition of shares repurchase and after repurchasing. Article of *the Provisional Regulations on the Administration of Stock Issuance and Transaction* stipulates that "Incorporated company may not repurchase its issued shares without approval in accordance with the relevant provisions of the State." The *Guidelines for the Articles of Association of Listed Companies* stipulate that a company shall cancel its treasury stock within a certain period of time. Therefore, there is no institutional space for treasury stocks in China.

After the repurchase, treasury shares may be (1) kept by the company, (2) reissued and (3) canceled. The accounting for these different possibilities is described as follows.

(1) Treasury shares are kept by the company

As long as the treasury shares are kept by the company (CFD Inc.), the equity reports a deduction of $110,000, as illustrated above. Treasury shares are not considered to be issued for voting rights, dividends, or other rights in conjunction with common shares.

(2) Treasury shares are reissued

Companies may reuse treasury shares to satisfy demand for options that have been exercised (e.g., in employee share option schemes) or resell them in the open market or to other investors. Since the proceeds on such resell may differ from the original cost of the treasury shares, a gain or a loss may arise. However, *IAS 32 Financial Instruments: Presentation* stipulates that recognition of such gains or losses in the income statement is not allowed. Instead, it should be recognized directly in reserves.

Assume CFD Inc. resells on the open market 10,000 treasury shares at $3 each. This generates a gain of $0.8 per share, or a total gain of $8,000. A typical entry to record this would be:

Dr. Bank Deposits	30,000	
Cr. Treasury Shares		22,000
Share Premium		8,000

If, on the other hand, CFD Inc. resells 10,000 treasury shares at $1.4 a share on the open market, a loss of $8,000 is generated. This will be recorded as follows:

Dr. Bank Deposits	14,000	
Share Premium	8,000	
Cr. Treasury Shares		22,000

Similarly, on occasions where the debit to the share premium account exceeds its opening balance, the difference may be debited to retained earnings, or to any other reserve account permitted by the relevant national regulations.

(3) Treasury shares are canceled

From an economic perspective, the write-off of repurchased shares amounts to a redistribution of wealth for owners. On this basis, retained earnings should be reduced appropriately when treasury shares are canceled. However, depending on the legal jurisdiction, other distributable reserves can be used. In addition, the original share capital should be canceled. Assume that prior to the purchase of the 10,000 treasury shares, CFD Inc. also had an asset revaluation surplus reserve of $20,000 that can be used for this purpose. The cancellation of 50,000 shares is therefore recorded as:

Dr. Share Capital	50,000	
Share Premium	27,000	
Revaluation Surplus	20,000	
Retained Earnings	13,000	
Cr. Treasury Shares		110,000

Corporate law in some countries requires the maintenance of capital as a means of protecting creditors (as is the case in the UK, for example), implying that a new non-distributable reserve in equity is also established at the amount of canceled share capital. Employing the previous example, this can be recorded as follows:

Dr. Share Capital	50,000	
Share Premium	27,000	
Revaluation Surplus	20,000	

                    Retained Earnings   63,000
                Cr. Treasury Shares   110,000

Creditors' protection is obtained through the larger debit to retained earnings, implying that CFD Inc.'s ability to further pay cash dividends in the future is reduced (by an additional $50,000).

Key Words and Expressions

sole proprietorship	独资企业
partnership	合伙企业
corporation	公司
individual business	个体工商户
enterprise legal person	企业法人
natural persons	自然人
corporate income tax	企业所得税
ordinary partnership	普通合伙企业
limited partnership	有限合伙企业
general partners	普通合伙人
limited liability company	有限责任公司
joint stock company limited	股份有限公司
share capital	股本
other reserves	其他综合收益
retained earnings	留存收益
financial instruments	金融工具
financial market	金融市场
dividend distribution	股利分配
owner's equity	所有者权益
paid-in capital	实收资本
common share	普通股
Shanghai Stock Exchange (SSE)	上海证券交易所
Shenzhen Stock Exchange (SZSE)	深圳证券交易所
listed corporations	上市公司
capital reserve	资本公积
cash basis	收付实现制
fair market value	市场公允价值
the board of directors	董事会
annual general meeting	年度股东大会
major issues	重大事项
liquidate	清算
shareholders' meeting	股东大会

net profit	净利润
bankruptcy	破产
dissolution	解散
incorporated company	股份有限公司
registered shares	记名股
unregistered shares	不记名股
sponsors	发起人
par value stock	面值股
non-par value stock	无面值股
preferred share	优先股
dividends	股利
creditor	债权人
corporate bonds	公司债券
bank loans	银行贷款
participating preferred stock	参与优先股
non-participatory preferred stock	非参与优先股
accumulated preferred stock	累积优先股
non-cumulative preferred shares	非累积优先股
convertible preferred shares	可转换优先股
non-convertible preferred stock	不可转换优先股
redeemable preferred stock	可赎回优先股
irredeemable preferred stock	不可赎回优先股
cash dividend	现金股利
the date of declaration	股利宣告日
the date of record	股权登记日
the date of payment	付息日
share dividend	股票股利
treasury stock	库存股
surplus reserve	盈余公积
earnings -per-share (eps)	每股收益
share premium	股本溢价
revaluation surplus	重估盈余
capital redemption reserve	偿还资本准备金

Exercises

Please select the best answer for the following questions or uncompleted sentences.

1. Preferred share may have priority over common share except in (   ).
   A. voting

B. conversion

C. dividends

D. liquidate assets

2."Earnings" is another name for net profit. If earnings haven't been distributed as dividends, it should have been retained in the company. The name of this portion of number listed in the balance sheet is ( ).

A. paid-in capital

B. retained earnings

C. dividend

D. cash

3. Retained earnings ( ).

A. represent an amount of cash available to pay shareholders

B. can only be appropriated by setting aside a cash fund

C. generally consists of a company's cumulative net income less any net losses and dividends declared since its inception

D. are never adjusted for anything other than net income or dividends

4. Each of the following is the characteristic of the common share except ( ).

A. voting rights in the election of the board of directors

B. after issuance, the market value of the share is unrelated to its par value

C. shares can be transferred from one investor to another without disrupting the community of business operations

D. a cumulative right to receive dividends

5. Companies often buy back their own stocks ( ).

A. to have shares available for a merger or acquisition

B. to maintain market value for the company stock

C. to avoid a hostile takeover

D. all above

第11章 所有者权益

企业一般有三种合法的组织形式：独资企业、合伙企业和公司制企业。
- 独资企业

个人独资企业又称个体工商户或个人独资企业，是自然人所有并经营的企业法人。在个人独资企业中，所有者与企业之间没有法律上的区别，个人和企业是一体的。个人独资企业的所有人直接掌管整个组织，对企业的债务、贷款和损失承担无限的法律责任。

个人独资企业的优点是设立容易，不需要缴纳企业所得税。同时它也有显著的缺点：企业所有者对其所有的损失和债务承担无限责任，这种风险是极高的。独资企业的存续受到其所有者的寿命的影响，而且筹资规模有限。

- 合伙企业

合伙企业是指两个或两个以上的合伙人根据合伙协议的条款汇集资金、技能和其他资源，并分享利润和亏损的一种商业组织形式。合伙企业又被分为普通合伙企业和有限合伙企业。

合伙企业的优势主要包括以下几点。首先，与独资企业相比，合伙企业的融资能力更强。第二，与法人企业相比，合伙企业中至少有一方承担无限责任，债权人的利益受到更多的保护。从理论上讲，在无限责任的压力下，企业的声誉可以得到更多的提升。第三，合伙企业只缴纳个人所得税，不缴纳企业所得税。合伙企业的一个主要缺点是无限责任，普通合伙人负有无限责任。合伙企业所承担的所有债务使得合伙企业在大多数情况下风险较大。而且合伙企业的存续受合伙人的寿命的影响，合伙企业可能会因为合伙人的退出或死亡而注销。

- 公司制企业

公司制企业是指依法由法定人数以上的投资者(或股东)出资设立、独立经营、自负盈亏、具有法人资格的经济组织。目前，我国公司有两种形式：有限责任公司和股份有限公司。

由于公司制为股东提供有限责任保护，公司已成为许多国家普遍采用的组织形式。这些公司的经营是由股权和债务混合出资的。本章的重点是公司的权益出资。公司权益资本的来源主要包括所有者投入的资本、其他综合收益、留存收益等。金融市场中发展的各种金融工具为投资者提供了一系列有风险回报的替代品，进而会对公司股本造成影响。每一种股票期权都有其自身的会计含义。储备的存在是由传统会计方法和现行会计准则的局限性所决定的。一般而言，公司财富的增加更多来自股权投入而不是当期收入。尽管所有者权益的各个组成部分之间有明显区别，但重要的是要认识到它们属于所有者权益，其区别包括对股息分配的管辖权不同，对税收的影响不同和对所有者权利的限制。《国际会计准则第1号——财务报表的列报》要求对所有者权益的每个组成部分进行详细披露。

根据《国际会计准则——概念框架》，所有者权益(也被称为"股东权益")被定义为："企业资产扣除负债后，由所有者享有的剩余权益"。所有者权益的定义清楚地表明，所有者权益不能脱离资产负债表中的其他因素。所有者权益的特征是：所有者权益是公司的一种剩余，它是账面价值的剩余金额，代表公司所有者实体的价值。用公式表示即：

$$所有者权益 = 资产 - 负债$$

所有者权益通常通过两种方式增加。一种是投资者以出资换取股本，称为实收资本；另一种是公司长期留存的利润,称为留存收益。如果企业出现亏损或所有者撤资等情况,会导致公司所有者权益减少。

在编制一般性财务报表时,所有者权益受到资产和负债计量方法以及资本和资本保全概念的影响,所有者权益是反映企业财务状况的要素之一。

11.1 股票

股票是股份公司发行的所有权凭证,股票又称股票股本。股份公司的经济基础是股东认购的金额或财产。股票发行时附有特定权利。不同类型的股票有不同的权利,通过他们的名字可以加以区分。股票一般可分为普通股和优先股。

11.1.1 普通股

1. 普通股概述

普通股是具有普通权利、承担普通义务的股份,是公司股份的最基本形式。普通股的股东对公司的管理、收益享有平等权利,根据公司经营效益分红,风险较大。普通股是公司资本的基础,是股份的基本形式,也是流通量最大且最重要的股份。目前,在上海证券交易所和深圳证券交易所交易的股票都是普通股。

股票通常不是以票面价值发行的,发行股票的价格与股票的票面价值没有必然的关系。如果一家公司以高于票面价值的价格发行股票,则该股票被称为溢价发行。如果公司以低于面值的价格发行有面值的股票,则该股票被称为折价发行。

在中国,所有上市公司的股票面值都是每股 1 元人民币,且不允许折价发行。出售股票的价格取决于公司历史收益水平、历史股利分配情况、宏观经济状况等多种因素。股票溢价发行时,现金或其他资产账户根据收到的金额增加。超过票面金额的部分也同样构成公司股东出资总额,这个数额通常记在一个叫做"资本公积"的账户里。在大多数情况下,发行股票适用于收付实现制记录。

HYX 股份有限公司发行 100,000 股普通股,每股票面面值为 1 元人民币,每股发行价格为 1.5 元人民币。记录该项经济业务的会计分录如下所示:

借:银行存款　　　　　　　　　　　　　　　　150,000
　　贷:股本——普通股　　　　　　　　　　　　　　　　100,000
　　　　资本公积——股本溢价　　　　　　　　　　　　　　50,000

当股票以现金以外的资产(如设备、建筑物、土地等)发行时,所取得的资产应按其市场公允价值记账。如果不能客观确定资产的市场公允价值,可以使用发行的股票的市场公允价值记账。

普通股股东在股利分配上没有决定权。是否分派股利息取决于董事会的决定。一些国家的法律法规可能会规定支付股息应记录在哪个权益类账户中,或者公司在支付股息前是否必须通过偿付能力测试。在某些情况下,董事可以在年底提出分配股利的建议,但决定权仍归属于年度股东大会。

2. 普通股股东的权利

普通股股东有如下权利:①对重大事项进行表决;②领取董事会宣布的股息;③公司清算时分派现金或其他资产的分配;④公司增发新股时,按照持股比例优先购买增资股份的权利。

(1) 一般而言，普通股股东有发言权和表决权，即对公司重大问题的发言权和表决权。普通股股东的表决权是一股一票。任何普通股股东都有资格参加公司的最高会议，即年度股东大会，如果普通股股东不能参加，也可以委托代理人代理他行使其表决权。

(2) 持有普通股的股东有权领取股息，但公司只有在偿还了债务和支付了优先股股利之后才能够给普通股股东分配股息。普通股的股利数额很大程度上取决于公司的净利润，这意味着它不是固定的。当公司经营良好，利润增加时，普通股可获得比优先股更多的股息，有时股息率甚至可以超过50%。但是，在公司管理不善的时期，普通股股东可能分不到分文，甚至还可能损失其投入的资本。

(3) 公司因破产、解散而清算时，普通股股东有权分享公司的剩余资产。但是，企业在将剩余财产分配给普通股股东之前，必须先偿还债权人和优先股股东的权利。如果在分配给债权人和优先股股东后没有剩余财产，普通股股东就不能从公司破产或解散中获得经济利益。由此可见，普通股股东与公司是血脉相连的。公司盈利时，普通股股东是主要受益者，公司亏损时，他们又是主要的亏损承担者。

(4) 普通股东一般都有优先认购权证。也就是说，当公司发行新的普通股时，现有股东有优先购买新股的权利，以维持其在企业原有的所有权比例不变，从而维护公司的权益。例如，如果一家公司共有10,000股普通股，而詹妮弗拥有100股，占股1%。公司决定再发行10%的普通股，即1,000股，那么詹妮弗有权购买1%即10股，以保持她的股份比例不变。

3. 普通股的种类

股份有限公司出于募集资金和投资者的需要可以根据相关规定发行不同类型的普通股。

(1) 记名股 VS 不记名股

根据股份是否登记，可分为记名股票和不记名股票。

记名股票是指股票票面上记载有股东姓名或名称的股票。除股票上所记载的股东外，其他人不得行使其股份对应的权利，且记名股票有严格的法定程序和股份转让程序，转让后还需办理过户手续。

无记名股票是指不记载股东姓名或名称的股票。持票人即股份所有人，具有股东资格，股份转让相对自由、方便，无须办理转让手续。

(2) 面值股票 VS 无面值股票

按照股票上是否标明确定的金额，可分为面值股票和无面值股票。

面值股票是在股票票面上标有一定金额的股票。持有这种股票的股东，对公司享有的权利和承担的义务大小，依其所持有的股票票面金额占公司发行在外股票总面值的比例而定。

无面值股票是指不在票面上标明金额，而只表明所占公司股本总额比例或股份数的股票。无面值股票的价值随公司财产的增减而变化，股东对公司的权利和义务的多少直接由股票票面标明的比例决定。

(3) 国有股票 VS 法人股票 VS 个人股票

根据投资者的不同，可分为国有股、法人股、个人股等。

国有股票是指有权代表国家投资的部门或机构所形成的股份。

法人股票是企业法人依法以其可支配的财产向公司投资，或者具有法人资格的机构、社会组织以国家允许经营的资产向公司投资形成的股份。

个人股份是由社会个人或者职工将其合法财产投资于公司而形成的。

11.1.2 优先股

优先股是指其股东相比于普通股股东享有一定优先权的股票。

1. 优先股通常具有以下四个主要特征

(1) 优先股按照规定的比例或者数额优先分配股利。

由于优先股的股息率是预先固定的,优先股的股利不会根据公司的经营状况而增减,一般不能参与公司的股利分配,但优先股可以在普通股前获得股利。对于一个公司来说,因为股利是固定的,所以不影响公司的利润分配。

(2) 优先股股东在公司清算时享有公司财产分配上的优先权。

如果公司股东大会需要讨论与优先股有关的债权,那么优先股的受偿权就优先于普通股,但是次于公司的债权人。

(3) 可由公司选择赎回。

公司需要向优先股股东支付固定股息,优先股实际上是一种举债形式。但是优先股不同于公司债券和银行贷款,这是因为优先股股东分享利润和公司资产的权利只能在公司满足债权人要求之后才能实现。

(4) 无表决权。

优先股股东一般没有选举权和被选举权,对公司的主要经营活动没有表决权。在财务管理中优先股股东的投票权受到严格限制。优先股股东在股东大会上的表决权有限。然而,在某些情况下,优先股股东可以享有表决权。当召开会议讨论与优先股股东利益相关的事项时,优先股股东享有表决权。

2. 优先股的种类

(1) 参与性 VS 非参与性

参与优先股:当企业利润增加时,除了享受固定利率外,还可以参与普通股的利润分配。

非参与优先股:指除已约定的股息外,不再参与利润分配的优先股。

一般而言,对于投资者来说,参与优先股比不参与优先股更有吸引力。

(2) 可累积 VS 不可累积

累积优先股是指在某一营业年度内,如果公司所获的盈利不足以分派规定的股利,日后优先股的股东对往年未给付的股息,有权要求如数补给。

对于非累积的优先股,虽然对于公司当年所获得的利润有优先于普通股获得分派股息的权利,但如该年公司所获得的盈利不足以按规定的股利分配时,非累积优先股的股东不能要求公司在以后年度中予以补发。

一般来讲,对投资者来说,累积优先股比非累积优先股具有更大的优越性。

(3) 可转换 VS 不可转换

可转换优先股是允许优先股股东在特定条件下将优先股转换为一定数额的普通股的股份。由于股息是固定的,当公司表现良好时,优先股的价值不会高于普通股的价值。为了使他们的股票对投资者更有吸引力,公司有时会增加一个转换比率。这意味着当某人购买可转换优先股时,如果普通股的价值上升,他/她可以选择把它们转换成一定数量的普通股。对于风险厌恶型投资者,这个功能是很有吸引力的。如果公司的表现好于预期,它将产生更高的回报。

不可转化优先股是指不能转换成普通股的优先股。

在实际生活中，可转换优先股比不可转换优先股更受投资者的青睐。

(4) 可赎回 VS 不可赎回

可赎回优先股是指允许发行该类股票的公司，按原来的价格再加上若干补偿金将已发生的优先股收回。当该公司认为能够以较低股利的股票来代替已发生的优先股时，就往往行使这种权利。

反之，就是不可赎回的优先股。

11.2 股利和留存收益

当一家公司产生利润时，管理层有两种选择：要么将其作为现金股利支付给股东，要么保留收益并将其再投资于企业。一部分利润以股息的形式分配给股东。剩下的被称为留存收益或留存资本。

11.2.1 股利

每当一家公司产生盈余收入时，一部分长期股东可能会希望以股息的形式获得一定的固定收益，作为他们将自有资金投入公司的奖励。为短期投资而持有的交易者可能也更希望获取即时收益，即希望公司支付股利。因为许多国家和地区允许股息作为免税收入，而买卖股票的收益则需要纳税。所以对投资者而言，股利也是优先考虑的。

股利是公司向股东分配现金或股本的行为。股利这一术语，在没有加任何限定词的时候，通常被理解为现金股利。股利必须经公司董事会批准后才能支付。以下将说明现金股利的形成和支付的整个过程。

20×1年3月1日，A公司董事会宣布上年的股利分配方案为每股派发1人民币的现金股利(公司共有股票100,000股)，股权登记日为3月5日，股息将于3月28日支付。

本公告包括三个重要日期：宣告日(20×1年3月1日)、股权登记日期(20×1年3月5日)、股息支付日期(20×1年3月28日)。在股权登记日和股息支付日之间，股票的价格是排除在股息之外的。这意味着，由于股权登记日已过，新投资者(20×1年3月5日以后购买的投资者)将不会收到股息。

在宣告日(2011年3月1日)，A公司应记载如下分录：

  借：留存收益   100,000
    贷：应付股利   100,000

在股息支付日(20×1年3月28日)，应记录以下分录：

  借：应付股利   100,000
    贷：银行存款   100,000

向股东分配股份称为股票股利。通常，这种是分配给普通股股东的。股票股利不会改变公司的资产、负债或所有者权益。同样，它也不会改变股东的权益比例。

股息按照发放的时间也可被分为中期股息和年末股息。中期股息是在财务年度中期支付的，而年末股息是由董事在财务年终宣布于财务年度期末的某一时间支付。在大部分公司中，年末股息的最终支付须经股东大会批准。对于年末股息，人们对公司何时应确认负债存在一些争论，特别是在股息支付须经股东批准的情况下。有的人认为，在获得批准之前，只存在或有负债，公司没有支付股息的现时义务。也有人认为在年终时，推定义务已经存在，根据惯例，公司在报告期末需要确认负债。

鉴于此，《国际会计准则第10号——报告期后的事件》明确：如果在报告期结束后，公司才宣布向权益工具持有人(权益工具持有人定义参见《国际会计准则第32号——金融工具》)支付股利，则在报告期末，公司不应将这些股利确认为负债。如果股息宣告处在报告期之后，财务报表被授权发表之前，股息在报告期结束时不被认作是负债，因为义务尚未产生。按照《国际会计准则第 1 号——财务报表的编制》需在当期财务报表附注中披露该事项。

如果股息在报告期末未宣告，则在报告期末不可确认负债。只有在股东大会批准股息后才能确认负债，因为在该日期之前，该公司不具有现时义务。在股东大会批准之前，宣布的股息只是或有负债。

11.2.2 留存收益

留存收益是指企业在向股东支付股息后留存的净收益额。企业产生的收益可以是正的(利润)，也可以是负的(亏损)。

一般而言，公司管理层认为如果盈余保留在公司内部，他们可以更好地利用这笔资金。同样，部分相信管理层能力的股东，可能更愿意将收益留在公司，希望能获得更高的回报(即使这部分收益需要被征税)。保留收益或在股东中分配收益的决定通常取决于公司的管理层。一个以增长为中心的公司可能根本不支付股利或支付非常少的金额，因为它可能更愿意使用留存收益来为扩张活动融资。

当评估一家公司的基本面时，投资者需要看股东持有多少资本。为股东谋利应该是公司的主要目标，同样，投资者往往最关注财务报告中的利润。利润固然重要，但公司用这笔钱做什么同样重要。投资者应该密切关注公司如何运用留存收益并使其产生回报。

11.3 库存股

公司可以通过回购自己的股票来减少发行在外的股票数量。因为公司回购股份可能会削弱其偿债能力，所以有关公司回购自身股票的法律法规的一个主要特点是保护债权人的利益。公司可进行股票回购的情况包括：

— 增加每股收益。
— 通过减持股权来调整资本结构。
— 最有效的将公司持有的盈余资金返还给股东的方式，某些时候比分派股息或再投资于其他企业更受投资者青睐。

被公司回购的股份称为库存股。《国际会计准则第 32 号——金融工具》规定：公司回购股票所花费的金额是从股本中扣除的。然而，该标准并未规定应减少哪项权益。

以 CFD 公司为例，该公司在过去几年里以每股面值 1 美元的价格发行了 50 万股股票。CFD 公司的所有者权益如下表所示：

所有者权益	金额 ($)
股本	500,000
股票溢价	270,000
留存收益	230,000
所有者权益总额	1,000,000

如果 CFD 公司现在以每股 2.2 美元的价格回购 50,000 股，则库存股的金额为 110,000 美元(50,000 股×2.2 美元/每股)。回购股份的会计分录如下：

借：库存股　　　　　　　　　　　　　　　　　110,000
　　贷：银行存款　　　　　　　　　　　　　　　　　　　110,000

CFD 公司回购其股票后的所有者权益如下表所示：

所有者权益	金额（$）
股本	500,000
股票溢价	270,000
留存收益	230,000
库存股	(110,000)
所有者权益总额	890,000

值得注意的是，库存股账户虽然是属于使用者权益类的账户，但其结构与一般所有者权益类账户的结构刚好相反，库存股是贷方登记减少，借方登记增加。正如其在权益表中所显示的那样，有一个负号表示库存股的增加。

对于是否允许公司回购股票，不同国家和地区有不同的法律法规。在美国，对股票回购的规定相对宽松，原则上允许公司回购股票。然而，美国各州的州公司法条文之间存在差异。在德国，除特殊情况外，法律原则上禁止企业回购本公司股份。根据德国法律，在某些情况下，公司可以回购低于公司原股份 10%的股份。具体情况包括：(1)避免重大损失；(2)向职工提供时；(3)基于减资决议注销股票时；(4)继承股票等。我国上市公司股份回购和持有股票存在法律障碍。《中华人民共和国公司法》不允许上市公司库存股份。《中华人民共和国证券法》没有就股份回购及回购后的处理方法作出规定。《股票发行与交易管理暂行条例》规定："未依照国家有关规定的批准，股份有限公司不得购回其发行在外的股票"。《上市公司章程指引》规定公司购回该公司股票必须在一定时间内注销该部分股份。据此而言，库存股并不存在制度上的生存空间。

回购后，库存股可(1)由公司保管；(2)重新发行；(3)注销。对这些不同可能性的会计处理如下所述。

(1) 公司保管

如果库存股被保留在公司中，则上文所述的 CFD 公司的股权报告中的所有者权益总额需要扣除 110,000 美元的库存股价值。和普通股不同，库存股股票既不分配股利，也不具有投票权。

(2) 重新发行

公司可以用库存股，以满足对已行使的期权(例如员工持股计划)的需求，或将其转售给公开市场或其他投资者。由于转售的收入可能与库存股的原始成本不同，因此可能会产生收益或亏损。《国际会计准则第 32 号——金融工具》规定：重新发行库存股的收益或亏损不允许直接在利润表中予以确认，而应在储备中确认。

假设 CFD 公司在公开市场转售 10,000 股库存股，每股售价为 3 美元，那么每股将产生 0.8 美元的收益，总计 8,000 美元。记录这一经济业务的会计分录如下所示：

借：银行存款　　　　　　　　　　　　　　　　　30,000
　　贷：库存股　　　　　　　　　　　　　　　　　　　22,000
　　　　股票溢价　　　　　　　　　　　　　　　　　　8,000

另一方面，如果 CFD 公司在公开市场上以每股 1.4 美元的价格出售 10,000 股库存股，就会损失 8,000 美元。记录这一经济业务的会计分录如下所示：

借：银行存款　　　　　　　　　　　　　　　　　14,000
　　股票溢价　　　　　　　　　　　　　　　　　　8,000
　　贷：库存股　　　　　　　　　　　　　　　　　　　22,000

在股票溢价账户借记超过其开立余额的情况下，差额可借记留存收益，或由相关国家规定准许的任何其他储备账户。

(3) 注销库存股

回购后注销库存股从经济角度等同于将财富再分配给所有者。根据这一观点，当库存股被注销时，应适当减少留存收益。但是，也可以使用其他可分配的准备金。此外，应冲销原股本。假设在购买10,000股库存股前，CFD公司还拥有可用于此目的的资产重估盈余准备金20,000美元。注销50,000股库存股的会计分录如下：

借：股本	50,000	
股本溢价	27,000	
重估盈余	20,000	
留存收益	13,000	
贷：库存股		110,000

一些国家的公司法为保护债权人的利益，要求公司在处理库存股时需要保持公司资本在一定水平(例如，在英国就是这样)。这意味着，新的不可分配权益准备金也按注销的股本数额设立。延续前面的例子，会计分录如下：

借：股本	50,000	
股本溢价	27,000	
重估盈余	20,000	
留存收益	63,000	
贷：库存股		110,000
偿还资本准备金		50,000

对债权人的保护是通过借记留存收益来反映企业的偿债能力被削弱。在这个例子中CFD公司在未来支付现金股利的能力下降了(公司的偿还准备金减少50,000美元)。

Chapter 12

Revenues

The new accounting standards adopt the principle of "transfer of control rights" instead of "transfer of risks and rewards" as the basic principle of revenue recognition, and use the "five-step method" model to unify the accounting treatment standards for revenues of different enterprises, industries, and sources.

12.1 Accounting for Revenue

An entity will recognize revenue to reflect the transfer of promised goods or services to customers, and its amount should reflect the consideration to which the entity expects to be entitled in exchange for those goods or services.

12.1.1 Definition of Revenue

Revenue refers to the total inflow of economic benefits that are formed in the daily business activities of an enterprise and will increase the owner's equity and have nothing to do with the capital invested by the owner.

Revenue may cause owners' equity to increase in accounting. It may manifest itself as an increase in assets or a decrease in liabilities, or both, i.e., an increase in owner's equity. Revenue only includes the inflow of the company's economic benefits, so it should not include payments collected for third parties or customers.

According to the nature of economic activities undertaken by enterprises, revenue can be mainly divided into income from sales of goods, the provision of services, royalties form property owned by the entity, and construction contracts.

12.1.2 Recognition and Measurement of Revenue

According to *IFRS 15 Revenue from Contracts with Customers*, where a contract between an enterprise and a customer simultaneously satisfies the following conditions, the enterprise shall recognize revenue. This core principle is implemented through a five-step model framework.

Step 1: Identify the Contract with the Customer

- Definition of Contract

A contract exists when an agreement is reached between the two or more parties, creating enforceable rights and obligations between the parties, and such agreement may be implied in writing, orally or in business practice.

The decision on whether a contractual right or obligation is enforceable is made within the relevant legal framework of the jurisdiction. As a result, whether a contract is enforceable will vary between jurisdictions.

In practice, fulfilling obligations may include a commitment that an entity is effectively expected to transfer goods or services to a customer, even if the law does not enforce those commitments.

- The Criteria of the Contract

IFRS 15 Revenue from Contracts with Customers specifies four criteria of contract that must be met before an entity recognizes revenue conditions.

(1) Both parties have completed the contract and promised to fulfill their obligations.
(2) Determine the rights and payment terms of the parties to the good or service to be transferred.
(3) The contract has commercial significance before revenue is recognized.
(4) The entity is likely to charge its due consideration.

Assessing the customer's credit risk is an important factor in determining whether the contract is valid but the customer's credit risk does not affect the measurement or reporting of income. The entity should evaluate the ability and intention to pay the consideration. Based on these criteria, the entity can continuously re-evaluate the contract to determine whether it subsequently meets the criteria.

Step 2: Identify the performance obligations in the contract

At the beginning of a contract, the entity shall evaluate the goods or services promised to the customer and determine that they are obligations to perform.

Goods or services are distinguishable if the customer can benefit from the goods or services by themselves or with other readily available resources; the entity's commitment to transfer the goods or services to the customer is determined separately from other commitments in the contract.

A series of different goods or services are transferred to the customer in the same way. If the entity promises to transfer each unique product or service in the series of products continuously to the customer, it is a long-term obligation; and a metric is used to measure the progress of an entity in fully fulfilling its obligations to transfer to customers each unique product or service in the series.

Step 3: Determine the transaction price

The transaction price is the amount to which the entity expects to be entitled by the transfer of goods and services. This amount does not include amounts received on behalf of third parties.

The transaction price may include variable or contingent consideration. It should be estimated as the expected value or the most likely amount of consideration to be received, whichever better predicts the amount of consideration to which the entity will be entitled. And management should adopt a method that reflects the best estimated amount and should be applied consistently throughout the contract.

When the consideration in a customer contract includes an amount that is variable, an entity is required to evaluate whether the amount of variable consideration included in the transaction price needs to be constrained. The objective of the constraint is to ensure that an entity recognizes revenue only to the extent it is highly probable that there will not be a significant reversal of revenue when associated uncertainties are resolved.

[Example 12-1] D.Z. Co supplies laptop computers to large businesses. On 1 July 2018, D.Z. Co entered into a contract with T Co., under which it was to purchase laptops at $500 per unit. The contract states that if T Co. purchases more than 500 laptops in a year, the price per unit is reduced retrospectively to $450 per unit. D.Z. CO.'s year-end is 30 June

(a) As at 30 September 2018, T Co. had bought 70 laptops from D.Z. Co therefore estimated that T Co.'s purchases would not exceed 500 in the year to 30 June 2019, and T Co. would therefore not be entitled to the volume discount

(b) During the quarter ended 31 December 2018 T Co. expanded rapidly as a result of a substantial acquisition, and purchased an additional 250 laptops from D.Z. Co. T Co. then estimated that T Co.'s purchases would exceed the threshold for the volume discount in the year to 30 June 2019.

Required:

Calculate the revenue D.Z. Co would recognize in

(a) Quarter ended 30 September 2018.

(b) Quarter ended 31 December 2018.

Solution:

(a) Applying the requirements of IFRS to T company's procurement model as of September 30, 2018, D.Z. company should conclude that when the uncertainty is solved, i.e., when the total procurement amount is known, the recognized cumulative revenue ($500 per laptop) is highly unlikely to have a significant reversal.

Therefore, D.Z. company shall recognize the first quarter revenue as of September 30, 2018 as 770 × $500=$35,000.

(b) In the quarter ended December 31, 2018, the procurement mode of T company has changed, so D.Z. company has reason to conclude that T company's procurement will exceed the threshold value of one-year volume discount as of June 30, 2019, so it is appropriate to reduce the price to 450 dollars per laptop computer retrospectively.

Therefore, D.Z. company shall recognize revenue of $109,000 for the quarter ended December 31, 2018. This amount is calculated from $112,500 (250 laptops × $450) less $3,500 (70 laptops × $50 price reduction) after the change in transaction price, which is the price reduction of laptops sold in the quarter ending September 30, 2018.

If the consideration is paid in advance or in arrears, the entity will need to consider whether the contract includes a significant financing arrangement, and if so, adjust the transaction price based on the time value of the currency which to reflect an amount for the selling price as though the customer had paid cash for the goods or services when they were transferred. Not required if the time between the transfer of goods or services and payment is less than one year.

[Example 12-2] D.Z. Co. enters into a contract with a customer to sell an existing printing machine such that control of the machine vests with the customer in two years' time. The contract has two payment options. The customer can pay $240,000 when the contract is signed or $300,000 in two years' time when the customer gains control of the machine. The interest rate implicit in the contract is 11.8% in order to adjust for the risk involved in the delay in payment. However, D.Z. Co.'s incremental borrowing rate is 5%. The customer paid $240,000 on 1 December 2017 when the contract was signed.

Date		Description	P.R.	Debit	Credit
Nov.30	2018	Finance cost (240,000 × 5%)		$12,000	
		Contract Liability			$12,000
Nov.30	2019	Finance cost [(240,000+12,000) × 5%]		$12,600	
		Contract Liability			$12,600
		To record two years finance cost.			

Date		Description	P.R.	Debit	Credit
Nov.30	2019	Contract Liability		$264,600	
		Revenue			$264,600
		To record the machine delivery			

As the consideration was received in advance, the contract contains important financing component because the time interval between the purchase of assets by the client and the transfer of assets to the client by D.Z. Co. is long.

In this case, the contract should be divided into revenue and a loan component, which should be equivalent to the accounting of loans with the same characteristics using the company's incremental borrowing rate.

If an entity's right to receive consideration is conditional on the occurrence or non-occurrence of a certain event, the promised consideration may also change

- Trade Discounts

Trade discounts are discounts based on market supply and demand or for different customers. The actual transaction price after deducting the commercial discount from the commercial quote is the book value of the receivables, so the commercial discount does not affect the measurement of sales revenue.

Trade discounts are one of the most commonly used promotional methods for businesses. In order to expand sales and occupy the market, companies often give commercial discounts to wholesalers, and use a sales strategy with selling more at a lower price.

[Example 12-3]D.Z. Co. offers a 25% trade discount on orders of 1,000 units or more of their popular product. Each popular product has a list price of $7.8.

Quantity sold	1,000
Price per unit	$7.80
Total	7,800
Less: 25% discounts	($1,950)
Invoice price	$5,850

Trade discounts are offered based on quantities purchased. In this example, a trade discount of 25% is offered when a customer orders 1,000 units or more. Trade discounts are not recorded in the accounting records. This transaction would be recorded at the price of $5,850, which reflects the trade discount granted.

- Sales Discounts

A sales discount is a way of offering customers a discount and encouraging them to pay in advance. Its main purpose is to increase the liquidity of corporate funds by reducing the amount of funds used in accounts receivable, and the discount are recorded in a revenue account. The credit period is the normal period for a company to allow customers to extend their accounts receivable, which is generally 30 or 60 days. The discount period is much shorter, typically 10 or 15 days. If payment is received during the discount period, it can be discounted. If payment is due after the discount period expires, payment shall be made in full at or before the end of the credit period.

"2/10, n/30" The first number represents discount percentage, the second number represents the discount period, the letter "n" represents word net, and the last number represents the entire credit period. In this case, if a customer makes payment within 10 days, there will be a 2% discount. If not, the entire payment amount will be due within 30 days.

[Example 12-4] On Nov.6, 2019, D.Z. Co. sold $1,500 of merchandise inventory on account to Frank, credit terms are 2/10, n/30. If Frank pays the account within the discount period, the amount will qualify for the discount of 2% because it is within the ten-day discount period. Frank paid the amount due on the purchase of Nov. 16, 2019.

Date		Description	P.R.	Debit	Credit
Nov.6	2019	Accounts receivable		$1,500	
		Revenue			$1,500
		Sold inventory on account.			
Nov.16	2019	Cash		$1,470	
		Sales discount		$30	
		Accounts receivable			$1,500
		To receive the payment			

- Sales Returns and Allowances

Sales returns and allowances refer to the products returned by the purchaser or the discounts given on the price due to unqualified products, wrong delivery, etc.

According to the direct write-off method, it is recognized when the sales are returned and allowance, regardless of whether it occurred in the current period of sales. The allowance method is commonly used in accounting treatment. According to the allowance method, the amount of sales returns and discounts should be reasonably estimated during the current period of revenue recognition and is included in the account of "Sales Returns and Allowances".

[Example 12-5] On Nov. 8, 2019, Frank returned $200 of defective products to D.Z. Co.

Date		Description	P.R.	Debit	Credit
Nov.8	2019	Sales returns and allowances		$200	
		Accounts receivable			$200
		Returned defective products.			
		Cash		$1,274	
		Sales discount		$26	
		Accounts receivable			$1,300
		To receive the cash			

A $200 allowance requires the same entry. In the sales revenue section of an income statement, the sales returns and allowances account are subtracted from sales because these accounts have the opposite effect on net income. As a result, "Sales Returns and Allowances" is considered a contra-revenue accountant usually have a debit balance.

Sales revenue	$1,500
Returns	($200)
Amount	1,300
Less: 2% sales discounts	($26)
Cash received	$1,274

Step 4: Allocate the transaction price to the performance obligations in the contracts

When a contract has multiple performance obligations, the entity will allocate the transaction price to the performance obligations in the contract with reference to its relatively independent selling price.

Any overall discount, as compared to the sum of the independent sale prices, is based on the distribution of the relatively independent sale prices among the obligations.

If independent selling prices cannot be observed directly, the entity will need to estimate them. The various approaches that may be used, including adjusted market assessment methods, expected cost plus margin method and residual method (allowed only in specific circumstances).

Step 5: Recognize revenue when a performance obligation is satisfied

Revenue is recognized as a transfer of control, which may occur over a period of time or at a point in time. Asset control refers to the ability to use the asset directly and obtain almost all residual income from the asset. This includes the ability to prevent others from directing and using the asset.

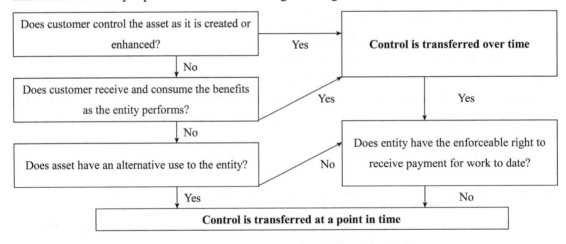

Figure 12-1   Determining the timing of transfer

Indicators of control at a point in time include that the entity has the current right to pay, that the customer has accepted or has legal ownership of the asset, and that the entity has transferred the actual ownership of the asset.

Over time, customers receive and consume the benefits provided by entity performance during entity execution. Revenue is recognized in accordance with the performance progress during this period, except where performance progress cannot be reasonably determined. Meanwhile, the entity will consider the nature of the commodity, and use the output or input methods to determine the appropriate performance progress. For similar performance obligations under similar circumstances, enterprises should adopt the same method to determine performance progress. If the performance progress cannot be reasonably determined and the costs incurred by the enterprise are expected to be compensated, the revenue shall be recognized at the cost amount until the performance progress can be reasonably determined.

12.1.3 Accounting for special transactions

1. Principal and Agent

The entity must establish its identity as principal or agent in any transaction.

It is a principal if it controls the promised goods or services and then transfers them to the customer. When the performance is realized, the entity recognizes revenue based on the gross consideration to which it is expected to be entitled.

If its obligation is to arrange another party to provide goods or services, it acts as an agent. The performance of the obligation will result in the recognition of revenue in the amount of any fees or commissions to which it is expected to be entitled in exchange for arranging another party to provide its goods or services.

[Example12-6] Revenue includes an amount of $200,000 for cash sales made through D.Z. Co.'s retail outlets during the year on behalf of Frank. Ytol, acting as agent, is entitled to a commission of 10% of the selling price of these goods. By 31 March 2019, Ytol had remitted to Frank $150,000 (of the $200,000 sales) and recorded this amount in cost of sales.

Date		Description	P.R.	Debit	Credit
Mar.31	2019	Revenue		$200,000	
		Cost of sales			$150,000
		Operating income			$20,000
		Trade payable			$30,000
		To cash received.			

The agency sales should be removed from revenue and their 'cost' from cost of sales. Instead, Ytol should report the commission earned of $20,000 as other operating income (or as revenue would be acceptable). This leaves a net amount of $30,000 owing to Frank as a trade payable.

2. Consignment

Consignment is the act of consigning or delivering the products to be sold to the dealer. The dealer sells the product on the market on behalf of the consignor in accordance with the conditions specified in the consignment agreement. Upon delivery, the dealer shall settle the payment for products with the consignor in the manner agreed stipulated in the agreement. Control of these products rests with the consignor until the goods are sold or personnel transferred.

When a product is delivered to a dealer under a consignment arrangement, the dealer does not obtain the control of the product at that point in time and therefore does not recognize revenue at delivery.

3. Sale and repurchase agreement

The seller also agrees to repurchase the same goods at a later date, or when the seller has a call option to repurchase or the buyer has a put option to require the seller to repurchase the goods.

When the seller retains the ownership of the assets other than the financial assets as well as the risks and rewards of the sale and repurchase agreement, it needs to analyze the terms of the agreement to determine whether it has substantially transferred the risks and rewards of the ownership to the buyer. T Thus, even if legal ownership has been transferred, the transaction is a financing arrangement and does not generate revenue.

4. Customer unexercised rights

When the customer pays in advance, the prepayment creates contractual liability, and the order is confirmed to be terminated when it is met.

If the customer makes a non-refundable prepayment, but does not exercise its right to receive good or services, if the pattern of rights exercised by the customer results in the entity's right to receive good or services, the breakage amount can be recognized as revenue.

If not applicable, customers can be recognized as revenue when the possibility of exercising its rights becomes remote.

12.1.4 Presentation in financial statements

Contracts with customers will be displayed in the form of contract liabilities, contract assets or receivables in the entity's statement of financial position, depending on the relationship between the entity's performance and the customer's payments.

Contract liabilities are reported in the statement of financial position, and the customer has paid a certain amount of consideration before the entity fulfills its obligations by transferring the relevant goods or services to the customer.

12.2 Contract cost

If the costs incurred in fulfilling a contract with a customer meet another criterion, the entity should calculate these costs in accordance with those criteria. If not, as long as all conditions in the adjacent table are met, the company recognizes an asset at that cost.

Costs are capitalized if the following conditions are met costs directly related to the contract include direct labor, direct material, allocation directly related to the contract or contract activity (for example, contract management and supervision costs and depreciation of tools), costs explicitly charged to the customer, other costs incurred by the entity only due to the signing of the contract, and the cost that generates or enhances the entity. These resources will be used to fulfill the obligations in the future, and the enterprise expects to recover the cost.

If an entity expects to recover these costs, it will capitalize the incremental costs of the contract. The incremental cost of acquiring a contract is a cost that an entity would not incur if it did not acquire the contract (for example, some sales commissions). An asset recognized as the cost of acquiring or performing a contract shall be systematically amortized according to the method of transfer of goods or services related to the asset.

However, if the amortization period of the asset does not exceed one year, it can be included in the current profit and loss when it occurs. In order to obtain the contract, the other costs incurred by the enterprise in addition to the expected recoverable incremental cost shall be included in the current profit and loss at the time of occurrence. Except for costs explicitly borne by the customer.

Take the incremental cost of obtaining the contract as the incurred expense, which includes the general and administrative expenses not explicitly charged to the customer, the cost of wasted materials, labor or other resources not reflected in the contract price, the cost related to the performance of obligations, and the cost related to the remaining performance of obligations, which cannot be distinguished from the cost related to the performance of obligations.

Key Words and Expressions

revenue	收入
performance obligation	履行义务
consideration	对价
contingent consideration	或有对价
transaction price	交易价格
stand-alone selling price	独立交易价格
expected value	预期价值
finance component	融资成分
trade discount	销售折扣
sales discount	现金折扣
revenue recognition	收入确认原则
sales returns and allowances	销售退回和折让
repurchase	回购
principal	委托人
agent	代理人
capitalize	资本化
expense	费用
contract cost	合同成本

Exercises

Ⅰ. **Please select the best answer for the following questions or uncompleted sentences.**

1. What is the definition of revenues? ( )

A. Decrease the owner's equity from the daily business activities of an enterprise.

B. Increase the owner's equity from the daily business activities of an enterprise.

C. Income.

D. Increase he owner's equity from regular operating activities.

2.What is the correct definition of a contract? (   )

A. A contract exists when an agreement between two parties results in enforceable rights and performance obligations.

B. The decision on the enforceability of contractual rights or obligations is made within the legal framework.

C. The performance obligation of the contract can be changed at any time.

D. The contract cannot be implied by written, oral or commercial practice.

3. Broom Co successfully receives a government grant of $1, 500,000 on 1 January 2019 allowing it to purchase an asset which costs $500,000, also on 1 January 2019. The asset has a ten-year useful life and is depreciated on a 20% reducing balance basis. Company policy is to account for all grants received as deferred income.

What amount of income will be recognized in respect of the grant in the year to 31 December 2015? (   )

A. $1,500,000

B. $500,000

C. $300000

D. $150,000

4. YL Co. entered into a contract in respect of which performance obligations are satisfied over time on 1 January 2019. The contract is expected to last 24 months. The price, which has been agreed for the contract, is $5 million. At 30 September 2019 the costs incurred on the contract were $1.6 million and the estimated remaining costs to complete were $2.4 million. On 20 September 2019, YL Co. received a calculates the stage of completion of its performance obligations on contracts on the basis of amounts invoiced to the contract price.

What amount would be reported in YL Co. s statement of financial position as at 30 September 2019 as the contract asset arising from the above contract? (   )

A. Nil

B. $1600,000

C. $800,000

D. $200,000

5. R Co, a company which sells photocopying equipment, has prepared its draft financial statements the year ended 30 September 2019. It has included the following transactions in revenue at the stated amounts below.

Which of these has been correctly included in revenue according to Revenue from Contracts with customers? (   )

A. Agency sales of $250,000 on which R Co is entitled to a commission.

B. Sale proceeds of $20,000 for motor vehicles that were no longer required by R Co.

C. Sales of $150,000 on 30 September 2019. The amount invoiced to and received from the customer was $180,000, which included $30,000 for ongoing servicing work to be done by R Co over the next two years.

D. Sales of $200,000 on 1 October 2018 to an established customer which, (with the agreement of Repro Co), will be paid in full on 30 September 2019 Repro Co has a cost of capital of 10%.

6. In what cost should be expensed in contract costs. (   )

   A. General and administrative costs that are not explicitly chargeable to the customer.

   B. Costs of wasted materials, labor, or other resources that were not reflected in the contract price.

   C. Costs that relate to satisfied performance obligations.

   D. Costs related to remaining performance obligations that cannot be distinguished from costs related to satisfied performance obligations.

7. Which of the steps for revenue recognition? (   )

   A. Identify the contract with the customer.

   B. Identify the performance obligations in the contract.

   C. Determine the transaction price.

   D. Allocate the transaction price to the performance obligations in the contracts.

   E. Recognize revenue when a performance obligation is satisfied

8. Which will affect the consideration? (   )

   A. Sales discount

   B. Sales return and allowance

   C. Trade discounts

   D. All of above

II. Finish the following tasks based on the information given.

Klevins is a retailer of caravan, dormer vans and mobile homes, with a year-end of 31 March 2019. It is now having trouble selling one model the $30,000 caravan and so is offering incentives for customers who buy this model before 31 March 2021:

Customers buying this model before 31 March 2019 will receive a period of interest free credit, provided they pay an installment of $18,000 and the balance of $12,000 on 31 March 2021.

A 3-year service plan, normally worth $1,500, is included free in the price of the caravan.

On 31 March 2019, a customer agrees to buy a caravan, paying the installment $18,000 and the delivery was arranged immediately.

Task:

Explain how to treat the contract in the financial statements for the years ended 31 March 2019 (assuming a 10% discount rate).

第12章 收入

新的会计准则采取"控制权转移"原则替代"风险和报酬转移"作为收入确认基本原则,并通过"五步法"模型统一了不同企业、不同行业、不同来源收入的会计处理标准。

12.1 收入的核算

企业将确认收入以反映承诺的商品或服务向客户的转移,其金额应反映该企业期望交换这些商品或服务有权获得的对价。

12.1.1 收入的定义

收入是指企业日常经营活动中形成的,会增加所有者权益,与所有者投入的资本无关的经济利益的总流入。

收入可能导致所有者权益增加。它可能表现为资产增加或负债减少,或两者兼而有之,即所有者权益的增加。收入仅包括公司经济利益的流入,因此不应包括为第三方或客户收取的资金。

根据企业从事的经济活动的性质,收入可分为商品销售收入、服务提供收入、企业所拥有财产的特许权使用费、建筑合同等。

12.1.2 收入的确认和计量

根据《国际财务报告准则第15号——客户合同收入》,当企业与客户之间的合同同时满足以下五个条件时,企业应当确认该收入。核心原则通过五步模型框架得以实施。

第1步:确定与客户的合同

- 合同的定义

当两方或多方之间的协议在双方之间产生可执行的权利和履约义务时,即存在合同,该协议可以是书面、口头或商业惯例暗示的。

合同权利或义务是否可执行的决定是在管辖权的相关法律框架内进行的。因此,合同是否可强制执行在不同司法管辖区之间会有所不同。

实际上,履约义务可能包括一些承诺,即使这些承诺不是法律强制执行的,也可以有效地期望该实体将向客户转移商品或服务。

- 合同的标准

《国际财务报告准则第15号——客户合同收入》规定了在主体确认收入条件之前必须满足的四个标准:

(1) 双方已完成合同并承诺履行其义务。
(2) 可以确定有关要转让的商品或服务的各方权利和付款条款。

(3) 在确认收入之前，合同具有商业实质。
(4) 该实体很可能会收取其应得的对价。

对客户的信用风险进行评估是确定合同是否有效的重要因素，但客户信用风险不影响收入的计量或呈报。主体应评估支付对价的能力和意图。根据这些标准，主体可以不断重新评估合同，以确定其随后是否符合标准。

第2步：确定合同中的履约义务

订立合同时，主体应评估已承诺给客户的商品或服务，并将其确定为履行义务。

商品或服务是可区分的，如果客户可以单独或与其他随时可用的资源一起从商品或服务中受益；实体将商品或服务转移给客户的承诺与合同中的其他承诺是分开确定的。

一系列不同的商品或服务以相同的方式转移给客户，如果主体承诺将一系列产品中的每一个独特的产品或服务持续地转移给客户，则随着时间的推移履行履约的义务；使用进度测量方法来测量整个履行的进度，其履行义务是将系列中的每一种独特产品或服务转让给客户。

第3步：确定交易价格

交易价格是该实体期望获得的用以交换货物和服务的转让价格。此金额不包括代表第三方收取的金额。

交易价格可能包括可变对价或者或有对价。应将其估计为预期价值或最有可能收到的对价，以能更好地预测该实体有权获得的对价为准。管理层应采用能反映最佳估计金额的方法，并在整个合同中始终如一地应用。

当客户合同中的对价包括可变金额时，实体需要评估交易价格中包含的可变对价金额是否需要受到约束。约束条件的目的是确保当相关不确定性被解决时，主体仅在很可能不会大幅度转回收益的范围内确认收益。

【例 12-1】D.Z.公司向大型企业提供便携式计算机。2018 年 7 月 1 日，D.Z.公司与 T 公司签订了一项合同，根据该合同，每台笔记本电脑的价格为 500 美元。合同规定，如果 T 公司一年购买超过 500 台笔记本电脑，则每台的价格将降至每台 450 美元。D.Z.公司的年终是 6 月 30 日。

(a) 截至 2018 年 9 月 30 日，T 公司已从 D.Z.购买了 70 台笔记本电脑，因此 D.Z.公司估计，在 2019 年 6 月 30 日之前的一年中，T 公司的购买量不会超过 500 台，因此 T 公司将无权享受批量折扣

(b) 在 2018 年 12 月 31 日结束的季度中，T 公司因进行了大量收购而迅速扩张，并从 D.Z.公司再购买了 250 台笔记本电脑。T 公司估计 T 公司的购买量将超过到 2019 年 6 月 30 日的一年中的批量折扣。

要求：
计算 D.Z.公司在以下时间中确认的收入
(a) 2018 年 9 月 30 日结束的季度。
(b) 截至 2018 年 12 月 31 日的季度。

解决方案：
(a) 将 IFRS 的要求应用于 2018 年 9 月 30 日的 T 公司的采购模型，D.Z.公司应得出结论，当不确定性得到解决时，即当总采购金额已知时，已确认的累计收入(每台笔记本电脑 500 美元)为极不可能出现重大逆转。

因此，D.Z.公司应将 2018 年 9 月 30 日的第一季度收入确认为 70 × $500 = $35,000。

(b) 在 2018 年 12 月 31 日结束的季度中，T 公司的采购方式发生了变化，因此 D.Z.公司有理由得

出这样的结论，即 T 公司的采购将超过 2019 年 6 月 30 日的一年批量折扣的门槛，因此，有必要将价格降低到每台笔记本电脑 450 美元。

因此，D.Z.公司应确认 2018 年 12 月 31 日结束的季度的收入为 109,000 美元。此金额是根据交易价格变更后的 112,500 美元(250 台笔记本电脑 × 450 美元)减去 3,500 美元(70 台笔记本电脑 × 价格降低 50 美元)后得出的，即交易价格在 2018 年 9 月 30 日结束的季度内的降低价格。

如果对价是预先支付或拖欠的，则主体将需要考虑合同是否包含重大融资安排，如果是，则根据反映交易金额的货币时间价值来调整交易价格，以此反映客户在转让商品或服务时已经支付现金的价格。如果商品或服务的转让与付款之间的时间少于一年，则不需要。

【例 12-2】D.Z.公司与客户签订了出售现有打印机的合同，以便在两年内将对打印机的控制权归客户所有。合同有两种付款方式。客户可以在签订合同时支付 240,000 美元，也可以在获得机器控制权后的两年内支付 300,000 美元。合同中隐含的利率为 11.8%，以调整延迟付款所涉及的风险。但是，D.Z.公司的增量借款利率为 5%。客户在 2017 年 12 月 1 日签订合同时支付了 24 万美元。

日期		摘要	过账参考	借方	贷方
11.30	2018	融资成本 (240,000 × 5%)		$12,000	
		合同负债			$12,000
11.30	2019	融资成本[(240,000+12,000) × 5%]		$12,600	
		合同负债			$12,600
		记录两年的融资成本			
11.30	2019	合同负债		$264,600	
		收入			$264,600
		记录机器的交付			

由于提前收到对价，合同中包含重要的融资内容，因为从客户购买资产到 D.Z. Co.将资产转让给客户之间的时间间隔很长。

在这种情况下，应将合同分为收入部分和贷款部分，该贷款部分应与使用公司增量借款利率对具有相同特征的贷款的会计核算相等。

如果主体获得对价的权利以某未来事件的发生或不发生为条件，已承诺的对价也可能改变。

- 商业折扣

商业折扣是指公司根据市场供求或针对不同客户的折扣。从商业报价中扣除商业折扣后的实际交易价格为应收账款的账面价值，因此商业折扣不影响销售收入的计量。

商业折扣是企业最常用的促销方式之一。为了扩大销售并占领市场，公司经常给批发商以商业折扣，并采用销售量更大、价格更低的销售策略。

【例 12-3】D.Z.公司对订购 1,000 个或更多其流行产品的订单提供 25%的贸易折扣。每个流行产品的标价为 7.8 美元。

销售量	1,000
单价	$7.80
合计	7,800
减:25%折扣	($1,950)
发票价格	$5,850

根据购买的数量得到商业折扣。在此示例中，当客户订购 1,000 个或更多数量时，提供 25%的商业折扣。商业折扣不记录在会计记录中。本例中该交易将以 5,850 美元的价格记录下来，该价格反映了给定的商业折扣。

- 销售折扣

销售折扣是指向顾客提供购买折扣，鼓励其提早付款，其主要目的是通过减少应收账款中占用的资金量来增加企业资金的流动性。销售折扣记录在另一个抵销收入账户中，使管理层能够监控公司折扣政策的有效性。信用期是公司允许客户延长其应收账款的正常期限，通常为 30 天或 60 天。折扣期要短得多，一般是 10 天或 15 天。如果在折扣期内收到付款，可以打折。如果在贴现期到期后付款，则应在信用期结束时或之前全额付款。

"2/10, n/30" 第一个数字代表折扣百分比；第二个数字代表折扣期；字母"n"代表单词 net；最后一个数字代表整个信用期。在这种情况下，如果客户在 10 天内付款，则可以享受 2%的折扣。如果不是，则应在 30 天内支付全部款项。

【例 12-4】2019 年 11 月 6 日，D.Z.公司通过账户向弗兰克出售了 1,500 美元的商品库存，信用条件为 2/10，n/30。如果弗兰克在折扣期(10 天)内付款，则他可以享受 2%的折扣弗兰克于 2019 年 11 月 16 日支付了应付款。

日期		摘要	过账参考	借方	贷方
11.6	2019	应收账款		$1,500	
		收入			$1,500
		赊销存货			
11.16	2019	现金		$1,470	
		销售折扣		$30	
		应收账款			$1,500
		记录支付额			

- 销货退回及折让

销货退回与折让是指企业由于售出商品的质量不合格或错发商品等原因，被购买方退回的商品或在价格上给予的折扣。

根据直接冲销法，在销货退回与折让时予以确认，不论其是否发生在销售的当期。在会计处理中，常用的方法是备抵法。根据备抵法，在确认收入当期合理估计销货退回与折让的数额计入"销货退回与折让"账户，该账户是"应收账款"的对销账户，在资产负债表中作为应收账款的减项。

【例 12-5】在 2019 年 11 月 8 日，弗兰克将 200 美元的有缺陷产品退还给 D.Z.公司

日期		摘要	过账参考	借方	贷方
11.8	2019	销售退回和折让		$200	
		应收账款			$200
		退回瑕疵商品			
		现金		$1,274	
		销售折扣		$26	
		应收账款			$1,300
		记录现金			

200 美元的津贴要求相同的科目。在损益表的销售收入部分中，从销售中减去销售退货和备抵金科目，因为这些科目对净收入有相反的影响。因此，"销货退回与折让"被视为对冲账户，通常有借方余额。

销售收入	$1,500
退回	($200)
金额	1,300
减：2%销售折扣	($26)
现金收入	$1,274

第 4 步：将交易价格分配给合同中的履约义务

合同具有多个履约义务时，主体将参照其相对独立的销售价格将交易价格分配给合同中的履约义务。与独立销售价格的总和相比，任何整体折扣均按相对独立销售价格在预期义务之间进行分配。

如果无法直接观察到独立的销售价格，实体将需要对其进行估计。IFRS 15 建议了可能使用的各种方法，包括：调整后的市场评估方法、预期成本加保证金方法、剩余方法(仅在有限情况下允许)。

第 5 步：在履行履约义务时确认收入

收入被确认控制权转移时，这种转移可以在一段时间内或一个时间点发生。资产控制是指直接使用资产并从资产中获得几乎所有剩余收益的能力，包括阻止他人指挥和使用资产的能力。

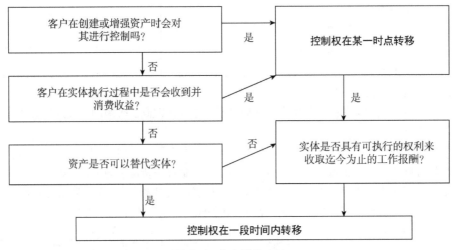

图 12-1　确定转移时间

在某一时点控制权转移的迹象包含：实体拥有付款的现时权利、客户已接受资产或对该资产具有合法所有权、实体已转让资产的实际所有权。

满足控制权在一段时间内转移的条件为：客户在实体执行过程中取得并使用其提供的利益收入。本期收入根据该期间的履行进度确认，但不能合理确定履行进度的除外。同时，实体将考虑商品的性质，采用输出法或输入法来确定适当的履行进度。对于类似情况下的履行义务，企业应采用相同的方法确定履行进度。如果无法合理确定履行进度，且企业发生的成本预计能够得到补偿，则在合理确定绩效进度之前，按照成本金额确认收入。

12.1.3 特珠交易的会计处理

1. 委托人和代理人

实体必须在任何交易中确立其作为委托人或代理人的身份。

如果它控制了承诺的货物或服务，然后将其转移给客户，则为委托人。当履行完义务时，该实体有权按其预期获得对价总额的确认收入。

如果其履行的义务是安排另一方提供货物或服务，则其作为代理人行事。义务的履行将导致收入的确认，其金额为其预期有权获得的费用或佣金，并安排另一方提供其货物或服务。

【例12-6】收入包括当年通过D.Z.公司的零售店代表弗兰克进行的现金销售200,000美元。作为代理人，Ytol有权收取这些商品售价的10%作为佣金。到2019年3月31日，Ytol已将20万美元的销售额中的15万美元汇给了弗兰克，并记录了这笔销售成本。

日期		摘要	过账参考	借方	贷方
3.31	2019	收入		$200,000	
		销售成本			$150,000
		其他营业收入			$20,000
		应付账款			$30,000
		现金收入			

代理商的销售应从收入中删除，其"成本"应从销售成本中删除。相反，Ytol应该将赚取的20,000美元的佣金报告为其他营业收入(或可以接受的收入)。剩下的净额30,000美元是欠弗兰克的应付账款。

2. 寄售

寄售是指寄售人将要出售的产品交付给代理商，代理商按照寄售协议中规定的条件代表寄售人在市场上销售产品。交付后，代理商将按照协议中规定的方式与发货人结清付款。这些物品的所有权保留在发货人手中，直到货物出售或人员变动为止。

当按照托运安排将产品交付给客户时，客户在该时间点尚未获得对该产品的控制权，因此在交付时不会确认任何收益。

3. 销售和回购协议

卖方同意在未来，或当卖方有回购的看涨期权，或买方有要求卖方回购货物的看跌期权时都会回购相同的货物。

当卖方保留金融资产以外的资产的所有权、出售和回购协议的风险和报酬时，需要分析协议的条款，以确定卖方是否实质上已将所有权的风险和报酬转移给买方，因此，即使合法所有权已经转让，交易也是一种融资安排，并不会产生收入。

4. 客户未行使的权利

当客户预付款时，预付款将具有合同责任，并在满足订单条件时终止确认。

如果客户垫付了不可退还的预付款，但没有行使其获得商品或服务的权利，则如果客户行使的权利模式导致实体有权获得商品或服务，则破损金额可以确认为收入。

如果不适用，则在行使权利的可能性微乎其微时，可以确认为收入。

12.1.4 财务报表的披露

与客户的合同将以实体的财务状况表中的合同负债、合同资产或应收款的形式显示，具体取决于实体的绩效和客户付款之间的关系。

合同负债在财务状况表中列报，客户在实体通过将相关商品或服务转让给客户而履行义务之前已经支付了一定对价。

12.2 合同成本

如果与客户履行合同所产生的费用符合另一项准则，则实体应按照这些准则来核算这些费用。如果不是，则只要满足相邻表中的所有条件，企业便会为该成本确认一项资产。

如果满足以下条件，则将成本资本化。与合同直接相关的成本包括：直接人工、直接材料、与合同或合同活动直接相关的分配(例如，合同管理和监督成本以及工具的折旧)，向客户明确收取的费用，主体仅因签订合同而产生的其他费用，成本产生或增强了实体的资源，这些资源将用于将来履行义务，企业预期能收回成本。

如果一个实体希望收回这些成本，它就将获得合同的增量成本资本化。获得合同的增量成本是一个实体如果没有获得合同就不会产生的成本(例如，一些销售佣金)，就取得或履行合同的成本而确认的资产，按照与该资产有关的货物或服务的转移方式相一致的系统性原则摊销。

但是该资产摊销期限不超过一年的，可以在发生时计入当期损益。企业为取得合同发生的除预期能收回的增量成本之外的其他支出，应在发生时计入当期损益。但是，明确由客户承担的支出除外。

获得合同的增量成本将作为已发生的费用，包括未明确向客户收取的一般和管理费用、未反映在合同价格中的浪费材料、劳动力或其他资源的成本，与履行义务相关的成本，剩余履行义务相关的成本，已履行义务相关的成本不能区分开来。

Chapter 13

Financial Statement

The purpose of the financial statements is to provide information about the entity's economic resources (assets), claims (liabilities, equity) on the entity, and changes in these economic resources and claims (income and expenditure). Users may use such information to assess the inflow prospects of the entity's net assets and management's right to manage the entity.

*The elements of financial statements refer to Chapter 2

13.1 Components of Financial Statements

Financial statements reflect the financial condition of an enterprise or budget unit at a point in time and the change of financial condition over a period of time. A complete set of financial statements should include:

Statement of profit and loss and other comprehensive income for the period.
Statement of changes in equity for the period.
A statement of financial position as at the end of the period.
Statement of cash flow for the period.
Notes, including significant accounting policies and other explanatory information.

13.2 Statement of Profit or Loss and Other Comprehensive Income

The statement of profit and loss and other comprehensive income uses the statement of profit and loss and is adjusted for certain profit and loss. The idea is to present all profits and losses, including those that are recognized in profit or loss and those that are recognized directly in equity, such as revaluation surpluses (in other comprehensive income).

The statement of profit and loss is a report of income (revenue), expenses as well as profits and losses incurred during the accounting period, which is prepared on an accrual basis. This means that revenue is recognized when it is earned, not when it is realized. Instead, expenses, once incurred, are recognized in the income statement, even if they have been paid in previous or future accounting periods.

And it does not report transactions with entity owners. As a result, dividends paid to common shareholders are not included as expenses in the income statement, and earnings from the issuance of shares are not considered income. Transactions between entities and their owners are accounted for separately in the statement of changes in equity.

13.2.1 The Objective of the Statement of Profit and Loss

The statement of profit and loss is a financial statement that reflects a company's business performance over a period of time. The objectives of the statement of profit and loss are as follows.

1. Explain, Evaluate and Forecast the Business Results and Profitability of the Enterprise

According to the business performance reflected by income statement, shareholders, creditors and management departments can explain, evaluate and predict the profitability of the enterprise, and make decisions on whether to invest or additional investment, where to invest, how much to invest, etc.

2. Investigate the Management Level of the Enterprise

By comparing and analyzing the various components, shareholders, creditors and management departments can get to know the growth and decline trends of various incomes, expenses and benefits, find issues in various work, expose shortcomings, identify gaps, improve business management, and strive to increase income, save costs, prevent losses, and make reasonable business decisions.

3. Provide the Rational Distribution Basis for Business Results

Shareholders, creditors and management departments can objectively evaluate the performance of various functional departments, production and operation units, and the relationship between the performance of these departments and personnel and the business performance of the entire enterprise so as to further evaluate the performance of management personnel in each department.

4. Predict the Solvency of the Enterprise

Creditors and management departments can indirectly explain, evaluate and predict the solvency, especially long-term solvency of a company by analyzing and comparing the relevant information of the income statement, reveal the changing trend of the solvency, make various credit decisions and improve business management decisions.

13.2.2 Statement of Profit and Loss

1. Items

The main items of the statement of profit and loss include revenue, cost, cost of goods sold, operating income and other income and expenses.

Revenue — Revenue is generated by selling the company's products or services, which are generated by its core business activities. It mainly includes sales revenue, service revenue, and net sales after sales discount, sales return and allowance are deducted.

Cost of Goods Sold — The statements will have an additional expense item called cost of goods sold. It is presented as a separate expense item on the statement of profit and loss and other comprehensive income. Net sales minus cost of goods sold equal gross Profit. Gross Profit is the profit generated to cover all other expenses after deducting the cost of inventory sold.

Operating expenses — Operating expenses are expenses incurred by an enterprise in the normal course of business, including sales, general and administrative expenses, depreciation or amortization, research and development (R&D), employee salaries, sales commissions, and utilities such as electricity and transportation. One of the responsibilities for management is to determine how to reduce operating expenses without significantly affecting the company's ability to compete with competitors.

Other revenue (gain) — Other income is income derived from non-operating activities. It includes income from disposal of fixed assets, interest on bank deposits, rental income from real estate, etc.

Other expense (loss) — Other expense is the expense incurred from non-operating activities and it includes interest paid on loans or debt, losses from the sale of an asset, etc.

2. Format

At present, there are two commonly used income statement formats in the world: one-step and multi-step. The one-step method is to add up the total income for the period and then add up the total amount of all expenses to calculate the current income in a lump sum. Its characteristic is that the information provided is raw data and easy to understand. Exhibit 13-1 is a one-step income statement.

Exhibit 13-1

SL Co.
Statement of Profit and Loss
For the Year End December 31, 2019

Revenue (Income):		
Sales		$5,243
Interest received		$33
Total revenue		$5,276
Expense:		
Cost of sales	$3,711	
Distribution costs	$281	
Administrative expenses	$464	
Interest costs	$75	
Income tax expense	$157	
Total expenses		$4,688
Net profit		$588

The multi-step method is to add up profits of all kinds. The multi-step method of obtaining net profit is convenient for users to compare and analyze the operating status and profitability of enterprises. Exhibit 13-2 is a multi-step statement of profit and loss.

Exhibit13-2

SL Co.
Statement of Profit and Loss
For the Year End December 31, 2019

Sales		$5,243
Cost of sales	$3,711	
Gross profit		$1,523
Other income:		
Interest received		$33
Distribution costs	$281	
Administrative expenses	$464	
Interest costs	$75	$820
Profit before tax		$745
Income tax expense		$157
Net profit		$588

The contents of the profit statement are divided into several categories. The multi-step profit statement takes sales as the starting point and displays the business results of the enterprise and its influencing factors in the following steps:

Sales revenue	=	price × quantity sold
Net sales	=	sales revenue − sales return and allowances − sales discount
Gross profit	=	net sales − cost of goods sold
Operating profit	=	gross profit − other indirect costs
PBIT	=	operating profit + non-operating income
PBT	=	PBIT - Interest payable
Net Profit	=	PBT − Tax

13.2.3 Statement of Comprehensive Income

According to the requirements of *IAS 1*, entities should include income statement and other comprehensive income statement as a single statement or two separate statements: the income statement and other comprehensive income statement.

Other comprehensive income includes unrecognized profits and losses in income and expense (including reclassification adjustments).

Reclassification adjustment refers to the amount recognized in other comprehensive income of the current or previous periods. For example, reclassification adjustment does not occur as a result of changes in the revaluation surplus or the determination of the measurement of the benefit plan. Exhibit 13-3 is a component of other comprehensive income statement.

Exhibit 13-3

××× Ltd.

Statement of comprehensive income

For the year ended 31 Dec, 20××

	$, 000
Profit for the year	X
Other comprehensive income after tax	
Changes in revaluation surplus	X
Re-measurements of defined benefit plans	X
Gains and losses arising from translating the financial statements of a foreign operation	X
Gains and losses from investments in equity instruments (FVTOCI)	X
Gains and losses from investment in debt instrument (FVTOCI)	X
Gains and losses on hedging instruments	X
Other comprehensive income for the year, net of tax	X
Total comprehensive income for the year	XX
Profit attributable to:	
Owners of the company	X
Non-controlling interests	X
	XX
Total comprehensive income attribution to:	
Owners of the company	X
Non-controlling interests	X
	XX

13.3 Statement of Changes in Equity

13.3.1 The Objective of the Statement of Changes in Equity

    The statement of changes in equity helps users of financial statements identify factors that cause changes in equity during an accounting period. While changes in capital or equity can be observed in the balance sheet, the statement of changes in equity discloses important information about the amount of equity that does not appear separately elsewhere in the financial statements and helps to understand changes in the amount of nature of equity. This information includes the capital invested in the current period, the issuance and redemption of equity in the current period, the impact of changes in accounting policies and previous period error corrections, the gains and losses recognized off-balance sheet, the declared dividends in the current period, and the bonus shares issued.

13.3.2 Presentation of the Statement of Changes in Equity

1. Items

The main items of the statement of changes in shareholders' equity are as follows:
- Opening Balance

This is the balance of shareholders' equity reflected in the statement of financial position for the previous period at the beginning of the comparative reporting period. The opening balance has not yet been adjusted because of the correction of errors prior to the current period and the impact of changes in accounting policies implemented during the current year, as these changes are shown separately in the statement of changes in equity.

- Changes in accounting policies

Since changes in accounting policies are applied retrospectively, equity needs to be adjusted at the beginning of the comparative reporting period to restate opening equity to the amount at which the new accounting policy always applies.

- Adjustments of prior-year errors

The effect of prior period error correction must be separately listed in the statement of changes in equity as an adjustment to the amount at the beginning of the period. The impact of the correction shall not be deducted from the opening balance of the equity amount, so that the amount listed in the statement of the current period can be easily verified and traced from the previous financial statements.

- Restated balance

This means that the equity attributable to shareholders at the beginning of the comparative period after the change in the above accounting policy and the adjustment of previous error corrections.

- Changes in share capital

Share capital reissued during this period must be added to the statement of changes in equity, and redeemed shares must be deducted from it. The effect of stock issuance and redemption must be expressed as equity and premium, respectively.

- Dividends

Dividend payments issued or announced during this period must be deducted from shareholders' equity because they represent the distribution of wealth attributable to shareholders.

- Profit and loss for the period

This represents the profit or loss attributable to shareholders during the period reported in the income statement.

- Revaluation of changes in reserve

The revaluation gains and losses recognized during this period must be presented in the statement of changes in equity. However, the revaluation gains recognized in the income statement as a result of the reversal of previous impairment losses should not be presented separately in the statement of changes in equity, as these gains have been included in the current profit and loss.

- Other profit or loss

Any other profit or loss not recognized in the income statement can be shown in the statement of

changes in equity, such as actuarial gains and losses.
- Closing balance

This is the balance of shareholders' equity at the end of the reporting period as reflected in the statement of financial position.

2. Format

In order to clearly show the increase and decrease of each component of the owner's equity in the current period, the statement of changes in equity should be presented in the form of a matrix: on the one hand, the transactions or events that cause the changes in the owner's equity have changed the way that the changes in the owner's equity were reflected only according to each component of the owner's equity in the past, but from the source of the changes in the owner's equity; on the other hand, the impact of transactions or events on the owner's equity is presented according to the components of the owner's equity (including share capital, share premium, revaluation surplus, and retained earnings) and their total amount. Exhibit 13-4 is a statement of changes in owners' equity.

Exhibit 13-4

SL Co.
Statement of Changes in Owners' Equity
For the year end 31 Dec. 2019

	Share Capital	Share Premium	Revaluation Surplus	Retained Earnings	Total
Balance at 1 Jan. 2019					
Changes in accounting policy					
Adjustments of prior errors					
Restated Balance					
Changes in equity for 2019					
Total comprehensive income					
Issue/Redemption of share capital					
Dividends					
Revaluation gain					
Balance at 31 Dec. 2019					

13.3.3 The Link Within the Financial Statement

The net profit in the income statement will affect the amount of undistributed profit in the owner's equity. Therefore, the net profit in the statement of changes in owner's equity is reflected by the net profit of the impact of the operation of the enterprise on the owner's equity in the current year.

At the same time, the statement of changes in owner's equity reflects the changes in the part of owner's equity in the balance sheet.

13.4 Balance Sheet

13.4.1 The Objective of the Balance Sheet

A statement of financial position helps users of financial statements to assess the financial position of an entity. The analysis of balance sheet in multiple accounting periods helps identify the potential trends in an entity's financial position and determine its risks in liquidity, finance, credit and operation. When analyzed in conjunction with the entity's other financial statements and those of its competitors, balance sheet helps identify its relationships and trends that indicate potential problems or areas for further improvement. Therefore, the analysis of the statement of financial position can help users of financial statements to predict the amount, time and volatility of the entity's future earnings.

13.4.2 Presentation of Balance Sheet

1. Items

Statement of financial position, also known as balance sheet, presents the financial position of an entity at a given date. It is comprised of three main components: assets, liabilities and equity.

- Assets

An asset is an economic resource controlled by the entity as a result of past events. Economic resources refer to the right to generate economic benefits. In the balance sheet, assets are classified into current assets and non-current assets according to their liquidity and the duration for which the reporting entity uses its expected economic benefits. Assets that can bring long-term economic benefits to the entity are classified as non-current assets, while those expected to be realized within one year after the reporting date are classified as current assets.

- Liabilities

Liabilities are the current obligations of a company to divert financial resources as a result of past events. Liabilities are classified as current liabilities or non-current liabilities in the balance sheet according to its liquidity, which depends on the period when the entity intends to pay off the liabilities. Long-term liabilities are classified as non-current liabilities, while those expected to be repaid within one year from the reporting date are classified as current liabilities.

- Equity

Equity is the residual interest in the assets of the entity after deducting all its liabilities. As a result, it represents a residual interest in the business that belongs to the owner.

2. Format

Using the concept of accounting equation, balance sheet divides the transactions of assets, liabilities and owner's equity into two parts: "assets" and "liabilities and owner's equity". Exhibit 13-5 is a statement of financial position.

Exhibit 13-5

SL Co.
Statement of Financial Position
As at 31 December 2019

	2019	2018
	$,000	$,000
Non-current assets		
Property, plant and equipment (PPE)	1,700	1,615
Intangible assets	425	375
Investments	0	95
Current assets		
Inventory	150	102
Trade receivables	1,010	315
Short-term investments	75	0
Cash at Bank	452	1
Total assets	3,812	2,503
Liability and equity		
Equity		
Share capital ($1 ordinary shares)	1,950	1,550
Share premium account	260	150
Revaluation surplus	70	51
Retained earnings	618	200
Non-current liability		
Long-term loans	170	50
Current liabilities		
Trade payables	289	119
Bank overdrafts	143	98
Taxation	312	285
Total liability and equity	3812	2503

13.5 Statement of Cash Flows

The cash flow statement provides important insights into a company's liquidity and solvency, which is vital to the survival and development of any organization. It also enables users of statements to use information about historical cash flow to forecast the entity's future cash flows and use them as a basis for economic decisions. The cash flow statement highlights the priorities of management by summarizing the major changes in financial conditions over a period of time. For example, an increase in capital expenditures and development costs may mean an increase in future revenue, while a trend of excessive short-term investment may mean a lack of viable long-term investment opportunities. In addition, comparing the cash flows of different entities may better reveal the relative quality of its returns, because cash flow information is more objective than the financial performance reflected in the income statement, and the income statement is prone to major changes due to the use of different accounting policies.

13.5.1　The Definition of Cash and Cash Equivalents

The cash flow statement uses cash or cash equivalents as the definition of cash. The statement should explain the changes in cash and cash equivalents during the period.

Cash is the most liquid asset, including coins, currency, checks, money orders, and currency deposits that can be freely withdrawn in banks or other financial institutions. Its main accounts include cash on hand, bank deposits, and other monetary funds.

Cash equivalents are short-term, highly liquid investments that can be quickly converted into known amounts of cash. Generally speaking, there is essentially no credit risk; the original maturity of the cash equivalent to the entity is three months or less. There is essentially no market (or interest rate) risk. Examples of cash equivalents include short-term treasury bills, commercial paper, and money market funds.

13.5.2　Business Activities of Statement of Cash Flows

Since the income statement and balance sheet are prepared on an accrual basis, it is necessary to adjust the amounts drawn from these financial statements in order to reflect the changes in cash inflows and outflows over a period of time. All cash flows are grouped into operating, investment and financing activities, as shown below.

- Cash flows from operating activities

Operating activities on the cash flow statement include the sources and uses of cash generated from operating a business and selling its products or services. Cash generated from operating activities includes any changes in cash, accounts receivable, depreciation, inventory and accounts payable. These transactions also include wages, income taxes, interest, rent and cash income from the sale of products or services.

Cash flows from operating activities

Inflows	Outflows
Receipts from the sales of goods or services	Payments for trade goods purchased for resale or for use in manufacturing
Receipts from the collection or sale of operating receivables	Payments for notes to supplies of trade goods
Interest received	Payments to other supplies and to employees
Dividend received	Cash paid for taxes, fees and fines
Other operating receipts	Interest paid to creditors
	Other operating cash payments

- Cash flows from investing activities

Investment activities include the sources and use of the company's investments in its long-term future. Cash flows from investing activities include changes in cash flows from the purchase or sale of assets, loans to sellers, loans received from customers, or any payments related to mergers and acquisitions.

Cash flows from investing activities

Inflows	Outflows
Receipt of loan repayments	Purchase debt instruments of other entities
Sale of equity investments, such as common or preferred stock	Payments made to buy an equity interest
Sale of productive assets (PPE)	Purchase productive assets (PPE)

- Cash flows from financing activities

The cash generated from financing activities includes the cash sources of investors or banks, and the use of cash paid to shareholders. Financing activities include debt issuance, equity issuance, stock buybacks, loans, dividend payments and debt repayment.

Cash flows from financing activities

Inflows	Outflows
Issuing of equity securities (such as common and preferred stock)	Repay principal on long and short-term debt
Receipt from borrowing (such as bonds, mortgages and notes)	Payments to reacquire common and preferred equity instruments, whether retired or placed in the treasury
Receipts from contributions and investment income donor restricted for endowments or buying, improving or constructing long-term assets	Dividend paid to common and preferred shareholders

13.5.3 Preparation of Statement of Cash Flows

The cash flow statement can be prepared using direct or indirect methods. Under the direct and indirect methods, the cash flow generated by investment and financing activities is the same, while the cash flow generated by business activities is the same, but the information format is different

1. Direct method

According to the direct method, the cash flow statement uses the actual cash inflows and outflows of the three major activities of the company: operation, investment and financing. Under the direct method, the operating part of the cash flow statement is presented on a cash basis, and the net cash flow in the accounting period is the difference between the actual cash inflow and outflow. The format of the direct method is as follows.

Exhibit 13-6　Format of Direct Method

	$
Cash flows from operating activities	
Cash receipts from customers (W1)	X
Cash paid to suppliers (W2)	(X)
Cash paid to employees (W3)	(X)
Cash paid to operating expenses (W4)	
Cash generated from operations	X
Interest paid　(W5)	(X)
Income taxes paid (W6)	(X)
Net cash from operating activities	X

Workings:

1.	Cash receipts from customers	= net sales + decrease accounts receivables/ (increase accounts receivable)
2.	Cash paid for supplies	= COGS + increase inventory/ (decrease inventory) + decrease accounts payable/(increase accounts payable)
3.	Cash paid to employees	= salaries expenses + decrease salaries payable / (increase salaries payable)
4.	Cash paid to operating expenses	= other operating expenses + increase prepaid expense / (decrease prepaid expense) + decrease in accrued expenses payable / (increase in accrued expenses payable)
5.	Interest paid	= interest expenses + decrease interest payable / (increase interest payable)
6.	Income taxes paid	= income tax expenses + decrease income tax payable / (increase income tax payable)

Notes: The depreciation should be excluded operating expense.

2. Indirect method

The indirect method is one of two accounting methods for preparing the cash flow statement. The indirect method uses changes in the balance sheet items to modify the operating part of the cash flows. Under the indirect method, the statement of cash flow starts from the profit before tax under the accrual basis, and then increases or decreases in non-cash income and expense items to generate cash flow from operating activities.

The format of the indirect method calculation is as follows. This method is more common in calculations.

Exhibit 13-7　Format of Indirect Method

	$
Profit before tax (statement of profit or loss)	X
Adjustments:	
Add: Depreciation/Amortization	X
Interest expense	X

	(Continued)
Loss (gain) on sale of non-current assets	X/(X)
(Increase)/decrease in receivables	(X)/X
(Increase)/decrease in inventories	(X)/X
Increase/(decrease) in payables	X/(X)
Cash generated from operations	X
Interest (paid)/received	(X) /X
Income taxes paid	(X)
Net cash flows from operating activities	X

It is important to understand why some items are added and others are subtracted. The following should be noted:

(1) Depreciation / amortization is not a cash expense but is deducted when calculating profit in the income statement. Therefore, eliminate it by increasing depreciation / amortization.

(2) Losses on disposal of non-current assets (arising from depreciation) need to be added to or subtracted from earnings.

(3) More inventory means less cash because companies spend cash on purchasing inventory.

(4) An increase in accounts receivable means that the company's accounts receivable is not paid as much, so the company's cash decreases.

(5) A decrease in accounts payable means that the company has already repaid, and therefore, the company's cash will decrease.

[Example 13-1] Additional information for the year ended 31 December 2019 is as follows:

(1) The proceeds of the sale of non-current asset investments amounted to $60,000.

(2) Fixtures and fittings with an original cost of $220,000 and net book value of $130,000 were sold during the year of $128,000.

(3) The following information relates to Property, Plant and Equipment (PPE)

	31 Dec. 2019	31 Dec. 2018
		(Figures in $, 000)
Cost	2,200	2,015
Accumulated depreciation	500	400

(4) During the year, 400,000 ordinary $1.00 shares were issued at a premium per share of 27.5 pence.

(5) The short-term investments are highly liquid and are close to maturity.

(6) Dividends paid during the year amounted to $200, 000

Required:

Prepare statement of cash flows for SL Co. for the year ended 31 December 2019 based on the company's income statement and balance sheet. Using the Indirect Method, as permitted by International Accounting Standards *IAS 7*.

Solution:

Taking the net profit before taxation under the accrual basis as the starting point, excluding the profit generated by non-operating activities, the "net profit" is adjusted to the net profit generated by operating activities. Add items recorded in profit reduction but not related to operation activities and items recorded in profit increase but not related to operation activities.

Step 1: Find the net profit before taxation from income statement.

SL Co.
Statement of Cash Flows
For the year ended 31 Dec. 2019

	$, 000
Cash flows from operating activities	
Net profit before taxation	$745

Step2: Determine the depreciation expense

The depreciation expense needs to be adjusted, because depreciation expense reduced net income but did not require an outflow of cash, it is added back to net profit before taxation. If it is not given on the income statement, sometimes it can be found by analyzing the accumulated depreciation account.

Working 1: Accumulated depreciation T-account

Accumulated deprecation			
Depreciation assets on sold (220-130)	$90	Balance b/d	$400
Balance c/d	$500	Depreciation expense	$190(bal.)
	$590		$590

Step3: Analyze any gains or losses from selling investing, equipment, etc.

The gain or loss was included in net profit, but did not represent an operating cash flow, the gain/loss would have been deducted/added to net income.

	$, 000
Cash flows from operating activities	
Net profit before taxation	745
Adjustments:	
Depreciation (W1)	190
Disposal loss of fixtures and fittings (128-130)	2
Disposal loss of PPE (60-95)	35
Interest received	(33)
Interest costs	75
Operating profits before working capital changes	1014

Step4: Working capital changes that impact cash flows.

The preparation of the cash flow statement is based on the cash basis. Therefore, it is necessary to adjust the working capital, which affects the cash flow according to the accrual basis.

Operating profits before working capital changes	1014
(Increase)/decrease of trade receivable	(695)
(Increase)/decrease of inventory	(48)
Increase/(decrease) of trade receivable	170
Cash generated from operations	441

Step5: Calculate the net cash from operating activities

Finally, in calculating the net cash flow generated by operating activities, it is necessary to consider the impact of paying taxes and interests on it.

Cash generated from operations	441
Interest paid	(75)
Tax paid (W2)	(130)
Net cash flow from operating activities	236

Working 2: Taxation T-account

The tax paid in the year is last year's year-end provision and calculate the charge as the balancing figure.

Taxation			
Tax paid (bal.)	$130	Balance b/d	$285
Balance c/d	$312	Income statement	$157
	$442		$442

Step6: Analyze and calculate the net cash from investing and financing activities

Cash flows from investing activities	
Purchase of intangible non-current assets (425-375)	(50)
Purchase of PPE (W3)	(386)
Receipt from sale of non-current assets (128+60)	188
Interest received	33
Net cash flow from investing activities	(215)
Cash flows from financing activities	
Proceeds from issue of share capital (400+400*0.275)	510
Long-term loan	120
Dividend paid	(200)
Net cash flow from financing activities	430

Working 3: Property, Plant and Equipment T-account

Property, Plant and Equipment			
Balance b/d	$2,015	Disposal	$220
Revaluation gain (70-51)	$19	Balance c/d	$2,200
Purchase	*$386 (bal.)*		
	$2,420		$2,420

To sum up, the cash flow statement prepared according to the indirect method is as follows:

SL Co.

Statement of Cash Flows

For the year ended 31 Dec. 2019

$, 000

	(Continued)
Cash flows from operating activities	
Net profit before taxation	745
Adjustments:	
Depreciation (W1)	190
Disposal loss of fixtures and fixtures (128-130)	2
Disposal loss of PPE (60-95)	35
Interest received	(33)
Interest costs	<u>75</u>
Operating profits before working capital changes	1014
(Increase)/decrease of trade receivable	(695)
(Increase)/decrease of inventory	(48)
Increase/(decrease) of trade receivable	<u>170</u>
Cash generated from operations	441
Interest paid	(75)
Tax paid (W2)	<u>(130)</u>
Net cash flow from operating activities	<u>236</u>
Cash flows from investing activities	
Purchase of intangible non-current assets (425-375)	(50)
Purchase of PPE (W3)	(386)
Receipt from sale of non-current assets (128+60)	188
Interest received	<u>33</u>
Net cash flow from investing activities	<u>(215)</u>
Cash flows from financing activities	
Proceeds from issue of share capital (500+500×0.275)	510
Long-term loan	120
Dividend paid	<u>(200)</u>
Net cash flow from financing activities	<u>430</u>
Net increase in cash and cash equivalent	451
Cash and cash equivalent at 1 Jan. 2019	(79)
Cash and cash equivalent at 31 Dec. 2019	372

13.6 Notes

The notes to the financial statements provide the users of the statements with information about the basis of preparing the financial statements and the specific accounting policies used in the statements of profit and loss and other comprehensive income, statement of financial position, statement of cash flow and statement of changes in equity, any information not listed in the financial statements in accordance with the disclosure requirements of the international financial reporting standards, and other information that is not provided elsewhere in the financial statements, but is related to understanding any of the information. It mainly includes: the main accounting treatment methods adopted by the enterprise, the accounting policies and their changes, the reasons for the changes, the impact on the financial situation and business performance, the non-recurrent items that have occurred, the obvious information of some important statement items, transaction of relevant parties, contingencies and subsequent events, and etc.

Key Words and Expressions

financial statement	财务报表
statement of profit or loss and other comprehensive income	损益及综合收益表
statement of changes in equity	权益变动表
a statement of financial position	资产负债表
statement of cash flows	现金流量表
solvency	偿债能力
operating expense	营业费用
income tax expenses	所得税费用
subtract	扣除
disposal	处置
interest rate	利率
cash inflows	现金流入
cash outflows	现金流出
operating activities	经营活动
investing activities	投资活动
financing activities	筹资活动
working capital	营运资本
general and administrative expenses	管理费用
accounting policy	会计政策
accounting estimate	会计估计
limited liability company	有限责任公司

Exercises

Ⅰ. **Please select the best answer for the following questions or uncompleted sentences.**

1. Which financial statement shows whether the business earned a profit and also lists the types and amounts of the income and expenses? (   )

   A. Balance sheet.

   B. Statement of changes in equity.

   C. Statement of cash flows.

   D. Income statement.

243

2. A business's bank balance increased by $750,000 during its last financial year. During the same period, it issued shares of $1 million and repaid a loan note of $750,000. It purchased non-current assets for $200,000 and charged depreciation of $100,000. Working capital (other than the bank balance) increased by $575,000. What was its profit for the year? (   ).

    A. $1,175,000

    B. $1,275,000

    C. $1,325,000

    D. $1,375,000

3. Which of the following headings is not a classification of statements of cash flows? (   )

    A. Operating.

    B. Investing.

    C. Administration.

    D. Financing.

4. A company has the following information about property, plant and equipment.

	2019	2018
	$, 000	$, 000
Cost	750	600
Accumulated depreciation	250	150
Carrying amount	500	450

Plant with a carrying amount of $75,000 (original cost $90,000) was sold for $30,000 during the year. What is the cash flow from investing activities for the year? (   ).

    A. $95,000 inflow

    B. $210,000 inflow

    C. $210,000 outflow

    D. $95,000 outflow

5. A company has the following extract from a statement of financial position.

	2019	2018
	$, 000	$, 000
Share capital	2000	1000
Share premium	500	0
Loan stock	750	1000

If there had been a bonus issue of 500,000 shares of $1 each during the year, from financing activities for the year? (   ).

    A. $1,250 inflow

    B. $750 inflow

    C. $750 outflow

    D. $1,250 outflow

6. Which of the following items may appear as current liabilities in a company's statement of financial position? (   ).

    A. Revaluation surplus

B. Loan due for repayment within one year

C. Taxation

D. Preference dividend payable on redeemable preference shares

7. Which of the following might appear as an item in a company's statement of changes in equity? (   )

A. Profit on disposal of properties.

B. Surplus on revaluation- of properties.

C. Equity dividends proposed after the reporting date.

D. Issue of share capital.

II. Finish the following tasks based on the information given.

1. ABC Co. had the following transactions during the year.

(1) Purchases from suppliers were $19,500, of which $2,550 was unpaid at the year ended. Brought forward payables were $1,000.

(2) Wages and salaries amounted to $10,500, of which $750 was unpaid at the year ended. The accounts for the previous year showed an accrual for wages and salaries of $1,500.

(3) Interest of $2,100 on a long-term loan was paid in the year.

(4) Sales revenue was $33,400, including $900 receivables at the year ended. Brought forward receivables were $400.

(5) Interest on cash deposits at the bank amounted to $75.

Task: Calculate the cash flow from operating activities using the direct method.

2. The following information relating a limited liability company called Jackie. This company is preparing financial statement for the year ended 31 March 2019.

Jackie Co.: Income Statement for the Year End 31 March 2019

	$,000
Sales	33,000
Cost of sales	6,266
Gross profit	26,734
Investment income	66
Distribution costs	3,423
Administrative expenses	1,144
Interest costs	535
Profit before tax	21,698
Income tax expense	4,480
Profit for the year	17,218

Jackie Co.: Statement of Financial Position as at 31 March 2019 and 2018

	2019	2018
	$,000	$,000
Non-current assets		
Property, plant and equipment (PPE)	65,838	52,175
Accumulated depreciation	12,470	11,963

	(Continued)	
	53,368	40,212
Current assets		
Inventory	11,332	10,939
Trade receivables	8,600	6,017
Cash at Bank	1,677	1,010
Total Assets	74,977	58,178
Current liabilities		
Trade payables	7,600	9,236
Bank overdrafts	2,515	3,170
Taxation	3,670	3,340
	13,785	15,746
Non-current liability		
Long-term loans	8,100	10,940
Equity		
Share capital	12,200	10,600
Share premium	6,622	4,900
Revaluation surplus	7,000	3,237
Retained earnings	27,270	12,755
Total Owner' Equity	53,092	31,492
Total liability and owners' equity	74,977	58,178

Addition information:

(1) During the year ended 31 March 2019, the company sold a piece of equipment for $1,380,000, realizing a profit of $700,000. There were no other disposals of non-current assets during the year.

(2) Deprecation of $2,660,000 has been charged.

(3) There were no amounts outstanding in respect of interest payable or receivable as at 31 March 2019 or 2019.

(4) There were no dividends paid or declared during the year.

Task: Calculate the cash flow from operating activities using the indirect method.

第13章　财务报表

财务报表的目的是提供有关实体的经济资源(资产)，对实体的债权(负债、权益)以及这些经济资源和债权(收入和支出)变化的信息。用户可以使用此信息来评估实体净资产的未来流入前景，并评估管理层管理实体的权利。

财务报表的要素请参考第二章

13.1　财务报表的构成

财务报表反映了某个时间点企业或预算部门的财务状况以及一段时间内财务状况的变化。完整的财务报表应包括：
- 损益表和其他综合收益表。
- 所有者权益变动表。
- 资产负债表。
- 现金流量表。
- 注释，包括重要的会计政策和其他解释性信息。

13.2　损益表和其他综合收益表

损益表和其他综合收益表使用损益表对某些损益进行调整。其理念是列示所有损益，包括损益中确认的损益和直接在权益中确认的损益，如重估盈余(在其他综合收益表中)。

损益表是会计期间收入、费用和由此产生的损益的报告。损益表以权责发生制为会计基础编制。这意味着收入是在赚取时确认的，而不是在实现收入时确认的。相反，费用在发生时在利润表中确认，即使是在以前或以后的会计期间支付的。

损益表不报告与实体所有者的交易。因此，支付给普通股股东的股息在利润表中不列为费用，发行股票的收益不确认为收入。实体与其所有者之间的交易在权益变动表中单独核算。

13.2.1　损益表的作用

损益表是反映企业一段时间内经营成果的会计报表。它的作用包括：

1. 解释、评估和预测企业的经营成果和盈利能力

根据损益表提供的经营成果信息，股东、债权人和管理部门可以对企业的盈利能力进行说明、评估和预测，并对是否投资或追加投资、投资地点、投资金额等做出决策。

2. 调查企业的管理水平

对损益表中的各项构成要素、股东、债权人和管理部门进行比较分析，可以了解各项收入、成本、费用、效益的增减趋势，发现工作中各方面存在的问题，发现不足，找出差距，改进经营管理，努力增加收入，节约成本，防止损失，做出合理的商业决策。

3. 为经营成果提供合理的分配依据

股东、债权人和管理部门可以客观评价各职能部门、生产经营单位的绩效，以及这些部门和人员的绩效与整个企业经营成果的关系，从而判断各部门管理人员的绩效。

4. 预测企业的偿付能力

债权人和管理部门可以通过对利润表的相关信息进行分析比较，间接解释、评价和预测公司的偿债能力，特别是长期偿债能力，揭示偿债能力的变化趋势，进而做出各种信贷决策，完善企业管理决策。

13.2.2 损益表的列报

1. 项目

损益表的主要项目包括收入、成本、销货成本、营业收入、其他收入和费用。

收入——收入是通过销售公司的产品或服务产生的，这些产品或服务是由公司的核心业务活动产生的，主要包括销售收入、服务收入、扣除销售折扣的净销售额、销售退回及折让。

销货成本——利润表将有一个额外的费用项目，称为销货成本。销货成本在利润表中作为单独的费用项目列示。净销售额减去销货成本等于毛利。毛利润是减去存货的销售成本后，用来支付所有其他费用和利润的金额。

营业费用——营业费用是指企业通过正常经营所发生的支出，包括销售费用、管理费用、折旧或摊销费用、研发费用、员工工资、销售佣金、水电费和交通费。管理层必须承担的责任之一是确定如何在不显著影响公司与竞争对手竞争能力的情况下降低运营费用。

其他收入(收益)——其他收入是从非经营活动中获得的收入。其他收入包括处置土地、车辆或子公司等长期资产所得收益、银行现金利息、物业租金收入、股息收入等。

其他费用(损失)——其他费用是指非经营活动产生的费用，包括支付贷款或债务的利息、出售资产的损失等。

2. 格式

目前国际上常用的利润表格式有两种：单步式和多步式。单步式是将当期收入总额相加，再加上各项费用总额，一次性计算当期收入。其特点是所提供的信息是便于理解的原始数据。表13-1展示的就是单步式损益表。

表 13-1

SL 公司
利润表
截至 2019 年 12 月 31 日

收入(利润)：		
销售收入		$5,243
利息收入		$50
收入总额		$5,293
费用：		
销货成本	$3,273	
销售费用	$281	
管理费用	$464	
利息费用	$113	
所得税费用	$236	
费用总额		$4,367
净利润		$9,26

多步式方法是增加各种利润。获取净利润的多步式计算方法，方便用户比较分析企业的经营状况和盈利能力。表 13-2 演示的就是多步式损益表。

表 13-2

SL 公司
损益表
截至 2019 年 12 月 31 日

销售收入		$5,243
销货成本	$3,273	
毛利		$1,970
其他收入：		
利息收入		$50
销售费用	$281	
管理费用	$464	
利息费用	$113	$858
税前利润		$1,162
所得税费用		$236
净利润		$926

多步式利润表将其内容分为多个类别。从销售额开始，多步式利润表按以下步骤显示企业的业务结果及其影响因素：

销售收入	=	单价 × 销售数量
销售净额	=	销售收入 − 销售退回和折让 − 销售折扣
毛利	=	销售净额 − 销货成本
营业利润	=	毛利 − 其他间接成本
息税前利润	=	营业利润 + 非营业利润
税前利润	=	息税前利润 − 利息支出
净利润	=	税前利润 − 所得税

13.2.3 其他综合收益表

根据 IAS 1 的要求，主体应包括损益表和其他综合损益表，并将其作为一个单独的报表或两个单独的报表(损益表和其他综合损益表)。

其他综合收益包括未在损益中确认的收支项目(包括重分类调整)。

重分类调整为当期重分类至损益的金额，并在当期或以前期间的其他综合收益中确认。例如，重新分类调整不会因重估盈余变化或确定的福利计划的计量而发生。表 13-3 是综合收益表的组成部分。

表 13-3

×××有限公司
其他综合收益表
截至20××年12月31日

	$,000
净利润	X
税后其他综合收益	
重估盈余变动	X
重新确定设定受益计划	X
国外业务的财务报表产生的汇兑损益	X
投资权益工具的损益(FVTOCI)	X
投资债务工具的损益(FVTOCI)	X
套期工具的损益	X
年度其他综合收益, 税后净额	X
其他综合收益总额	XX
利润归属于:	
公司所有者	X
非控制性权益	X
	XX
综合总收益归属于	
公司所有者	X
非控制性权益	X
	XX

13.3 权益变动表

13.3.1 权益变动表的目的

权益变动表有助于财务报表使用者识别会计期间导致权益变动的因素。虽然资本或权益的变动可以从资产负债表中观察到，但权益变动表披露了有关权益金额的重要信息，这些信息在财务报表中没有单独列示，有助于理解权益性质的变动。这些信息包括本期投入资本、本期发行和赎回权益、会计政策变更和前期差错更正的影响、资产负债表外确认的损益、本期宣告分派的股利和发行的红利等。

13.3.2 权益变动表的列报

1. 项目

权益变动表的主要内容如下：
- 期初余额

这是上期财务状况表中反映的比较报告期开始时权益的余额。期初余额未因本期更正的前期差错以及本年度执行的会计政策变更的影响而调整，因为这些变更已在权益变动表中单独列示。

- 会计政策变更

由于会计政策的变更是追溯适用的，因此需要在比较报告开始时对股本进行调整，以将期初权益重报至新会计政策始终适用时的金额。

- 前期差错更正

前期差错更正的影响必须在权益变动表中单独列示，作为期初金额的调整。更正的影响不得从权益金额的期初余额中扣除，以便本期报表中列示的金额可以很容易地从上期财务报表中核对和追溯。

- 重估余额

这表示在上述会计政策变更和前期差错更正调整后的比较期开始时归属于股东的权益。

- 股本变动

在此期间再发行的股本必须加入权益变动表，而赎回股份则必须从中扣除。股票发行和赎回的效果必须分别列示为股本和股本溢价。

- 股息

在此期间发行或宣布的股息支付必须从股东权益中扣除，因为它们代表了归属于股东的财富分配。

- 本期损益

这表示损益表中报告的期间内归属于所有者或股东的损益。

- 重估损益变动

在此期间确认的重估损益必须在权益变动表中列报。但是，由于以前减值损失的转回而在损益表中确认的重估损益不应在权益变动表中单独列报，因为这些损益已经计入当期损益。

- 其他损益

损益表中未确认的任何其他损益，可在权益变动表中列示，例如精算损益。

- 期末余额

这是财务状况表中反映的报告期末股东权益余额。

2. 结构

为了清楚地表明构成所有者权益的各组成部分当期的增减变动情况，权益变动表应当以矩阵的形式列示：一方面，列示导致所有者权益变动的交易或事项，改变以往仅仅按照所有者权益的各组成部分反映所有者权益变动情况，而是从所有者权益变动的来源对一定时期所有者权益的变动情况进行全面反映；另一方面，按照所有者权益各组成部分及其总额列示交易或事项对权益的影响。表 13-4 是所有者权益变动表。

表 13-4

SL 公司
所有者权益变动表
截至 2019 年 12 月 31 日

	股本	股本溢价	重估盈余	留存收益	总额
2019 年 1 月 1 日余额					
会计政策变动					
前期差错调整					
重估余额					
2019 权益变动					
综合收益总额					
发行/回购股本					
股利					
重估收益					
2019 年 12 月 31 日余额					

13.3.3　所有者权益变动表与财务报表之间的联系

利润表中的净利润会影响所有者权益中的未分配利润金额。因此，所有者权益变动表中净利润反映为本年度企业经营情况对所有者权益的影响。

同时，所有者权益变动表是资产负债表中的所有者权益部分的变动情况体现。

13.4　资产负债表

13.4.1　资产负债表的作用

财务状况表帮助财务报表使用者评估一个实体的财务状况。在多个会计期间进行分析时，分析财务状况表有助于确定实体财务状况的潜在趋势以及确定实体的流动性风险、财务风险、信用风险和业务风险的状况。当与该实体的其他财务报表及其竞争企业的财务报表一起分析时，财务状况表有助于确定其关系和趋势，这些关系和趋势表明潜在的问题或需要进一步改进的领域。因此，对财务状况表的分析可以帮助财务报表使用者预测实体未来收益的金额、时间和波动性。

13.4.2 资产负债表的列报

1. 项目

财务状况表，也称为资产负债表，反映了一个实体在给定日期的财务状况。它由三个主要部分组成：资产、负债和所有者权益。

- 资产

资产是由于过去事件而由实体控制的经济资源。经济资源是指产生经济利益的权利。资产根据其流动性在资产负债表中分为流动资产或非流动资产，具体取决于报告实体使用该资产所产生的预期经济利益的持续时间，能够为主体带来长期经济利益的资产为非流动资产，而预期在报告日期后一年内实现的资产为流动资产。

- 负债

负债是公司的一项现行义务，该义务由过去的事件导致公司转移经济资源。负债根据其流动性在资产负债表中分为流动负债或非流动负债，具体取决于该实体打算还清负债的时期。长期负债为非流动负债，预计于报告日起一年内偿还的长期负债为流动负债。

- 所有者权益

所有者权益是实体的资产减去所有负债后的剩余权益。因此，它代表了在企业中属于所有者的剩余权益。

2. 格式

资产负债表使用会计平衡原则，将资产、负债和所有者权益的交易分为"资产"和"负债与所有者权益"两部分。表 13-5 演示的是资产负债表。

表 13-5

SL 公司
资产负债表
2019 年 12 月 31 日

	2019	2018
	$,000	$,000
非流动资产		
房屋，厂房和设备	1,700	1,615
无形资产	425	375
投资	0	95
流动资产		
存货	150	102
应收账款	1,010	315
短期投资	75	0
银行存款	452	1
资产总额	3,812	2,503

(续表)

负债和所有者权益		
所有者权益		
股本(普通股面值1美元)	1,950	1,550
股本溢价	260	150
重估盈余	70	51
留存收益	<u>618</u>	<u>200</u>
非流动负债		
长期债券	<u>170</u>	<u>50</u>
流动负债		
应付账款	289	119
银行透支	143	98
税费	<u>312</u>	<u>285</u>
负债和所有者权益总额	<u>3812</u>	<u>2503</u>

13.5　现金流量表

现金流量表提供了公司流动性和偿付能力这一重要观点，这对任何组织的生存和发展都至关重要。它还使报表使用者能够利用有关历史现金流的信息，形成对实体未来现金流的预测，以此为基础进行经济决策。现金流量表通过总结一段时期内财务状况的主要变化，突出管理层的工作重点。例如，资本支出和发展成本的增加可能意味着未来收入流的增加，而短期投资过度的趋势可能意味着缺乏可行的长期投资机会。此外，比较不同实体的现金流量可能更好地揭示其收益的相对质量，因为现金流量信息比损益表中反映的财务业绩更为客观，而损益表很容易因采用不同的会计政策而产生重大变化。

13.5.1　现金及现金等价物的概念

现金流量表中使用现金或现金等价物作为现金的定义。报表应说明该期间现金及现金等价物的变动情况。

现金是流动性最强的资产，包括硬币、纸币、支票、汇款单以及可以在银行或其他的金融机构自由提取的货币存款，其主要账户有库存现金、银行存款和其他货币资金三个部分。

现金等价物是短期、高流动性的投资，可以很快转换为已知金额的现金。一般来说，基本上没有信用风险；现金等价物对实体的原始到期日为三个月或三个月以下。基本上不存在市场(或利率)风险。现金等价物包括短期国库券、商业票据和货币市场基金。

13.5.2 现金流量表的商业活动

由于损益表和资产负债表是根据权责发生制会计编制的,因此有必要调整从这些财务报表中提取的金额,以便只反映一段时期内现金流入和流出的变动。所有现金流均按经营、投资和融资活动分类,如下所述:

- 经营活动产生的现金流

现金流量表上的经营活动包括经营企业和销售其产品或服务所产生的现金的来源和用途。经营活动产生的现金包括现金、应收账款、折旧、存货和应付账款的任何变动。这些交易还包括工资、所得税、利息、租金和销售产品或服务的现金收入。

经营活动产生的现金流

现金流入	现金流出
销售商品或服务的收入	购买用于转售或用于制造贸易商品的支出
收取或出售经营性应收款的收入	支付贸易物资票据
利息收入	其他物资和员工支出
股利收入	现金支付的税金、费用和罚款
其他经营性收入	利息支出
	其他经营性支出

- 投资活动产生的现金流

投资活动包括公司投资于公司长期未来的现金来源和用途。投资活动产生的现金流包括购买或出售资产、向卖方提供的贷款、从客户处收到的贷款或与并购有关的任何付款产生的现金流变动。

投资活动产生的现金流

现金流入	现金流出
贷款收入	购买其他实体的债务工具
出售股权投资,例如普通股或优先股	购买股权所支付的款项
出售生产性资产	购买生产性资产

- 融资活动产生的现金流

筹资活动产生的现金包括投资者或银行的现金来源,以及支付给股东的现金使用情况。融资活动包括债务发行、股权发行、股票回购、贷款、股息支付和债务偿还。

融资活动产生的现金流

现金流入	现金流出
发行权益证券(例如普通股和优先股)	偿还长期和短期债务本金
借款收入(例如债券、抵押和票据)	重新购买普通和优先股工具的付款
捐赠或购买,改善或建造长期资产的捐款和投资收入捐助方的收款	支付给普通股和优先股股东的股息

13.5.3 现金流量表的编制

现金流量表可以采用直接法或间接法编制。在间接法和直接法下,来自投资和融资活动部分的现金流是相同的，经营活动产生的现金流也是相同的，但信息的格式不同。

1. 直接法

根据直接法，现金流量表采用公司经营、投资和筹资三大活动的实际现金流入和流出。直接法下，现金流量表的经营部分以收入实现制为基础列示，会计期间的现金流量净额为实际现金流入与流出的差额。表 13-6 给出了直接方法的格式。

表 13-6 直接法计算的格式

	$
经营活动现金流	
收取客户的现金(W1)	X
付给供应商的现金(W2)	(X)
付给员工的现金(W3)	(X)
支付营业费用的现金(W4)	
经营产生的现金	X
已付利息(W5)	(X)
已付所得税(W6)	(X)
经营活动产生的现金净额	X

工作原理：

1.	收取客户的现金	= 销售净额 + 应收账款减少额/(应收账款增加额)
2.	付给供应商的现金	= 销货成本 + 存货增加额/(存货减少额) + 应付账款减少额/(应付账款增加额)
3.	付给员工的现金	= 应付工资薪酬 + 应付职工薪酬减少额/(应付职工薪酬增加额)
4.	支付营业费用的现金	= 其他经营费用 + 预付费用增加额 /(预测费用减少额) + 应急费用减少额/(应急费用增加额)
5.	已付利息	= 利息费用 + 应付利息减少额 /(应付利息增加额)
6.	已付所得税	= 所得税费用 + 应付税费减少额 /(应付税费增加额)

批：经营费用不包含折旧额。

2. 间接法

间接法是编制现金流量表的两种会计方法之一。间接法利用资产负债表项目的变动来修改现金流的经营部分。间接法下，现金流量表的编制以权责发生制下的净损益为基础，随后增加或减少非现金收支项目，形成经营活动产生的现金流量。

间接法计算的格式如表 13-7 所示，这种方法在计算中较为常见。

表 13-7 间接法计算的格式

	$
税前利润(利润表)	X
调整项：	
增加：折旧/摊销	X

	(续表)
利息费用	X
出售非流动资产损益	X/(X)
(增加)/减少应收账款	(X)/X
(增加)/减少存货	(X)/X
增加/(减少)应付账款	X/(X)
经营产生现金流	X
利息支出/收入	(X)/X
所得税费支出	(X)
经营活动产生净现金流	X

重要的是要理解为什么有些项目是加的，而其他项目是减的。应注意以下几点：

(1) 折旧/摊销不是现金支出，而是在损益表中计算利润时扣除的。因此，通过调增折旧/摊销来消除它的影响。

(2) 处置非流动资产的损失(由于折旧准备计提而产生)需要加回，并扣除利润。

(3) 存货增加意味着现金减少，因为企业将现金花在购买库存上了。

(4) 应收账款增加意味着公司的应收账款并没有支付那么多，因此，企业的现金减少。

(5) 应付账款减少意味着公司已经还款，因此，企业的现金会减少。

【例 13-1】截至 2019 年 12 月 31 日，其他业务信息如下：

(1) 出售非流动资产的投资收益为 60,000 美元。

(2) 年内出售的固定装置和配件原价为 22 万美元，账面净值为 13 万美元，售价为 12.8 万美元。

(3) 以下信息与财产、厂房和设备有关。

	2019年12月31日	2018年12月31日
	(数字单位：万美元)	
成本	2,200	2,015
累计折旧	500	400

(4) 年内，以每股 27.5 便士的溢价发行了 40 万股 1.00 美元的普通股。

(5) 短期投资流动性强，接近到期日。

(6) 年内支付股息总计 20 万美元。

要求：

根据公司的损益表和资产负债表，编制 SL 公司截至 2019 年 12 月 31 日的年度现金流量表。采用国际会计准则 IAS 7 允许的间接法。

解决方案：

以权责发生制下的税前净利润为起点，剔除非经营活动产生的利润，将"净利润"调整为经营活动所产生的净利润。加上曾经减少利润但与经营活动无关的项目和减去曾经增加利润但与经营活动无关的项目。

第1步：从利润表中获取税前净利润

SL 公司
现金流量表
截至 2019 年 12 月 31 日

	$,000
经营活动现金流	
税前净利润	$745

第2步：确定折旧费用

折旧费用需要调整，因为折旧费用使净收入减少，但现金未实际流出，它应被加回到税前净利润中。如果未在损益表中列示，有时可以通过分析累计折旧账户找到。

工作表1：累计折旧 T 型账户

累计折旧			
出售资产的折旧额 (220-130)	$90	期初余额	$400
期末余额	$500	*折旧费用*	*$190(差额)*
	$590		$590

第3步：分析出售投资、设备等产生的损益

损益包含在净利润中，但不代表是经营现金流，损益将被扣除/计入净利润。

	$,000
经营活动现金流	
税前净利润	745
调整：	
折旧(W1)	190
处置固定设施损失(128-130)	2
处置物业、厂房及设备损失(60-95)	35
利息收入	(33)
利息支出	75
营运资本变动前的营业利润	1014

第4步：影响现金流变动的营运资本

现金流量表的编制以现金收付制为基础。因此，有必要根据权责发生制调整影响现金流的营运资本。

营运资本变动前的营业利润	1014
(增加)/减少应收账款	(695)
(增加)/减少存货	(48)
增加/(减少) 应付账款	170
经营活动产生现金	441

第 5 步：计算经营活动净现金流量

最后，在计算经营活动产生的净现金流量时，有必要考虑纳税和利息对其产生的影响。

经营活动产生的现金	441
利息支付	(75)
已付税项(W2)	(130)
经营活动产生的现金流量净额	236

工作表 2：税金 T 型账户

本年度缴纳的税款为去年的年终准备金，并计算税费作为差额。

税金

已付税项(差额)	*$130*	期初余额	$285
期末余额	$312	损益表	$157
	$442		$442

第 6 步：分析和计算投资和筹资活动净现金流量

投资活动现金流	
购买无形资产(425-375)	(50)
购买物业、厂房及设备(W3)	(386)
出售非流动资产的收入(128+60)	188
利息收入	33
投资活动产生的现金流量净额	(215)
筹资活动现金流	
发行股本的收益(400+400*0.275)	510
长期贷款	120
股利支付	(200)
筹资活动产生的现金流量净额	430

工作表 3：物业、厂房及设备 T 型账户

物业、厂房及设备

期初余额	$2,015	处置	$220
重估收益(70-51)	$19	期末余额	$2,200
购买	*$386(差额)*		
	$2,420		$2,420

综上所述，采用间接法编制的现金流量表如下：

SL 公司
现金流量表
截至 2019 年 12 月 31 日

	$,000
经营活动现金流	

(续表)

税前净利润	745
调整：	
折旧(W1)	190
处置固定设施的损失(128-130)	2
处置物业、厂房及设备的损失(60-95)	35
利息收入	(33)
利息支出	<u>75</u>
营运资本变动前的营业利润	1014
(增加)/减少应收账款	(695)
(增加)/减少存货	(48)
增加/(减少)应付账款	<u>170</u>
经营活动产生的现金流量净额	441
利息支付	(75)
已付税项(W2)	<u>(130)</u>
经营活动净现金流	<u>236</u>
投资活动现金流	
购买无形资产(425-375)	(50)
购买物业、厂房及设备(W3)	(386)
出售非流动资产的收入(128+60)	188
利息收入	<u>33</u>
投资活动产生的现金流量净额	<u>(215)</u>
筹资活动现金流	
发行股本的收益(400+400×0.275)	510
长期贷款	120
股利支付	<u>(200)</u>
筹资活动产生的现金流量净额	<u>430</u>
现金及现金等价物净增加额	451
2019年1月1日现金及现金等价物	(79)
2019年12月31日现金及现金等价物	372

13.6 附注

    财务报表附注为报表使用者提供了有关损益及其他全面收益表，财务状况表，现金流量表和权益变动表中有关财务报表编制基础和所用具体会计政策的信息，按照国际财务报告准则披露的要求，财务报表中未列出的任何信息，以及其他信息，这些信息在财务报表的其他地方未提供，但与理解其中的任何信息有关。主要包括：企业所采用的主要会计处理方法、会计政策及其变更情况、变更的原因以及对财务状况和经营业绩的影响、发生的非经常性项目、一些重要报表项目的明显情况、或有事项以及期后事项。

Chapter 14

Financial Statement Analysis

14.1 Purpose of Financial Statement Analysis

Financial statement analysis refers to the systematic analysis and evaluation of the past and present operating results, financial status and changes of enterprises with special methods based on financial statements and other data. Its most basic function is to transform a large number of report data into useful information for specific decision-making so that relevant decisions are more accurate.

The main purpose of financial statement analysis is to evaluate the solvency, profitability and risk resistance of an enterprise. After the financial statement is analyzed, it is necessary to compare the analysis results with those of competitors, counterparts and general financial market standards, find out existing issues and propose corresponding strategies and measures, so as to further enhance its strengths, avoid its weaknesses and improve the economic benefits in operation and management. The main purposes of financial analysis for internal and external users are as follows:

Judge the financial situation of the enterprise

By calculating, analyzing and comparing indicators, it can be determined whether asset structure and debt level of the enterprise are reasonable or not, so as to better identify its financial strength such as such as solvency, operating ability and profitability, and reveal its financial situation and potential issues. External analysts, especially creditors, pay particular attention to such content.

Evaluate business performance

By calculating, analyzing and comparing indicators, an enterprise can evaluate its profitability and asset turnover rate, reveal all aspects and links of enterprise management, find out gaps and draw conclusions from analysis results.

Evaluate the development trend of enterprises

Through a variety of financial analysis, analysts can judge the development trend of the enterprise, predict its production and operation prospects and solvency, so as to provide important basis for the enterprise leadership to make decisions on production and operation, investors to make investment decisions and creditors to make credit decisions and to further avoid significant losses caused by wrong decisions.

14.2 Basic Analytical Procedures

14.2.1 Horizontal Analysis

Horizontal analysis is a financial analysis method, which compares the information reflecting the financial status of the reporting period with the information reflecting the financial status of the enterprise in an earlier period or a certain period, and studies its development and changes, as well as various business performance or financial status of the enterprise. The basic requirement of horizontal analysis is to compare the same data in different periods of financial statement resources.

In the analysis, the first problem is to determine the base year and then calculate the changes based on the base year. In a horizontal analysis, the oldest year shown is used as the base year and the change in the amount between the base year and the current year is determined. For Liam Co., 2018 is the base year.

After setting the base year, the change between the current year and the base year is calculated after the base year is established, and then the change is divided by the number of base year and multiplied by 100 to further calculate the change in percentage. In such context, the balance sheet of Liam Co., is used for case study.

For changes in Cash at Bank, subtract $778 in the base year from $683 in the current year and determine a cash change of $95. To determine the change in percentage, we divided $95 by the base year balance of $683 and multiply by 100%. The change in percentage was a 13.91% increase in Cash at Bank. Thus, the company's total assets increased by 12.66%, which may affect some of the ratios calculated later in the presentation.

Exhibit 14-1　Comparative Statement of Financial Position-Horizontal Analysis

Liam Co.

Comparative Statement of Financial Position

31 December 2019 and 2018

	2019 $, 000	2018 $, 000	Increase/Decrease Amount	Increase/Decrease Present
Non-current assets				
Property, plant and equipment (PPE)	2,150	1,942	208	10.71
Intangible assets	638	563	75	13.32
Investments	360	289	71	24.57

				(continued)
Current assets				
Inventory	634	522	112	21.46
Accounts receivables	925	886	39	4.40
Short-term investments	113	84	29	34.52
Cash at Bank	778	683	95	13.91
Total Assets	5,598	4,969	629	12.66
Liability and Equity				
Equity				
Common stock ($5 par)	2,325	2,325	-	-
Preferred stock ($100 par, 5%)	300	300	-	-
Revaluation surplus	205	177	28	15.82
Retained earnings	1,127	924	203	21.97
Non-current liability				
Long-term loans	486	338	148	43.79
Current liabilities				
Trade payables	442	330	112	33.94
Bank overdrafts	215	147	68	46.26
Taxation	498	428	70	16.36
Total Liability and Equity	5,598	4,969	629	12.66

14.2.2 Vertical Analysis

Vertical analysis is to compare the data of each project in the financial statement with the data of the whole project to obtain the position, importance and changes of the whole project. We can learn from vertical analysis about whether the enterprise is making progress in its operation, and its degree and speed. Generally speaking, all items in the balance sheet are expressed as a percentage of total assets, and all items in the income statement are expressed as a percentage of net sales.

Take the assets of Liam Co.'s balance sheet as an example for comparative analysis. Total assets represent all items on the financial statements, so the total assets are set equal to 100%. Calculate the percentage of Cash at Bank in total assets. Divide the total Cash at Bank in 2019 by the total assets in 2019 and multiply the result by 100%. As of the end of 2019, Cash at Bank accounted for 13.90% of total assets. The percentage in 2018 was calculated to be 13.75% in the same manner.

Exhibit 14-2   Comparative Statement of Financial Position-Vertical Analysis

Liam Co.

Comparative Statement of Financial Position

31 December 2019 and 2018

	2019		2018	
	$, 000		$, 000	
	Amount	Present	Amount	Present
Non-current assets				
Property, plant and equipment (PPE)	2,150	38.41	1,942	39.08
Intangible assets	638	11.40	563	11.33
Investments	360	6.43	289	5.82
Current assets				
Inventory	634	11.33	522	10.51
Accounts receivables	925	16.52	886	17.83
Short-term investments	113	2.02	84	1.69
Cash at Bank	778	13.90	683	13.75
Total Assets	5,598	100.00	4,969	100.00
Liability and Equity				
Equity				
Common stock ($5 par)	2,325	41.53	2,325	46.79
Preferred stock ($100 par, 5%)	300	5.36	300	6.04
Revaluation surplus	205	3.66	177	3.56
Retained earnings	1,127	20.13	924	18.60
Non-current liability				
Long-term loans	486	8.68	338	6.80
Current liabilities				
Trade payables	442	7.90	330	6.64
Bank overdrafts	215	3.84	147	2.96
Taxation	498	8.90	428	8.61
Total Liability and Equity	5,598	100.00	4,969	100.00

Take Liam's income statement as an example for comparative analysis. All items on the income statement are expressed as net sales, so the net sales are set equal to 100%. Calculate the cost of goods sold as a percentage of net sales. Divide the total cost of goods sold in 2019 by the total net sales in 2019 and multiply by 100%. As of the end of 2019, the cost of goods sold accounted for 69.54% of the total net sales. The proportion in 2018 was calculated to be 69.73% in the same manner.

Exhibit 14-3 Comparative Income Statement - Vertical Analysis

Liam Co.
Comparative Income Statement
31 December 2019 and 2018

	2019		2018	
	$, 000		$, 000	
	Amount	Present	Amount	Present
Net Sales	5,423	100	4,830	100
Cost of Sales	3,773	69.57	3,368	69.73
Gross Profit	1,650	30.43	1,462	30.27
Distribution Costs	341	6.29	295	6.11
Administrative Expenses	404	7.45	375	7.76
Total Operating Expense	745	13.74	670	13.87
Profit before Interest and Tax (PBIT)	905	16.69	792	16.40
Interest Expense	264	4.87	218	4.51
Profit before Tax (PBT)	641	11.82	574	11.88
Income Tax Expense	262	4.83	239	4.95
Profit after Tax (PAT)	379	6.99	335	6.94

14.3 Current Analysis

14.3.1 Working Capital

Working capital is the general term for the current assets and liabilities of an enterprise. The difference between current assets and current liabilities is net working capital. The current assets on a company's balance sheet include cash, accounts receivable, inventory and other assets that are expected to be realized or converted into cash within one year. Current liabilities include accounts payable, wages, taxes payable and current long-term debt.

$$\text{Working Capital} = \text{Current Assets} - \text{Current Liabilities}$$

Working capital can be used to measure the short-term solvency of a company or an enterprise. The larger the amount is, the more adequately the company or enterprise is prepared for payment obligations, and the better the short-term solvency is. When there is a negative working capital, that is, the current assets of an enterprise are less than the current liabilities, its operation may be interrupted at any time due to poor turnover.

14.3.2 Current Ratio

The current ratio is the ratio of total current assets to total current liabilities. It is a measure of a company's ability to convert its current assets into cash before repaying its debt at maturity. Generally speaking, the higher the ratio, the stronger the liquidity of the corporate assets and the stronger the short-term solvency; otherwise, it is weak. However, too large proportion indicates that the current assets occupy more, which will affect the turnover efficiency of working capital and profitability. The generally considered minimum liquidity ratio is two.

$$\text{Current Ratio} = \frac{\text{Current Assets}}{\text{Current Liabilities}}$$

For Liam Co. working capital and current ratio for 2019 and 2018 are as followings:

	2019	2018
Current assets	$2,450	$2,175
Current liability	$1,155	$905
Working capital	$1,295	$1,270
Current ratio	2.12	2.40

14.3.3 Acid-Test Ratio

When using current ratios to analyze a company's solvency, it does not take into account the structure of current assets. In calculating the liquidity ratios of Liam Co. And Sami Co., we know that the working capital of the two companies is the same, with the current ratio of 2.12. However, the two companies' capabilities in repaying debts are quite different. Liam's current assets are mainly concentrated on accounts receivable and cash. These assets are relatively easy to liquidate and are under less pressure to repay. Sami's current assets are mainly concentrated on inventory, which means that the company has to sell most of its inventory and collect money to repay its debt on schedule. In comparison, Sami's liquidity is relatively weak. Therefore, an indicator that excludes these inventories' poor liquidity is needed to measure the short-term solvency of an enterprise.

The data of Liam Co. and Sami Co.'s current position on December 31, 2019 are as follows:

	Liam Co.	Sami Co.
Current assets:		
Inventory	$634	$1192
Accounts receivables	$925	$410
Short-term investments	$113	$57
Cash at Bank	$778	$791
Total current assets	$2,450	$2,450
Current liabilities	$1,155	$1,155
Working capital	$1,295	$1,295
Current ratio	2.12	2.12

The acid test ratio is also called quick ratio. It compares a company's fast assets with its current liabilities and measures the company's ability to liquidate its current assets immediately to pay off short-term debts and other direct liabilities. In some cases, this measure is more useful than liquidity ratios because it excludes assets, such as inventories, that may be difficult to liquidate quickly.

$$\text{Quick Ratio} = \frac{\text{Quick Assets}}{\text{Current Liabilities}} \quad \text{(Quick Assets = Current Assets - Inventory)}$$

Liam's quick ratio calculation process is as follows:

	2019	2018
Quick assets:		
Accounts receivables	$925	$886
Short-term investments	$113	$84
Cash at Bank	$778	$683
Total quick assets	$1,816	$1,653
Current liability	$1,155	$905
Quick ratio	1.57	1.83

For most industries, acid test ratio should exceed 1. And too high ratio is not always favorable. It may indicate that cash has accumulated and is not being used, rather than being reinvested, returned to shareholders, or otherwise used for production. The acceptable range of acid test ratios varies from industry to industry, so a comparative analysis of companies in the same industry is necessary before any assessment can be made.

14.4 Solvency

14.4.1 Debt Ratio

The debt ratio is an indicator used to measure the ability of a company to use creditors to provide funds for operating activities, and reflect the degree of security of creditors' loans. By comparing a company's total liabilities with its total assets, it is possible to determine the proportion of debt financing in a company's assets.

A debt ratio greater than 1 indicates that a company has more liabilities than assets and is at risk of being insolvent. Meanwhile, high debt ratios suggest that companies could be at risk of defaulting on their loans if interest rates suddenly rise. A debt ratio less than 1 indicates that a significant portion of the company's assets are provided by equity and financial risk is relatively small.

Debt ratios in different industries are very different, so a reasonable analysis needs to be combined with other financial indicators. The debt ratio may greatly vary among different industries, so it needs to be analyzed reasonably in combination with other financial indicators.

$$\text{Debt Ratio} = \frac{\text{Total Liabilities}}{\text{Total Assets}}$$

The debt data for Liam Co. are as follows:

	2019	2018
Total liability	$1,641	$1,243
Total assets	$5,598	$4,969
Debt ratio	0.29	0.25

According to the calculations, the debt-to-asset ratio in 2019 was higher than in 2018, mainly due to an increase in long-term borrowing in 2019.

14.4.2 Times Interest Earned (TIE)

The times interest earned reflect a multiple of debt interest payable by a company's operating income. It is not only the premise basis of an enterprise's debt management, but also an important indicator to measure the long-term solvency of an enterprise. The times interest earned should be at least greater than 1, and the higher the ratio, the stronger the company's ability to pay interest expenses, which means that the company has enough cash to continue investing in other businesses after repaying debt. If the interest protection multiple is too low, the enterprise will face the risk of loss and the security and stability of debt service will also be reduced.

The formula for the times interest earned is the profit before interest and taxes divided by the total interest payable on bonds and other debts.

$$\text{Times Interest Earned} = \frac{\text{Profit before Interest and Tax (PBIT)}}{\text{Interest Expense}}$$

The times interest earned data for Liam Co. are as follows:

	2019	2018
Profit before tax	$641	$574
Add: Interest expense	$264	$218
Profit before Interest and tax	$905	$792
Times interest earned (times)	3.43	3.63

It can be seen from the calculation results that the times interest earned in 2018 and 2019 were greater than 1, the times interest earned in 2019 was lower than that in 2018.

14.5 Assets Efficiency

14.5.1 Accounts Receivable

Accounts receivable is an important asset in enterprises and they can even be current assets. If a company's accounts receivable can be recovered in a timely manner, its fund utilization efficiency can be greatly improved.

1. Accounts Receivable Turnover

Accounts receivable turnover rate is the ratio between a company's net credit sales income (the balance of sales income after deducting current sales and sales returns, sales discounts and discounts) and average accounts receivable balance in a certain period, and it is used to quantify the effectiveness of the company in collecting accounts receivable or amounts outstanding from customers. It is an indicator to measure the turnover and management efficiency of corporate receivables. If the company has notes receivable, the two should be analyzed together.

A high receivables turnover rate can indicate that it has high recovery efficiency and can quickly repay

Chapter 14 Financial Statement Analysis

debts. The low receivables turnover rate may be caused by insufficient credit policies of the company or poor financial status of the customers or untrustworthy reputation.

$$\text{Accounts Receivable Turnover} = \frac{\text{Net Sales}}{\text{Average Net Accounts Receivable}}$$

The accounts receivable turnovers for Liam Co. are as follows:

	2019	2018
Net sales	$5,423	$4,830
Accounts receivables		
Beginning of year	$886	$830
End of year	$925	$886
Total	$1,811	$1,716
Average net accounts receivables (Total/2)	$905.5	$858
Accounts receivable turnover	5.99	5.63

According to the calculation and analysis, the total asset turnover rate in 2019 was slightly better than that in 2018, mainly due to the increase of net sales.

2. Numbers of day's Sales in Receivable

The turnover rate of accounts receivable represented by time is the number of days of accounts receivable turnover, which represents the time required for the company to obtain the right to account receivables to recover the amounts and become cash.

$$\text{Numbers of day's Sales in Receivable} = \frac{\text{Average net accounts receivables}}{\text{Net sales}} \times 365$$

$$= \frac{365}{\text{Accounts Receivable Turnover}}$$

The numbers of day's sales in receivable for Liam Co. are as follows:

	2019	2018
Accounts receivables		
Beginning of year	$886	$830
End of year	$925	$886
Total	$1,811	$1,716
Average net accounts receivables (Total/2)	$905.5	$858
Net sales	$5,423	$4,830
×360		
Numbers of day's Sales in Receivable	60.11	63.95

14.5.2 Inventory Turnover

Inventory is of great significance in business operation and management decisions. Enterprises should maintain sufficient inventory to meet customers' purchase and business needs. However, the longer the inventory items are stored, the higher the storage cost, the more funds they occupy, and the worse the liquidity of the enterprise's funds. Therefore, for the inventory turnover speed, the enterprise can evaluate the inventory turnover rate and period.

1. Inventory Turnover

Inventory turnover is a supplementary explanation of the turnover rate of current assets. Through calculation and analysis of inventory turnover, it can be measured whether an enterprise's inventory liquidity and inventory capital occupation are reasonable, and its ability to put into production, inventory management, and sales recovery can also be determined. Generally speaking, the faster the inventory turnover, the lower the inventory occupancy level, the stronger the liquidity, and the faster the inventory is converted into cash or receivables. Therefore, a company's ability in cash liquidity can be improved by increasing its inventory turnover.

The inventory turnover rate can be calculated in two ways. One is to divide the sales by the average inventory balance (the sum of the opening inventory and the ending inventory divided by 2). And the other method uses the cost of goods sold instead of the sales, which is the ratio of the cost of goods sold over a certain period to the average inventory balance. The cost of goods sold instead of sales used for calculating inventory turnover is intended to make inventory turnover calculation results more accurate because sales include cost additions. In both cases, average inventory is used to help eliminate seasonal effects.

When inventory turnover is calculated, "revenue from sales" or "cost of sales" is used as the turnover rate for the purposes of the analysis. If the purpose of the analysis is to determine short-term solvency, sales revenue should be used. If the purpose of the analysis is to evaluate inventory management performance, cost of sales should be used.

$$\text{Inventory Turnover} = \frac{\text{Cost of Good Sold}}{\text{Average Inventories}}$$

The inventory turnovers for Liam Co. are as follows:

	2019	2018
Cost of goods sold	$3,773	$3,368
Inventory		
Beginning of year	$522	$478
End of year	$634	$522
Total	$1,156	$1,000
Average (Total/2)	$578	$500
Inventory turnover	6.53	6.74

According to calculations, Liam's inventory turnover has not changed much since 2018. For businesses, a low turnover rate means weak sales and a backlog of inventory, which may indicate a problem with the goods being offered for sale or the result of too little marketing; a high ratio means either strong sales or insufficient inventory. The former is desirable, while the latter may result in a loss of business opportunity.

2. Numbers of Day's Sales in Inventory

The days of inventory turnover can be calculated by dividing the number of days (360 days) during this period by the inventory turnover to calculate the number of days from inventory acquisition to consumption and sales.

The fewer days of inventory turnover, the more the number of inventory turnovers, the less the average inventories. However, too few days of inventory turnover cannot meet the needs of circulation, and too many days will occupy more funds and cause a waste of resources. Therefore, an enterprise needs to consolidate the receivables turnover days to obtain a suitable cash turnover period.

$$\text{Numbers of day's Sales in Inventory} = \frac{\text{Average Inventories}}{\text{Cost of Good Sold}} \times 365$$

$$= \frac{365}{\text{Inventory Turnover}}$$

The numbers of day's sales in inventories for Liam Co. are as follows:

	2019	2018
Inventory		
Beginning of year	$522	$478
End of year	$634	$522
Total	$1156	$1,000
Average (Total/2)	$578	$500
Cost of goods sold	$3,773	$3,368
*360		
Numbers of day's Sales in Inventory	55.15	53.44

14.5.3 Total Assets Turnover

The total asset turnover ratio is an indicator of the ratio between the scale of asset investment and the level of sales. It can be used as an indicator of a company's use of assets to generate income efficiency. It reflects the transfer speed of all assets of the company from input to output during the operating period, and the management quality and utilization efficiency of all assets of the company this year and in previous years. In general, the higher the asset turnover rate, the faster the company's total asset turnover, the stronger its sales capacity, and the higher its asset utilization efficiency.

The calculation of the asset turnover rate means that the numerator represents the net sales on the company's income statement, and the denominator represents the total assets on the company's balance sheet. The total assets should be averaged during the evaluation period. For example, if a company uses total assets in 2019 for calculating asset turnover, it should average its total assets at the beginning and end of 2019.

$$\text{Total Assets Turnover} = \frac{\text{Net Sales}}{\text{Average Total Assets}}$$

The Liam's total asset turnover ratio is calculated as follows:

	2019	2018
Net sales	$5,423	$4,830
Assets:		
Beginning of year	4,969	4,385
Ending of year	5,598	4,969
Total	10,567	9,354
Average (Total/2)	5283.5	4,677
Total assets turnover	1.026	1.033

Through calculation and analysis, it is found that the turnover rate of total assets in 2019 was lower than in 2018, mainly due to the increase in total assets and sales. Before evaluating Liam's asset turnover, it is necessary to make a comparative analysis with that of the same industry or similar companies.

14.6 Profitability

14.6.1 Profit Margin

Profit margin is one of the commonly used profitability ratios to measure the profitability of a company. It shows the percentage of sales converted to profit, that is, how much net profit each dollar of sales can bring. The higher the ratio, the stronger the profitability of the enterprise.

Profit margins are divided into gross profit, operating profit margin, pre-tax profit margin and net profit margin. However, in daily use, it usually refers to the net profit margin, which is the net profit divided by the net sales.

$$\text{Gross Profit Margin} = \frac{\text{Net sales} - \text{Cost of Goods Sold}}{\text{Net Sales}}$$

$$\text{Operating Profit Margin} = \frac{\text{Profit before Interest and Tax}}{\text{Net Sales}}$$

$$\text{Pretax Profit Margin} = \frac{\text{Profit before Tax}}{\text{Net Sales}}$$

$$\text{Net Profit Margin} = \frac{\text{Profit After Tax}}{\text{Net Sales}}$$

According to Liam Co.'s statement data, its profit margin is calculated as follows:

	2019	2018
Profit after tax	$379	$335
Net sales	$5,423	4830
Profit margin	6.99%	6.94%

Liam Co. achieved a profit margin of 6.99% in 2019, which means it had a net income of 6.99 cents for every dollar of sales. According to the calculation results, the profitability of Liam Co. was enhanced.

14.6.2 Return on Total Assets (ROA)

Return on assets is a profitability indicator used to measure how much net profit is created per unit of assets. When calculating the return on assets, interest expenses are added to the net profit to obtain the operating return before deducting financing costs. Since total assets are financed by shareholders and creditors, the return on assets is a measure of the business, regardless of the source of funds and the ability to create value for shareholders and creditors. The return on assets is expressed as a percentage. The higher the ratio, the more efficiently the company's management can manage its balance sheet and generate profits.

$$\text{Return on Total Assets} = \frac{\text{Profit after Tax} + \text{Interest Income}}{\text{Average Total Assets}}$$

Liam Co.'s return on total assets is calculated as follows:

	2019	2018
Profit after tax	$379	$335
Add: Interest expense	$264	$218
Total	$643	$553
Assets:		
Beginning of year	$4,969	$4,385
Ending of year	$5,598	$4,969
Total	$10,567	$9,354
Average (Total/2)	$5283.5	$4,677
ROA	12.17%	11.82%

According to the calculation results, the return on assets in 2019 was higher than that in 2018. Before evaluating Liam's profitability, it is necessary to compare and analyze the indicators of relevant companies in the industry.

14.6.3 Return on Capital Employed (ROCE)

Return on capital is a financial ratio that measures a company's profitability and the efficiency with which it uses its capital. The higher the return on capital, the more efficiently a company can use its available capital to generate profits. A company's good return on capital should always be above its average rate of return on capital. Return on capital is an important profit ratio that investors often use for selecting suitable investment candidates.

$$\text{Return on Capital Employed} = \frac{\text{Profit before Interest and Tax}}{\text{Capital Employed}}$$

(Capital Employed = Total Assets – Current Liability)

The calculation of Liam's return on capital employed is as follows:

	2019	2018
Profit before Interest and tax	$905	$792
Total Assets	$5,598	$4,969
Minus: Current liability	$1,155	$905
Capital employed	$4,443	$4,064
Return on capital employed	20.37%	19.49%

The return on capital employed used in 2019 has slightly improved. Before the evaluation, it needs to be compared with the return on capital employed used in the current year (risk-free return plus risk return) to draw a conclusion.

14.6.4 Return on Equity (Rate Earned on Total Assets)

Return on equity is a profitability indicator that measures how effectively management uses the company's assets to generate profits. The result indicates how much profit each dollar of common stockholders' equity generates. The return on equity is calculated by dividing net profit (entitled by ordinary shareholders, deducting preferred stock dividends) by shareholders' equity. Since shareholder equity is equal to the assets of a company minus debts, return on equity is also known as return on net assets.

$$\text{Returned on Equity} = \frac{\text{Profit after Tax} - \text{Preferred Dividends}}{\text{Average Total Owners' Equity}}$$

Liam's return to equity is calculated as follows:

	2019	2018
Profit after tax	$379	$335
Preferred dividends	$15	$15
Remainder – identified with common stock	$364	$320
Equity		
Beginning of year	3,726	3,483
Ending of year	3,957	3,726
Total	7,683	7,209
Average (Total/2)	3841.5	3604.5
ROE	9.48%	8.88%

Liam's return on equity was improved in 2019. But the return on equity depends on the conditions of the industry or company peers. Therefore, it makes more sense to compare one company with another similar company before making an assessment.

14.6.5 Earnings Per Share on Common Stock

Earnings per share is a market-expected ratio, which is used to indicate the net profit or the net loss of a company that every common shareholder can enjoy. It reflects the company's operating results, and measures the profitability and investment risk of common stocks. It is one of the important financial indicators for investors and other information users to evaluate the profitability of the company and predict its growth potential for more effectively making relevant decisions.

Earnings per share is calculated by dividing the company's net profit by number of shares. The higher the ratio, the more profit it creates. If the company only has common shares, the net income is net profit after tax. The number of shares requires the use of the balance sheet and income statement to identify the number of common shares issued at the end of the period. If the company has preferred shares, dividends distributed to preferred shareholders should be deducted from after-tax net profits.

Companies typically report earnings per share (EPS) adjusted for special projects and potential share dilution. The higher the company's EPS, the higher the company's profits, and the more profits the company has for distributing to shareholders.

$$\text{Earnings Per Share} = \frac{\text{Profit after Tax} - \text{Preferred Dividends}}{\text{Shares of Common Stock Outstanding}}$$

Liam's earnings per share is calculated as follows:

	2019	2018
Profit after tax	$379	$335
Preferred dividends	$15	$15
Remainder – identified with common stock	$364	$320
Shares of common stock outstanding ($ 5 par)	465	465
Earnings per share on common stock	$0.78	$0.68

Earnings per share of 2019 were $ 0.78, which means that each share of Liam's stock would enjoy a net profit of $ 0.78. The earnings per share indicator is one of the most important variables in determining stock prices. It is also the main component used to calculate the P/E ratio, where E in the P/E ratio represents EPS. By dividing the company's share price by earnings per share, investors can see the value of a stock based on how much the market is willing to pay for each dollar of earnings.

14.6.6　Price to Earnings Ratio

The P/E ratio is a measure of a company's current share price relative to earnings per share. The P/E ratio usually refers to the static P/E ratio, which is used as an indicator to compare whether stocks with different prices are overvalued or undervalued. The lower ratio, the lower the profitability of the market price relative to the stock, indicating that the shorter the investment recovery period, the smaller the investment risk, and the greater the investment value of the stock; a high ratio may mean that a company's stock is overvalued and that investors expect high growth rates in the future.

$$\text{Price to Earnings Ratio} = \frac{\text{Market Price per Share of Common Stock}}{\text{Earnings per share}}$$

Assume that the market price per share of Liam's common stock in 2018 and 2019 are $ 6.8 and $ 11.5, respectively.

Liam's P/E ratio is calculated as follows:

	2019	2018
Market price per share of common stock	$11.5	$6.8
Earnings per share on common stock	$0.78	$0.68
P/E ratio	14.74	10

Liam's P/E ratio in 2019 was 14.74, which translated to 14.74 times the company's profit on sales. When investors use the price-earnings ratio to compare the value of different stocks, they should choose stocks of the same industry for comparative research, because the earnings per share of the same industry are relatively close and comparable.

Key Words and Expressions

horizontal analysis	水平分析(横向分析)
vertical analysis	垂直分析(纵向分析)
asset management	资产管理
working capital	营运资本
current ratio	流动比率
quick/acid test ratio	速动比率
current position analysis	流动性分析
liquidity	流动性
solvency	偿债能力
debt ratio	资产负债率

times interest earned	利息保障倍数
efficiency	营运能力
accounts receivable turnover	应收账款周转率
number of days' sales in receivables	应收账款周转期
inventory turnover	存货周转率
number of days' sales in inventory	存货周转期
total assets turnover	总资产周转率
profitability	盈利能力
profit margin	销售利润率
profit before interest and tax	息税前利润
return on total assets	资产回报率
profit before tax	税前利润
profit after tax	税后利润
common stock	普通股
preferred stock	优先股
earnings per share on common stock	普通股每股收益
preferred dividend	优先股股利
price earnings ratio	市盈率
market price	市场价值

Exercises

Please select the best answer for the following questions or uncompleted sentences.

1. Zin has the following working capital ratios:

	2019	2018
Current ratio	1.3:1	1.5:1
Receivable days	60 days	35 days
Payables days	30 days	45 days
Inventory turnover	40 days	32 days

Which of the following statements is correct? (   )

A. Zin's liquidity and working capital has improving in 2019.

B. Zin is taking longer to pay supplies in 2019.

C. Zin is suffering from a worsening liquidity position in 2019.

D. Zin is receiving cash from customers more quickly in 2019 than in 2018.

2. The following figures are taken from statement of financial position of ABC Co.

	$,000
Inventory	360
Receivables	400
Cash	180
Payables	400
Bank loan repayable in 5 years' time	400

What is ABC Co.'s current ratio? (   )

A. 2.35

B. 1.175

C. 1.4

D. 0.725

3. A company's quick ratio has increased from 1.1:1 on 31 December 2018 to 1.5:1 on 31 December 2019. Which of the following events could explain this increase?

A. A reduction in payables

B. Improved inventory control

C. An increasing payable

D. The refinancing of a long-term loan

4. The following information has been taken or calculated from XYZ Co.'s financial statements for the year ended 31 March 2019:

Cash cycle on 31 March 2019	80 days
Inventory turnover	Six times (360days)
Year-end trade payables on 31 March 2019	$200,000
Credit purchases for the year ended 31 March 2019	$2,000,000

What is XYZ Co.'s trade receivables collection period as on 31 March 2019? (   )

A. 44 days   B. 56 days   C. 96 days   D. 104 days

5. T Co. had 30,000 shares in issue on 1 January 2019. On 1 July 2019 it made a 1 for 5 rights issue at a price of $1.5. The market value immediately prior to the issue was $2.0. Profit for the year ended 31 December 2019 was $78,000.

What is EPS for the year? (   )

A. 2.36   B. 2.55   C. 1.16   D. 2.32

6. The following information relating a limited liability company called Jackie. This company is preparing financial statement for the year ended 31 March 2019.

Jackie Co.: Income Statement for the Year End 31 March 2019

	$,000
Sales	33,000
Cost of sales	6,266
Gross profit	26,734
Investment income	66
Distribution costs	3,423

	(Continued)
Distribution costs	3,423
Administrative expenses	1,144
Interest costs	535
Profit before tax	21,698
Income tax expense	4,480
Profit for the year	17,218

Jackie Co.: Statement of Financial Position as on 31 March 2019 and 2018

	2019	2018
	$, 000	$, 000
Non-current assets		
Property, plant and equipment (PPE)	65,838	52,175
Accumulated depreciation	12,470	11,963
	53,368	40,212
Current assets		
Inventory	11,332	10,939
Trade receivables	8,600	6,017
Cash at Bank	1,677	1,010
Total Assets	74,977	58,178
Current liabilities		
Trade payables	7,600	9,236
Bank overdrafts	2,515	3,170
Taxation	3,670	3,340
	13,785	15,746
Non-current liability		
Long-term loans	8,100	10,940
Equity		
Share capital	12,200	10,600
Share premium	6,622	4,900
Revaluation surplus	7,000	3,237
Retained earnings	27,270	12,755
Total Owner' Equity	53,092	31,492
Total liability and owners' equity	74,977	58,178

Task:

Calculate for the financial year ended 31 March 2019 the following rations:

(1) Net profit margin

(2) Return on capital employed
(3) Current ratio
(4) Quick ratio
(5) The numbers of day's sales in receivable
(6) Debt ratio

第14章 财务报表分析

14.1 财务报表分析的目的

财务报表分析是指基于财务报表和其他材料并以其为出发点,使用特殊方法对企业过去和现在的业务结果、财务状况和变更进行系统的分析和评估。财务报表分析的最基本功能是将大量的报告数据转换成对特定决策有用的信息,并减少决策的不确定性。

财务报表分析的主要目的是评估企业的偿债能力、盈利能力和抵抗风险能力。分析完成后,有必要将获得的结果与竞争对手、同行业其他公司的结果以及一般金融市场标准进行比较,找出存在的问题,提出解决这些问题的策略和措施,以达到发展优势、避免劣势、提高经营管理水平的经济效益的目的。内部和外部用户进行财务分析的主要目的如下:

判断企业财务状况

通过对指标的计算、分析和比较,可以了解企业的资产结构和债务水平是否合理,从而判断企业的财务实力,如偿债能力、营运能力及获利能力,并揭示出企业的财务状况以及企业财务状况中可能存在的问题。外部分析者,尤其是债权人,对此内容尤其关注。

评估企业的业务绩效

通过对指标的计算、分析和比较,可以评价和评估企业的盈利能力和资产周转率,揭示企业经营管理的各个方面和各个环节,找出差距,得出分析结论。

评估企业的发展趋势

通过各种财务分析,可以判断企业的发展趋势,预测企业的生产经营前景和偿债能力,为企业领导制定生产经营决策,投资者做出投资决策和债权人做出信用决策提供重要依据,避免因决策错误而造成重大损失。

14.2 基本分析程序

14.2.1 水平分析

水平分析法是一种财务分析方法,将反映报告期财务状况的信息与反映企业在较早时期或一定时期内财务状况的信息进行比较,研究其发展和变化以及企业的各种业务绩效或财务状况。水平分析的基本要求是比较财务报表资源不同时期的相同数据。

在进行分析时，第一个需要面临问题是确定基准年，然后根据基准年计算变化。在水平分析中，使用显示的最早年份作为基准年，并确定基准年与当前年度之间的数额变化。对于 Liam 公司而言，2018 年就是基准年。

设定基准年后，计算出当前年度和基准年度之间的变化额，再将变动数额除以基准年数再乘以 100，计算出百分比变化。在这种背景下，以 Liam 公司资产负债表为案例展开分析。

对于银行现金变动，从当年的 778 美元减去基准年的 683 美元，确定现金变动 95 美元。为了确定百分比变化，我们将 95 美元的变化除以 683 美元的基年余额，再乘以 100%。银行现金为 13.91%。总的来说，公司的总资产增加了 12.66%，这可能会影响到稍后在报告中计算的一些比率。表 14-1 所示为 Liam 公司 2018 年及 2019 年 12 月 31 日的资产负债表对比情况。

表 14-1

Liam 公司
资产负债表的对比
2019 年及 2018 年 12 月 31 日

	2019 $,000	2018 $,000	增长/减少 数额	百分比
非流动资产				
不动产、厂房和设备	2,150	1,942	208	10.71
无形资产	638	563	75	13.32
投资	360	289	71	24.57
流动资产				
存货	634	522	112	21.46
应收账款	925	886	39	4.40
短期投资	113	84	29	34.52
银行存款	778	683	95	13.91
资产总额	5,598	4,969	629	12.66
负债和所有者权益				
所有者权益				
普通股(面值 5 美元)	2,325	2,325	-	-
优先股(面值 100 美元 5%股利)	300	300	-	-
重估盈余	205	177	28	15.82
留存收益	1,127	924	203	21.97
非流动负债				
长期债券	486	338	148	43.79
流动负债				
应付账款	442	330	112	33.94
银行透支	215	147	68	46.26
税费	498	428	70	16.36
负债和所有者权益总额	5,598	4,969	629	12.66

14.2.2 垂直分析

垂直分析是指将财务报表中每个项目的数据与整个项目的数据进行比较，以获取整个项目的位置、重要性和所做的变化。通过垂直分析可以了解企业的经营是否有发展进步及其发展进步的程度和速度。通常而言，资产负债表中的所有项目均以占总资产的百分比表示，利润表中的所有项目均以营业收入的百分比表示。

以 Liam 公司资产负债表的资产部分为例来进行比较分析。以总资产表示财务报表上的所有项目，因此将总资产设置为等于100%。计算银行存款占总资产的百分比。将 2019 年银行存款总额除以 2019 年资产总额，再乘以 100%。截至 2019 年底，银行存款占总资产的 13.90%。同样的数据显示，2018 年的这一比例为 13.75%。表 14-2 所示为用垂直法制作的 Liam 公司的财务状况比较表。

表 14-2

Liam 公司

财务状况比较表

2019 年、2018 年 12 月 31 日

	2019 $, 000 数额	百分比	2018 $, 000 数额	百分比
非流动资产				
不动产、厂房和设备	2,150	38.41	1,942	39.08
无形资产	638	11.40	563	11.33
投资	360	6.43	289	5.82
流动资产				
存货	634	11.33	522	10.51
应收账款	925	16.52	886	17.83
短期投资	113	2.02	84	1.69
银行存款	778	13.90	683	13.75
资产总额	5,598	100.00	4,969	100.00
负债和所有者权益				
所有者权益				
普通股(面值 5 美元)	2,325	41.53	2,325	46.79
优先股(面值 100 美元 5%股利)	300	5.36	300	6.04
重估盈余	205	3.66	177	3.56
留存收益	1,127	20.13	924	18.60
非流动负债				
长期债券	486	8.68	338	6.80

(续表)

	2019		2018	
流动负债				
应付账款	442	7.90	330	6.64
银行透支	215	3.84	147	2.96
税费	498	8.90	428	8.61
负债和所有者权益总额	5,598	100.00	4,969	100.00

以 Liam 公司利润表为例进行比较分析。以销售净额表示利润表上的所有项目，将销售净额设置为等于 100%，计算销货成本占销售净额的百分比。将 2019 年销货成本总额除以 2019 年销售净额总额，再乘以 100%。截至 2019 年底，销货成本占总销售净额的 69.54%，而 2018 年的这一比例为 69.73%。表 14-3 所示为用垂直法制作的 Liam 公司 2018 年、2019 年 12 月 31 日的利润表对比情况。

表 14-3

Liam 公司
利润表比较
2019 年、2018 年 12 月 31 日

	2019		2018	
	$,000		$,000	
	数额	百分比	数额	百分比
销售净额	5,423	100	4,830	100
销货成本	3,773	69.57	3,368	69.73
毛利	1,650	30.43	1,462	30.27
销售费用	341	6.29	295	6.11
管理费用	404	7.45	375	7.76
经营费用总额	745	13.74	670	13.87
息税前利润(PBIT)	905	16.69	792	16.40
利息费用	264	4.87	218	4.51
税前利润	641	11.82	574	11.88
所得税费用	262	4.83	239	4.95
税后利润(PAT)	379	6.99	335	6.94

14.3　流动性分析

14.3.1　营运资金

营运资金是企业流动资产和负债的总称。流动资产与流动负债之间的差额为净营运资金。企业资产负债表上的流动资产包括现金、应收账款、存货和其他预期在一年内变现或转换为现金的资产。流动负债包括应付账款、工资、应付税款和长期债务的当期部分。

$$\text{营运资金} = \text{流动资产} - \text{流动负债}$$

营运资金可用于衡量公司或企业的短期偿付能力。金额越大，公司或企业准备支付债务的能力就

越充分，短期偿付能力也就越好。当营运资金为负数时，即企业的流动资产少于流动负债，由于营业额不佳，企业的经营可能随时中断。

14.3.2 流动比率

流动比率是指流动资产总额与流动负债总额的比率。它用于衡量企业在短期债务到期前偿还其债务之前将其流动资产转换为现金的能力。一般来说，比率越高，企业资产的流动性强，短期偿债能力越强；否则，就较弱。但该比例过大，表明流动资产占用较多，将影响流动资金周转效率和盈利能力。通常认为合理的流动资金比率为2。

$$流动比率 = \frac{流动资产}{流动负债}$$

Liam 公司 2019 年和 2018 年的营运资本和流动比率如下：

	2019	2018
流动资产	$2,450	$2,175
流动负债	$1,155	$905
营运资本	$1,295	$1,270
流动比率	2.12	2.40

14.3.3 速动比率

使用流动比率分析企业偿债能力时，并没有考虑流动资产的结构。在 Liam 公司和 Sami 公司流动比率的计算过程中，可知两家公司的营运资本相同，流动比率均为 2.12，但这两家公司偿还到期债务的能力却有很大的差异。Liam 公司的流动资产主要集中在应收账款和现金上，这些资产较容易变现，还款压力较小。而 Sami 公司的流动资产主要集中在存货上，这意味该公司必须出售大部分存货并收回款项才能如期偿还债务，相比较而言，Sami 公司的资产的流动能力相对较弱。因此，需要一个排除存货这些变现能力较差的指标来衡量企业的短期偿债能力。

Liam 公司和 Sami 公司 2019 年 12 月 31 日的财务状况如下：

	Liam Co.	Sami Co.
流动资产：		
存货	$634	$1192
应收账款	$925	$410
短期投资	$113	$57
银行存款	$778	$791
流动资产总额	$2,450	$2,450
流动负债	$1,155	$1,155
营运资本	$1,295	$1,295
流动比率	2.12	2.12

酸性测试比率，也被称为速动比率。它将公司的速动资产和流动负债进行比较，用以衡量企业流动资产中可以立即变现用于偿还短期债务等直接负债的能力。这一指标在某些情况下比流动比率更实用，因为它排除了存货等可能难以迅速变现的资产。

$$速动比率 = \frac{速动资产}{流动负债} \quad (速动资产 = 流动资产 - 存货)$$

Liam 公司速动比率计算过程如下：

	2019	2018
速动资产：		
应收账款	$925	$886
短期投资	$113	$84
银行存款	$778	$683
速动资产总额	$1,816	$1,653
流动负债	$1,155	$905
速动比率	1.57	1.83

对于大多数行业，酸性测试比率应超过 1。另一方面，太高的比率并不总是好的。它可能表明，现金已经积累并闲置，而不是用于再投资、返还给股东或以其他方式用于生产。酸性测试比率的可接受范围在不同的行业中会有所不同，因此有必须在做出评价之前，在同一行业的同行公司之间做出比较分析。

14.4 偿债能力

14.4.1 资产负债率

资产负债率是用以衡量企业利用债权人提供的资金进行经营活动的能力，以及反映债权人发放贷款的安全程度的指标。通过将企业的期末负债总额与资产总额相比较，可以得出，一个公司的资产中债务融资的比例。

资产负债比率大于 1，表示公司负债多于资产，有资不抵债的风险。同时，资产负债比率高还表明，一旦利率突然上升，公司可能会面临贷款违约的风险。资产负债比率小于 1，表示公司资产的很大一部分由股本提供，财务风险相对较小。

不同行业的资产负债率差异很大，因此需要结合其他财务指标进行合理分析。

$$资产负债率 = \frac{负债总额}{资产总额}$$

Liam 公司的债务数据如下：

	2019	2018
负债总额	$1,641	$1,243
资产总额	$5,598	$4,969
资产负债率	0.29	0.25

通过计算结果可知，2019 年的资产负债率高于 2018 年，主要是由于 2019 年的长期借款增多。

14.4.2 利息保障倍数

利息保障倍数反映了企业经营收益为所需支付的债务利息的倍数。它既是企业举债经营的前提依据，也是衡量企业长期偿债能力大小的重要标志。利息保障倍数至少应大于 1，且比值越高，说明企业支付利息费用的能力越强，这意味着企业在偿还债务后有足够的现金继续投资于其他业务。如果利息保障倍数过低，企业将面临亏损、偿债的安全性与稳定性下降的风险。

利息保障倍数的计算公式为息税前利润除以债券和其他债务的应付利息总额。

$$利息保障倍数 = \frac{息税前利润}{利息费用}$$

Liam 公司利息保障倍数的数据如下：

	2019	2018
税前利润	$641	$574
加：利息费用	$264	$218
息税前利润	$905	$792
利息保障倍数	3.43	3.63

通过计算结果可知，2018 年和 2019 年的利息保障倍数均大于 1，2019 年的利息保障倍数与 2018 年相比有所下降。

14.5 资产效率

14.5.1 应收账款

应收账款是企业乃至流动资产中一项重要的资产。企业的应收账款如能及时收回，资金使用效率便能大幅提高。

1. 应收账款周转率

应收账款周转率就是反映企业应收账款周转速度的比率。它说明一定期间内企业应收账款转为现金的平均次数。应收账款周转率是企业在一定时期内赊销收入净额(销售收入中扣除了现销及销货退回、销货折扣与折让后的余额)与平均应收账款余额之间的比值，用于量化企业在收取应收账款或客户欠款方面的有效性。它是衡量企业应收账款周转速度及管理效率的指标。如果企业存在应收票据，则应将两者结合一起进行分析。

较高的应收账款周转率可以说明其回收效率高，能够快速偿还债务。应收账款周转率低可能是因为企业的信用政策不够完善或客户在财务上状况不好或信誉不值得信任等。

$$应收账款周转率 = \frac{销售净额}{应收账款平均余额}$$

Liam 公司应收账款周转情况如下：

	2019	2018
销售净额	$5,423	$4,830
应收账款		
期初余额	$886	$830
期末余额	$925	$886
总额	$1,811	$1,716
平均额(总额/2)	$905.5	$858
应收账款周转率	5.99	5.63

通过计算分析得出，2019 年的总资产周转率较 2018 年稍有改善，主要在于销售净额的提升。

2. 应收账款周转天数

用时间表示的应收账款周转速度为应收账款周转天数，它表示企业从获得应收账款的权利到收回款项、变成现金所需要的时间。

$$应收账款周转天数 = \frac{应收账款平均余额}{销售净额} \times 365$$

$$= \frac{365}{应收账款周转率}$$

Liam 公司应收账款周转天数情况如下：

	2019	2018
应收账款		
期初余额	$886	$830
期末余额	$925	$886
总额	$1,811	$1,716
平均额(总额/2)	$905.5	$858
销售净额	$5,423	$4,830
乘以 365		
应收账款周转天数	60.11	63.95

14.5.2　存货

存货在企业营运及管理决策中有着重要的意义。企业应保有足够的存货，以满足顾客的购买需要及企业的经营需求。但是，库存的物品存放时间越长，其存放成本就越高，占用的资金就越多，企业的资金流动性就更差。因此，对于存货的周转速度，企业可以通过存货周转率以及存货周转期来进行评价。

1. 存货周转率

存货周转率是对流动资产周转率的补充说明，通过对存货周转率的计算与分析，衡量企业存货的流动性及存货资金占用量是否合理，可以测定企业投入生产、存货管理水平、销售收回的能力。一般来讲，存货周转速度越快，存货的占用水平越低，流动性越强，存货转换为现金或应收账款的速度越快。因此，提高存货周转率可以提高企业的变现能力。

存货周转率的计算有两种方法，一种是销售额除以平均存货余额(期初库存和期末库存之和除以2)。另一种方法用销货成本代替销货额，是一定时期销货成本与平均存货余额(期初库存和期末库存之和除以 2)的比率。计算存货周转率时用销货成本代替销售额，目的在于提高库存周转率计算的准确性，因为销售额包括成本加成。在这两种情况下，平均存货被用来帮助消除季节性影响。

计算存货周转率时，使用"销售收入"还是"销售成本"作为周转额，看分析的目的。如果分析的目的是判断短期偿债能力，应采用销售收入。如果分析的目的是评估存货管理业绩，应当使用销售成本。

$$存货周转率 = \frac{销货成本}{存货平均余额}$$

Liam 的存货周转率情况如下：

	2019	2018
销货成本	$3,773	$3,368
存货		
期初余额	$522	$478
期末余额	$634	$522
总额	$1,156	$1,000
平均额(总额/2)	$578	$500
存货周转率	6.53	6.74

通过计算可得，Liam 公司的存货周转率较 2018 年变化不大。对于企业而言，低周转率意味着销售疲软和库存积压，这可能表明所提供销售的货物有问题，或者是市场营销太少导致的；高比率意味着要么销售强劲，要么库存不足。前者是大家希望的，而后者则可能导致业务流失。

2. 存货周转天数

存货周转天数可以用这段时间内的天数(360 天)除以存货周转率来计算出存货取得至消耗、销售为止所经历的天数。

存货周转天数越少，表明存货周转次数越多，平均存货越少。但是，存货周转天数过少不能满足流转需要，天数过多则占用资金多，造成资源浪费。因此，企业需要结合应收账款的周转天数得出一个适合的现金周转期。

$$存货周转天数 = \frac{存货平均余额}{销货成本} \times 365$$

$$= \frac{365}{存货周转率}$$

Liam 的存货周转天数情况如下：

	2019	2018
存货		
期初余额	$522	$478
期末余额	$634	$522
总额	$1156	$1,000
平均额(总额/2)	$578	$500
销货成本	$3,773	$3,368
乘以 365		
存货周转天数	55.15	53.44

14.5.3　总资产周转率

总资产周转率是衡量资产投资规模与销售水平之间配比情况的指标，可以作为企业利用资产创造收入效率的指标。它体现了企业在经营期间全部资产从投入到产出的流转速度，反映了企业本年度以及以前年度全部资产的管理质量和利用效率。一般情况下，资产周转率越高，表明企业总资产周转速度越快，销售能力越强，资产利用效率越高。

资产周转率的计算公式中，分子表示企业利润表上的销售收入净额，分母表示企业资产负债表上的总资产，总资产应在评估期内取平均值。例如，企业在计算资产周转率的公式中使用的是 2019 年的资产，则应平均 2019 年初和年末的总资产。

$$总资产周转率 = \frac{销售净额}{总资产平均余额}$$

Liam 公司的资产周转率计算过程如下:

	2019	2018
销售净额	$5,423	$4,830
资产:		
期初余额	4,969	4,385
期末余额	5,598	4,969
总额	10,567	9,354
平均额(总额/2)	5283.5	4,677
总资产周转率	1.026	1.033

通过计算分析得出，2019 年的总资产周转率低于 2018 年，主要是因为总资产的增幅较大。在评价 Liam 公司的资产周转率前，有必要与同一行业或类似公司进行比较分析。

14.6 盈利能力

14.6.1 利润率

利润率是衡量企业盈利程度的常用盈利能力比率之一。它说明销售额转化为利润的百分比，即每一美元的销售额可以带来多少净利润。该比率越高，企业的盈利能力越强。

利润率有毛利率、营业利润率、税前利润率、净利润率。然而，在日常使用中，它通常指的是净利润率，即净利润除以销售净额。

$$毛利率 = \frac{销售净额 - 销货成本}{销售净额}$$

$$营业利润率 = \frac{息税前利润}{销售净额}$$

$$税前利润率 = \frac{税前利润}{销售净额}$$

$$净利润率 = \frac{税后利润}{销售净额}$$

根据 Liam 公司的资料，其利润率计算如下:

	2019	2018
税后利润	$379	$335
销售净额	$5,423	4830
销售利润率	6.99%	6.94%

在 Liam 公司中，它在 2019 年度实现了 6.99%的利润率，这意味着它每销售一美元就有 6.99 美分的净收入。从计算结果可知，Liam 公司的盈利能力有所上升。

14.6.2 资产回报率

资产回报率是用来衡量每单位资产创造多少净利润的盈利能力指标。在计算资产回报率时用净收入加上利息开支，得出扣除融资成本前的营运回报率，因为总资产的资金来源于股东和债权人，所以资产回报率衡量的是企业(不论资金来源)为股东和债权人共同创造价值的能力。资产回报率以百分比表示，比率越高，企业管理层管理资产负债表以产生利润的效率就越高。

$$资产回报率 = \frac{净利润 + 利息费用}{总资产平均余额}$$

Liam 公司的总资产回报率计算如下：

	2019	2018
净利润	$379	$335
加：利息费用	$264	$218
总利润	$643	$553
资产：		
期初余额	$4,969	$4,385
期末余额	$5,598	$4,969
总额	$10,567	$9,354
平均额(总额/2)	$5283.5	$4,677
资产回报率	12.17%	11.82%

通过计算结果可知，2019 年的资产回报率与 2018 年相比有所提升，在对 Liam 公司的盈利能力做出评价之前，有必要与同行业的相关企业的指标进行对比分析。

14.6.3 资本使用回报率

资本使用回报率是衡量公司盈利能力和资本使用效率的财务比率。资本使用回报率越高，公司利用可用资本创造利润的效率就越高。一个好的资本使用回报率对于企业来说应该总是高于它的平均融资利率。资本使用回报率是一个重要的盈利比率，投资者在筛选合适的投资候选人时经常使用它。

$$资本使用回报率 = \frac{息税前利润}{使用资本额}$$

(使用资本额 = 资产总额 — 流动负债)

Liam 公司的资本使用回报率计算过程如下：

	2019	2018
息税前利润	$905	$792
资产总额	$5,598	$4,969
减：流动负债	$1,155	$905
使用资本额	$4,443	$4,064
资本使用回报率	20.37%	19.49%

2019 年的已动用资本回报率稍有提升，在进行评价前，还需要与当年的收益率(无风险收益率加风险收益率)进行比较，以得出结论。

14.6.4 股东权益收益率(净资产收益率)

股本收益率是衡量管理层如何有效地利用企业资产创造利润的盈利能力指标,其结果表示每一美元普通股股东权益产生多少利润。股本收益率计算方法是将净利润(普通股股东所享有,需扣除优先股股利)除以股东权益,因为股东权益等于一家公司的资产减去债务,所以净资产收益率也被认为是净资产的收益率。

$$股东权益收益率 = \frac{净利润 - 优先股股利}{净资产平均余额}$$

Liam 公司的股东权益收益率计算如下:

	2019	2018
净利润	$379	$335
减:优先股股利	$15	$15
余额——普通股可用	$364	$320
权益		
期初余额	3,726	3,483
期末余额	3,957	3,726
总额	7,683	7,209
平均额(总额)/2)	3841.5	3604.5
净资产收益率	9.48%	8.88%

Liam 公司 2019 年的股本收益率有所提升。但股本回报率的好坏取决于行业或公司同行的正常情况。因此,在做出评价前,将公司与另一家类似公司比较更有意义。

14.6.5 每股收益

每股收益是一种市场预期比率,用来表明普通股股东每持有一股所能享有的企业净利润或需承担的企业净亏损。它反映了企业的经营成果,衡量普通股的获利水平及投资风险,是投资者等信息使用者据以评价企业盈利能力、预测企业成长潜力、进而做出相关经济决策的重要的财务指标之一。

每股收益计算方式用企业的净利润除以股数来计算,比率越高,表明所创造的利润越多。若只有普通股,净收益是税后净利润,股份数需要使用资产负债表和损益表来查找期末发行在外的普通股股数。如果还有优先股,应从税后净利中扣除分派给优先股东的股利。

企业通常会报告针对特殊项目和潜在股份稀释而调整的每股收益。企业的每股收益越高,则意味着利润越高,有更多的利润分配给股东。

$$每股收益 = \frac{净利润 - 优先股股利}{发行在外的普通股股数}$$

Liam 公司的每股收益率计算如下:

	2019	2018
净利润	$379	$335
减:优先股股利	$15	$15
余额——普通股可用	$364	$320
发行在外普通股股数(面值 5 美元)	465	465
普通股每股收益	$0.78	$0.68

2019年每股收益为0.78美元，意味着每持一股Liam公司的股票，将享有0.78美元的净利润。每股收益指标是确定股票价格时最重要的变量之一。它也是用于计算市盈率的主要组成部分，其中市盈率中的E表示每股收益。通过将企业的股价除以每股收益，投资者可以根据市场愿意为每美元收益支付多少美元来查看股票的价值。

14.6.6　市盈率

市盈率是衡量公司当前股价相对于每股收益的比率。市盈率通常指的是静态市盈率，用来作为比较不同价格的股票是否被高估或者低估的指标。市盈率越低，市价相对于股票的盈利能力越低，表明投资回收期越短，投资风险就越小，股票的投资价值就越大；高市盈率可能意味着一家公司的股票被高估，或者说明投资者期望未来有高增长率。

$$市盈率 = \frac{普通股每股市价}{普通股每股收益}$$

假定2018年、2019年Liam公司的普通股每股市价分别为6.8美元及11.5美元。

Liam公司的市盈率计算如下：

	2019	2018
普通股每股市价	$11.5	$6.8
普通股每股收益	$0.78	$0.68
市盈率	14.74	10

2019年Liam公司的市盈率为14.74，意味着公司的股票是以盈利的14.74倍出售的。投资者利用市盈率比较不同股票的价值时，应选择同行业的股票进行比较研究，因为同行业的每股收益比较接近，具有可比性。

参考文献

[1] 侯立新，崔刚. 会计英语[M]. 北京：机械工业出版社，2013.
[2] 孙坤. 会计英语[M]. 上海：上海财经大学出版社，2013.
[3] 郭梅，郭丽芳. 实用会计英语[M]. 北京：机械工业出版社，2017.
[4] 张其秀. 会计英语——财务会计[M]. 上海：上海财经大学出版社，2010.
[5] 耿江云. 会计专业英语[M]. 北京：人民邮电出版社，2018.
[6] 叶建芳，孙红星，叶建平. 会计英语[M]. 大连：东北财经大学出版社，2014.
[7] 黄东坡，李伟，范实秋. 会计英语[M]. 北京：清华大学出版社，2016.
[8] 秦戈雯，池昭梅. 财务会计[M]. 成都：西南财经大学出版社，2018.
[9] 刘建华. 会计英语[M]. 北京：清华大学出版社，2017.
[10] 马建威，何玉润. 会计专业英语[M]. 大连：东北财经大学出版社，2014.
[11] 张国华，王晓巍. 财会专业英语[M]. 北京：科学出版社，2013.
[12] Carl S. Warren, James M. Reeve, Philip E. Fess. *Accounting* (20th Edition). 北京：机械工业出版，2003.
[13] Harrison Horngren. *Financial Accounting* (4th Edition). 北京：清华大学出版社，2004.
[14] Warren, C. S. *Survey of Accounting* (2nd Edition). 北京：高等教育出版社，2005.
[15] IFRS Foundation (2018). *IFRS.* https://www.ifrs.org/
[16] International Public Sector Accounting Standards Board (2013) *Conceptual Framework for General Purpose Financial Reporting by Public Sector Entities.* www.ipsasb.org/piblications-resources
[17] International Accounting Standards Board (2018). *Conceptual Framework for Financial Reporting.* https://www.ifrs.org/
[18] International Accounting Standards Board (2003). *Inventories.* https://www.ifrs.org/
[19] International Accounting Standards Board (2003). *Property, Plant and Equipment.* https://www.ifrs.org/
[20] International Accounting Standards Board (2004). *Intangible Assets.* https://www.ifrs.org/
[21] International Accounting Standards Board (2003). *Earning per share.* https://www.ifrs.org/
[22] International Accounting Standards Board (2014). *Revenue from contracts with customers.* https://www.ifrs.org/
[23] International Accounting Standards Board (2010). *Presentation of Financial Statements.* https://www.ifrs.org/
[24] International Accounting Standards Board (2003). *Statement of Cash Flow.* https://www.ifrs.org/